The

New Trek
Programme Guide

The New Trek Programme Guide

Paul Cornell, Martin Day
and Keith Topping

Virgin

First published in 1995 by
Virgin Books
an imprint of Virgin Publishing Ltd
332 Ladbroke Grove
London W10 5AH

Cover illustration by Adrian Mitchell

Typeset by Mark Stammers Design, London

Printed and bound in Great Britain by
BPC Paperbacks Ltd

ISBN 0 86369 922 7

CONTENTS

ACKNOWLEDGEMENTS

We would like to thank the following for their help with this book: Ian Abrahams, Ian Atkins, Bernard Atkinson, Pete Barras, Anthony Brown, Nick Cooper, Mark Cullen, Keith and Karen Dunn, Ken Ford-Powell, Dave Hughes, David Owen, Graeme Topping, Steve Walker, the staff of Newcastle upon Tyne Central Library, and the staff of Forbidden Planet, Newcastle, for their kind help in providing miscellaneous items otherwise unavailable in this country.

Acknowledgement is also made to the following books and periodicals: *DWB/DreamWatch*; Clive James, *Clive James on Television*; Stephen Fry, *Paperweight*; Thomas Maxwell, *The Trek Universal Index*; Larry Nemecek, *The Star Trek: The Next Generation Companion*; Michael Okuda, Denise Okuda and Debbie Mirek, *The Star Trek Encyclopedia*; the *Radio Times*; *Star Begotten*; *TV Zone*.

Dedicated to John McLaughlin.

Introduction

Soon after being cast as Captain Jean-Luc Picard in *Star Trek: The Next Generation*, Patrick Stewart was asked how it felt to be part of 'an American icon'. The question is a valid one, and Stewart came to realise that *Star Trek* was more than a mere TV programme.

Whatever one's perception of the 1960s *Star Trek* series, there's no doubt that it can claim a place in cultural history. Despite an occasional tendency towards hands-on-hips moralising, the show did examine many important and dramatic issues within an optimistic framework that millions of Americans were immediately attracted to.

Star Trek proved quite capable of conquering British audiences, too. In 1973, Clive James professed his love for the programme in his regular TV review column for the *Observer*, believing that its appeal lay in the 'classic inevitability of its repetitions. As surely as Brünnhilde's big moments are accompanied by a few bars of the Valkyries' ride, Spock will say that the conclusion would appear to be logical, Captain. Uhura will turn leggily from her console to transmit information conveying either (a) that all contact with Star Fleet [sic] has been lost, or (b) that it has been regained. Chekhov will act badly. Bones ("Jim, it may seem unbelievable, but my readings indicate that this man has . . . *two hearts*") will act extremely badly . . .' Most importantly, *Star Trek* 'has the innocence of belief'. Stephen Fry wrote in *The Literary Review* that *Star Trek* shows 'the fight between Apollo and Dionysus that Nietzsche saw as being at the centre of Greek tragedy'. More simply, the programme was of 'remarkable quality'.

By the late 1980s, *Star Trek* as an episodic TV series, a big budget film saga and a corporate merchandising empire, had become a phenomenon.

Star Trek: The Next Generation was the logical next step in that phenomenon. Gene Roddenberry had tried to revive his concept in 1977 with *Star Trek II*, but the cinematic splash of *Star Wars* ensured that some of this concept ended up on the big screen. By the mid-1980s Paramount TV executives came to believe that the fan following that had so vociferously attacked the decision to axe the original series might be converted to watch a new one. Although there was no question of using the original characters, the new show clearly had to be an evolution out of what had gone before, rather than a revolution that threw away all of Roddenberry's core precepts. After months of hard work, 'Encounter at Farpoint' premiered across America in the autumn of 1987.

After a shaky first season, *Star Trek: The Next Generation* matured into a satisfying reworking of the original programme's ethos. More important even than the special effects and the moral dilemmas were the new characters: to many, Kirk, Spock, et al., could never be replaced, but *The Next Generation* team became accepted in its own right. By 1990 *The Next Generation* had passed the original series' seventy-nine episodes.

The BBC acquired first option on *The Next Generation* that year, and put the series in their autumn schedules. They had only bothered to secure the series for two years (rumour has it that the BBC executive who purchased the series saw only the pilot and was unimpressed). Given an 18.00 Wednesday slot, the episodes up to 'The Best of Both Worlds 2' were shown and gained a following very quickly. Writing in the *NME*, Angus Batey described the series' 'excellent labyrinthine plot structures' as '*Back to the Future* with a Kurt Vonnegut screenplay' and noted the presence in *The Next Generation* of 'reliable old transporter beams, photon torpedoes and that split infinitive – so fans of the originals are well catered for.'

Despite this, the series was sometimes dropped to make way for sporting events, and one episode was postponed because of programme overrun, which caused a fan outcry. The BBC's decision to transmit the series in an early evening time slot also brought casualties: the *Alien*-influenced 'Conspiracy' was hacked to pieces by the censors (although ten seconds of cut footage was left intact in 'Shades of Gray'), and 'The High Ground', with its allusions to contemporary events in Northern Ireland, was banned completely. The BBC objected, amongst other things, to the character of Finn having an Irish name.

In 1992, the rights to the series transferred to the Astra satellite company BSkyB, which came up with the novel idea of turning *The Next Generation* into a daily soap. Scheduling episodes at 17.00 (with a 22.30 repeat) Monday to Friday, Sky One began re-broadcasting the series from episode one. (Despite the fact that there were rarely links between episodes, the previously-mentioned *NME* article suggested that *Star Trek: The Next Generation* made a great deal more sense in this fashion. 'Don't let the SF trappings put you off – this is basically *Neighbours* in outer space with less implausible stories and several times more addictive.')

Such was the confidence surrounding *The Next Generation* that by 1993 it was able to produce a sibling of its own, *Star Trek: Deep Space Nine*, a much darker area of the *Star Trek* universe. Thirty years after it all began, *Deep Space Nine* is carrying the concepts of Roddenberry and his successors forward towards a new century. As this book was being completed, *The Next Generation* had already been turned into the first of a probable series of feature films (*Star Trek: Generations*). Additionally, the new TV spin-off *Star Trek: Voyager* is returning the concept to its original roots in space exploration.

The New Trek Programme Guide is a book aimed at the casual viewer and the dedicated fan alike, a companion to *The Next Generation* and *Deep Space Nine* videotapes and a concise work of reference. Our aim is to highlight the elements that make both series so popular, whilst also giving a general guide to the quality of the individual episodes themselves.

In this guide we have used the American transmission order: although we want the book to reflect a British approach to *The Next Generation* and *DS9*, UK transmission dates are, as indicated below, less than straight-forward. Stardates are of little help (take a close look at the first season), and production order comes a cropper in stories like 'Unification', where the second episode was filmed first. Very occasionally the American transmission order clashes with that of the video releases, but we feel that the sequence we have is the most sensible compromise.

The American dates given are those on which Paramount transmitted the episodes by satellite to the various US TV stations for transmission during the following week. Although this usually occurred on the following Saturday, these have become accepted as the de facto transmission dates for *The Next Generation* and *Deep Space Nine*.

All of the UK transmission dates we quote from 'Family' onwards pertain to the Sky transmissions. A couple of special cases are 'The High Ground', which received its British TV debut on Sky out of sequence with the rest of the series, and 'Unification' parts one and two, which were first shown in truncated form on Sky's Movie channel. *Deep Space Nine* made its UK debut on Sky in a Sunday early evening slot (also used for season seven of *The Next Generation*).

UK transmission dates were taken from the *Radio Times* and more recent US dates (including the information in the Appendix) were derived from *TV Zone* and *DreamWatch*. We use American spellings for the episode titles and on-screen credits (so don't write in to say that isn't how you spell 'honour'), but British conventions elsewhere. Our production credits, cast lists and all other information has been taken from what featured on the screen, with one or two exceptions. Occasionally we have mentioned the pseudonyms used by writers, as noted in Larry Nemecek's book (see Acknowledgements). *The Star Trek Encyclopedia* was our 'bible' for spellings. We would like to state, however, that the substance and the majority of the content of this book came through watching the episodes themselves: our primary interest is what actually appeared on screen.

Although the end of the final season of *The Next Generation* and the second season of *Deep Space Nine* provides our theoretical cut-off point, so much is happening in the *Trek* universe that we felt we should at least try to reflect this, and bring our book as up-to-date as possible. Therefore, we have an appendix which features as much information on the third season of *Deep Space Nine* and the first of *Star Trek: Voyager* as we could glean before this book went to press. Be warned if you haven't seen these episodes and want the surprises left intact.

The factual information is self-explanatory, although it's worth pointing out that the regular cast lists come in two sections. The first covers those who get a standard credit during the title sequence; the second covers characters like Pulaski, Guinan, Q, Lwaxana Troi and any crossovers between *The Next Generation* and *Deep Space Nine*.

The categories are as follows (a variation on this format is used for the *Deep Space Nine* episodes):

Stardate: In this, we note the first Stardate given in each episode and, where applicable, how this is relates to 'real' dating. 'The Neutral Zone' provides an exact date for the era in which these events take place (2364 and beyond).

Strange New Worlds: The names of planets, stars, or other cosmic bodies visited or mentioned during an episode.

New Life Forms: Alien life forms encountered or alluded to, including extra facts about races already known.

Introducing: The first story of semi-regular characters.

Technology: Brief snippets about the gadgets and scientific achievements of the Federation and her allies and enemies.

Technobabble: American fandom coined this term to cover the meaningless pseudo-science that the writers seem to take great pleasure in having characters (especially Geordi) say.

Poker Game: A plot device first used in 'The Measure of a Man'. Often these events can be very illuminating, with hidden character traits (such as Riker's mean streak) bubbling to the surface.

Picard Manoeuvre: Patrick Stewart's habit of tugging at his uniform when sitting down or standing up in early episodes became a running joke on the show, with other actors performing the same nervous twitch, usually when in charge of the ship.

Riker's Conquests: You don't really need this one explained, do you?

Deanna Underused?: The poor counselor was usually the first character to get cut out of an episode if there wasn't enough action to go round.

Data's Jokes: A major focus of the early episodes was Data's role as the comic relief (a substitute Spock as noted by just about everyone). Later seasons somewhat transferred this role to Worf, but we do note here Data's funny lines – intentional or otherwise.

Dialogue Triumphs: Those little glimmers that can make a tired hack reach for the notebook. (Occasionally we'll list an absolute stinker or a line that sums up the tone of the whole episode.)

Future History: References to the development of the politics and culture of Earth (and the Federation) after 1988.

Notes: A collection of facts too detailed or too trivial for the other headings.

As with our previous books we also provide short reviews of the episodes. It's worth stressing that all things are in the eye of the beholder and that whilst our opinions are as valid as anyone else's, they aren't the Holy Writ. So, come *Star Trek* Judgement Day, don't have us cast into the pit just because we don't appreciate your favourite episode as much as you do.

Remember, it takes all sorts to make a universe.

First Season

24 45-minute and one 90-minute episode

Created by Gene Roddenberry

Executive Producer: Gene Roddenberry (7–9, 11–2
Co-Executive Producers: Rick Berman (18–25),
Maurice Hurley (18–25) **Producer:** Maurice Hurley (2–1)
Co-Producers: Robert Lewin, Herbert Wright (1–20, 22)
Supervising Producers: Rick Berman (1–17), Robert H.
Justman (1–17) **Associate Producers:** D.C. Fontana (1–12),
Peter Lauritson **Consulting Producer:** Robert H. Justman
(18–25) **Line Producer:** David Livingston (18–25)
Executive Story Editors: Hannah Louise Shearer
(16, 18–25), Tracy Tormé (20–25) **Story Editors:** Hans
Beimler (18–23), Johnny Dawkins (2–3, 5, 15), Richard
Manning (18–23) **Creative Consultant:** Greg Strangis
(11–13)

Regular Cast: Patrick Stewart (Captain Jean-Luc Picard),
Jonathan Frakes (Commander William Riker), LeVar Burton
(Lt Geordi La Forge), Denise Crosby (Lt Tasha Yar), Michael
Dorn (Lt Worf), Gates McFadden (Dr Beverly Crusher), Ma-
rina Sirtis (Counselor Deanna Troi), Brent Spiner (Lt Com-
mander Data), Wil Wheaton (Wesley Crusher) Colm Meaney
(Ensign[1], 1, 6), John de Lancie (Q, 1, 9), Majel Barrett (Lwaxana
Troi, 10)

[1]See notes below.

The debate as to whether Colm Meaney's appearance in 'Lonely Among Us'
(credited as First Security Officer) constitutes another sighting of O'Brien is a
long and complex one, but we list both roles here for the sake of completeness.

1: 'Encounter at Farpoint'
90 Minutes
US Transmission: 28 September 1987
UK Transmission: 26 September 1990
Writers: D.C. Fontana, Gene Roddenberry
Director: Corey Allen
Cast: Michael Bell, DeForrest Kelley, Cary-Hiroyuki,
Timothy Dang, David Erskine, Evelyn Guerrero,
Chuck Hicks, Jimmy Ortega

Taking command of the USS *Enterprise*, Captain Picard's first mission is to 'solve the mystery of Farpoint station'. Travelling to the outpost the ship is pursued by a powerful entity, Q, who places mankind on trial for its alleged crimes. Picard offers to prove his race's worth at Farpoint and, discovering that the station's power source is an enslaved life form, releases it. A fascinated Q tells Picard that the *Enterprise* has not seen the last of him.

Stardate: 41153.7

Strange New Worlds: Deneb 4 ('beyond which lies the great unexplored mass of the galaxy').

New Life Forms: The Bandi of Deneb 4. The nameless energy creatures. The Ferengi are mentioned.

Introducing: Q, a powerful entity with shape-shifting abilities and a curiosity about humans in general and Picard in particular.

Technology: Warp 9.3 is described as 'the red line'.

Technobabble: The bridge viewscreen uses 'high resolution multi-spectral imaging sensors'.

Riker's Conquests: Riker and Deanna are former lovers.

Dialogue Triumphs: 'You've got a lot to learn about humanity if you think you can torture or frighten us into silence.'

Future History: In the mid 21st century, 'the post
ror' was a period during which diplock courts dis
tice on a 'guilty until proved innocent' basis and go
appeared to control their military with drugs.

In 2036 the new United Nations decreed that no hum
be made to answer for the crimes of his forebears. By
however, the new UN had been abolished.

These events take place in the late 24th century (Picard
scribes the Cold War as having taken place '400 years ago': se
'The Neutral Zone').

Notes: 'Let's see what's out there.' This pilot begins very well,
with a great OTT performance from John de Lancie, some good
'get to know us' dialogue for the regulars and a charming scene
featuring DeForrest Kelley linking *The Next Generation* to its
predecessor. However, the ending is mawkish and obvious with
much padding. Picard is different from his later character, in
places nervy and unsure of himself. Colm Meaney's unnamed
conn ensign is revealed to be O'Brien in 'All Good Things'.

Admiral McCoy is 137 years old, which means that *The Next
Generation* is set approximately 75 years after the events of
Star Trek VI. Picard was a former crewmate of Dr Crusher's
dead husband. He quotes Shakespeare and is nervous of children. Riker, who recently served aboard the USS *Hood*, refused
to let his former captain DeSoto beam into a dangerous situation on Altair 3. Data is an android who has been programmed
with a complete human vocabulary. He graduated from the
Starfleet class of '78 (presumably a Stardate rather than a year),
with honours in exo-biology and probability mechanics. Geordi
says he was born blind. Deanna is half-Betazoid (a telepathic
race). Her father was an Earth Starfleet officer. The *Enterprise*
(NCC 1701-D) has two sections, the stardrive (which includes
the battle bridge) and the saucer.

2: 'The Naked Now'

US Transmission: 5 October 1987
UK Transmission: 3 October 1990
Writers: J. Michael Bingham (a pseudonym for
D.C. Fontana), from a story by John D.F. Black,
J. Michael Bingham (D.C. Fontana)
Director: Paul Lynch
Cast: Brooke Bundy, Benjamin W.S. Lum, Michael Rider,
David Rehan, Skip Stellrect, Kenny Koch

Disaster strikes the research vessel SS *Tsiolkovsky*, observing a collapsing star. When the *Enterprise* investigates, its crew begin to exhibit signs of intoxication and frivolity. Riker works out that the legendary Psi 2000 virus is at work. When the known cure fails to work, it seems that the *Enterprise* will plunge into the star, but Data's speed and coordination saves the ship.

Stardate: 41209.2

Data's Jokes: 'There was a young lady from Venus, whose body was shaped like a . . .'
'If you prick me, do I not . . . leak?'

Notes: 'I think we shall end up with a fine crew if we avoid temptation.' A sequel to (and virtual remake of) the original series classic 'The Naked Time' with the story set entirely on board the ship. Continuity references to these events ('complex strings of water molecules acted with the carbon in the body to produce an effect similar to intoxication') and to Captain James Kirk are pleasing. Wesley is particularly irritating in this episode, although he does save the ship. A Beverly/Picard relationship is briefly alluded to, and there are several fine comedy set pieces for some of the regulars (Brent Spiner is exceptional).

Tasha was abandoned as a five-year-old and survived the rape gangs on her planet before escaping when aged fifteen.

Deanna calls Riker 'Bill' on one occasion. Worf does
stand Earth humour. Data is listed in several bio-me
text books. He is capable of intercourse ('I am program
multiple techniques') as Tasha discovers (to her later
rassment). The ship's chief engineer is Sarah MacDouga

3: 'Code of Honor'

US Transmission: 12 October 1987
UK Transmission: 10 October 1990
Writers: Katharyn Powers, Michael Baron
Director: Russ Mayberry
Cast: Jessie Lawrence Ferguson, Karole Selomn,
James Louis Watkins, Michael Rider

The search for a vaccine to the anchilles fever takes the *Enterprise* to Ligon 2. The Ligonian leader, Lutan, is impressed with Tasha Yar and wants her to be his 'First One'. Thus, following Ligonian tradition, he kidnaps her and says she must fight to the death with his current First One, Yareena. Picard, knowing he is unable to break either the Ligonian's code of honour or the Prime Directive to get Tasha back, uses the ship's transporters to provide a novel way out of the stalemate. Beverly cures Yareena from deadly poisoning, and honour is satisfied.

Stardate: 41235.25

Strange New Worlds: Ligon.
   The anchilles fever seems to be confined to Styris 4.

New Life Forms: The Ligonians, a race with a culture implied to be similar to the American aboriginals and the Chinese Sung dynasty.

Technobabble: Data on the Ligonians' transporter technology: 'It uses the Hegelian shift to convert energy and matter.'

Picard Manoeuvre: First appearance: Jean-Luc hitching down

11

s uniform in frustration on two occasions.

Data's Jokes: The 'includeling the kidelies' tongue-slip.

Future History: Data describes the French language as 'obscure', much to Picard's chagrin.

Notes: 'Honour is everything.' Worthy, but plodding (and with a twist at the end that is so obvious it's painful). Tasha's fight with Yareena is stagey but curiously effective. Denise Crosby seems very uncomfortable with much of her dialogue.

Tasha is an expert in aikido.

4: 'The Last Outpost'

US Transmission: 19 October 1987
UK Transmission: 31 October 1990
Writers: Herbert Wright,
from a story by Richard Krzemien
Director: Richard Colla
Cast: Armin Shimerman, Jake Dengel, Tracey Walter,
Darryl Henriques, Mike Gomez

The *Enterprise* and the Ferengi ship it is chasing find themselves caught in a trap, suspended above an unknown planet, once part of the long-dead Tkon Empire. Both crews agree on a joint expedition to the surface, but this collapses into conflict, only halted by the appearance of the humanoid Portal, last remnant of the Empire. He tests Riker's wisdom and, when he passes, allows the *Enterprise* to leave. Portal also accepts Riker's plea for mercy for the Ferengi, allowing them to leave once they return the T-9 energy unit that they stole from the Federation.

Stardate: 41386.4

Strange New Worlds: The Delphi Ardu system (which contains eleven unexplored planets). There is a crewless monitor post on Gamma Tauri 4.

New Life Forms: Portal, the humanoid guardian of the Tkon Empire, which died out 600,000 years ago, when their sun went supernova, in their age of Makto. The Guardian is from the age of Bastu, with the ages of Cimi and Xora also preceding Makto.

The Ferengi, previously unseen by the Federation. Their technology is equal to Starfleet's (including transporters). They use power-flinging whips, and have very sensitive ears. They are dishonoured by unconditional surrender, and visual communication is against their custom, the Ferengi Code. Deanna can sense nothing from them.

Dialogue Triumphs: 'Merde,' mutters Picard.

Ferengi comment on Yar: 'You work with your females, arm them, and force them to wear clothing. Sickening.'

Future History: Riker's ancestors were American. The military theories of Sun Tzu are taught at the Academy.

Notes: Watch out for a huge anti-climax, Geordi's jive dialogue, and many longueurs. Very poor.

5: 'Where No One Has Gone Before'

US Transmission: 26 October 1987
UK Transmission: 17 October 1990
Writers: Diane Duane, Michael Reaves,
Maurice Hurley (uncredited)
Director: Rob Bowman
Cast: Biff Yeager, Stanley Kamel, Eric Menyuk, Herta Ware,
Charles Dayton, Victoria Dillard

Lt Kosinski, a Starfleet propulsion expert, and his alien assistant arrive to increase the *Enterprise*'s engine output, but Kosinski's theories don't make sense. Wes befriends the assistant, and distracts him during an experiment, sending the ship 2.7 million light years across space. An attempt to get the ship home sends the *Enterprise* to an even stranger place, an area where thoughts become real. Wesley discovers that the assistant, the Traveler, is responsible for the journeys, and the alien agrees to try to return the ship home. He does so, seemingly destroying himself in the process, but not before he has told Picard of Wesley's vast potential, leading to his promotion as acting ensign.

Stardate: 41263.1 (and a point when a Stardate would be 'meaningless').

Strange New Worlds: Galaxy M33, on the far side of Triangulum, 2,700,000 light years from Earth (which would take 300 years to get back to at maximum warp (so maximum warp is about one light year per hour) or 51 years ten months for a subspace message). Then a strange place one billion light years from the Milky Way.

New Life Forms: The Klingon Targ, a pig-like pet.
 The Traveler, a being from (not exactly) a different time. He focuses thought to travel through space, and his race have never visited humans before. (He's said to be a native of Tau Alpha C, a very distant planet.) He's a blank to Deanna.

Technobabble: 'I applied the power asymptomatically,' says Kosinski (he means asymptotically), but since he talks nonsense, this might be a clever joke.

Notes: Wil Wheaton acts really well in this episode.
 The USS *Ajax* and USS *Fearless* are two starships older than the *Enterprise* who've had their engines adjusted by Kosinski. Eleven per cent of the galaxy has been charted. Picard likes his tea strong. His mother is dead. The Traveler thinks Wesley is going to be a great genius, so he's given the rank of acting ensign. Unusually, Data uses the contraction 'it's'.

6: 'Lonely Among Us'

US Transmission: 2 November 1987
UK Transmission: 24 October 1990
Writers: D.C. Fontana,
from a story by Michael Halpern
Director: Cliff Bole
Cast: John Durbin, Kavi Raz

While taking representatives of the warring Antican and Selay races to Parliament, the *Enterprise* passes through a strange cloud. A bolt of energy secretly passes through several crew members in turn, possessing them as it goes, and finally enters the ship's computer. Several systems fail, including warp power. The energy bolt kills investigating Chief Engineer Singh and Data, acting as Sherlock Holmes, deduces that the ambassadors weren't responsible. Troi hypnotises Beverly and Worf, and discovers their recent 'possession'. The energy bolt enters Picard, causing him to turn the ship around and go back to the cloud. Revelling in the power to explore, he beams into the cloud, but finds that he can't be one with it, and returns to the ship, himself once more.

Stardate: 41249.3

Strange New Worlds: Parliament, this sector's neutral conference planet. Selay and Antica, worlds which have had contact with the Ferengi. Two planets in the Beta Renna system are home to the Anticans and Selay.

New Life Forms: The cat-like Anticans and reptilian Selay, warring species, and the sentient energy being from the cloud.

Technobabble: A lot of silliness about Picard floating around as energy.

Dialogue Triumphs: Beverly's greeting to Wes: 'Solve any new problems today?'

Selay's excuse for netting a crewmember: 'Sorry, wrong species.'

Notes: One fun, interesting plot, and one gallopingly stupid babblethon. Obviously, the latter gets centre stage.

Humans create meat in the replicator, and no longer keep animals for food. Dr Channing's theory concerns forcing dilithium into more useful crystals. The *Enterprise* is a year out of spacedock. Argyle, from the last episode, is still chief engineer. Riker regards Sherlock Holmes as an historical character.

7: 'Justice'

US Transmission: 9 November 1987
UK Transmission: 28 November 1990
Writers: Worley Thorne, Gene Roddenberry (uncredited), from a story by Ralph Wills (a pseudonym for John D.F. Black), Worley Thorne, Gene Roddenberry (uncredited)
Director: James L. Conway
Cast: Brenda Bakke, Jay Louden, Josh Clark, David Q. Combs, Richard Lavin, Judith Jones, Eric Matthew, Brad Zerbst, David Michael Graves

The *Enterprise* crew beam down to the paradise world of Rubicun 3 only for Wesley to be sentenced to death for a trivial offence. When Picard, despite the Prime Directive, argues against the punishment, the 'god' of the Edo (actually a number of multi-dimensional beings in a sort of spaceship) appears next to the *Enterprise*. Through Data the *Enterprise* is warned to leave its children alone. Picard brings an Edo on to the ship to see the reality of her 'god', but the sentence against Wesley still stands. Picard is forced to order the rescue of the boy from the unresisting Edos, but the 'god' creature stops the away team beaming back to the ship. Picard's impassioned speech on the injustice of such stringent laws saves the day.

Stardate: 41255.6

Strange New Worlds: The *Enterprise* comes to Rubicun 3 after delivering Earth colonists to a similar class M planet in the nearby Strnad system.

New Life Forms: Rubicun 3 is inhabited by the fun-loving Edos. The women are busty and the men wear daft costumes. They run everywhere, and their society is free from crime, as any committed in the randomly-selected punishment area is automatically punishable by death.

The Edos are watched over by a protective 'god' spacecraft. It is suggested the creatures in the craft once had a 'normal' existence.

Worf says that he would have to restrain himself if having sex with a human: compared to Klingons they are 'quite fragile'.

Riker's Conquests: We dread to speculate. His comment on the Edo women – 'They certainly are fit' – says it all.

Dialogue Triumphs: Geordi: 'They make love at the drop of a hat.' Yar: 'Any hat.'

Worf, after being embraced by an Edo female: 'Nice planet.'

Picard (exasperated at the sensor's vague information about the object off the starboard bow): 'Why has everything become a "something" or a "whatever"?!'

'Sharing an orbit with god is no small experience.'

Future History: Picard believes that Earth law now 'works' as the seeds of criminal behaviour can be detected. Capital punishment no longer takes place.

Notes: 'There can be no justice so long as laws are absolute. Even life itself is an exercise in exceptions.' Poorly directed, with Wil Wheaton seemingly out of his depth (although some of the lines he is given – 'You're not involved in this decision, boy.' 'I'm sorry, sir, but it seems like I am.' – would be a challenge to any actor). Although the Edo god spaceship is good, the rest of the story looks cheap. The resolution is awful, with the Prime Directive casually broken and the Edo 'god' convinced with two or three lines of horrible dialogue. Like a number of *Trek* episodes this story argues that religious belief is just a stage that humans (should) evolve out of.

Picard calls Data his friend and Wes 'the Crusher boy'.

8: 'The Battle'

US Transmission: 16 November 1987
UK Transmission: 7 November 1990
Writers: Herbert Wright,
from a story by Larry Forrester
Director: Rob Bowman
Cast: Frank Corsentino, Doug Warhit, Robert Towers

Ferengi DaiMon Bok has found the *Stargazer*, Picard's old ship, and wants to give it to the Federation. It was damaged and abandoned during the 'Battle of Maxia', where a Ferengi ship launched an unprovoked attack on the *Stargazer*. Only Picard's use of warp engines – in a procedure now known as the Picard Manoeuvre – ensured the destruction of the Ferengi ship. However, Picard, suffering from excruciating headaches, is incriminated by the ship's log, which indicates that the Federation ship fired first. Picard, under Bok's influence, relives the battle on the bridge of the *Stargazer* – and this time he will destroy the *Enterprise*. He is prevented from doing so, and Bok's fabrication of the records is revealed: the whole plan was Bok's revenge for the death of his son, who captained the Ferengi ship. Bok is taken away in disgrace by the other Ferengi.

Stardate: 41723.9

Strange New Worlds: The events are set in the Xendi Sabu star system, the *Stargazer*'s original battle having taken place in the Maxia Zeta system.

New Life Forms: DaiMon Bok's 'gift' of the *Stargazer* for no profit is termed 'very ugly' by the other Ferengi.

Technology: The hugely-expensive and illegal Ferengi mind-control device (known as a Thought Maker), used against Picard.

Picard Manoeuvre: An early instance of tunic-tugging and, of course, the real thing (see plot summary).

Dialogue Triumphs: A Ferengi: 'As you humans say, "I'm all ears."'

Future History: Medical science has eliminated headaches and the common cold (presumably in the previous century, as it was still present in the original series episode 'The Omega Glory': see also 'Angel One').

Notes: Some excellent nightmarish scenes on the *Stargazer* help to disguise an obvious plot.

Whilst captain of the Constellation-glass USS *Stargazer* (NCC 2893) some nine years previously Picard was forced to attack the unidentified (Ferengi) ship. Picard's weapons officer was called Vigo.

9: 'Hide and Q'

US Transmission: 23 November 1987
UK Transmission: 21 November 1990
Writers: C.J. Holland (a pseudonym for Maurice Hurley),
Gene Roddenberry,
from a story by C.J. Holland (Maurice Hurley)
Director: Cliff Bole
Cast: Elaine Nalee, William A. Wallace

The *Enterprise* is interrupted on its way to help a Federation colony by Q, who transports crewmembers to a surreal Napoleonic world. Worf and Wesley are killed, and Riker is offered Q's god-like powers to restore them to life. Picard is worried by Riker's new abilities, but his granting of the wishes of Wes, Data, Geordi and Worf is rejected by them. Q's wild claims about the unresistible nature of his powers are shown to be false, and, humiliated, he is called home by the continuum.

Stardate: 41590.5

Strange New Worlds: The Federation colony on Quadra Sigma 3 needs medical help after an accidental explosion in the mines.

New Life Forms: Q appears as an Aldebaran serpent (an orb with three heads).

According to Worf, the Klingon code maintains 'Drink not with thine enemy' (see 'Redemption 2').

Technology: Typically of the first season, the *Enterprise* here seems a little primitive: Crusher is hailed by the Bridge with a Naval-type whistle, and she responds via a wall panel.

Picard Manoeuvre: As he sits before a meeting with Riker.

Deanna Underused?: She does not appear. (Her absence is, at least, explained.)

Data's Jokes: To Picard, on the monsters in Napoleonic uniform: 'You may find it aesthetically displeasing, sir. I could just file a computer report on that.'

Dialogue Triumphs: Q (as a monk): 'Let us pray for understanding and for compassion.' Picard: 'Let us do no such damn thing!'

Worf (when confronted by a snarling Klingon woman): 'No! She is from a world now alien to me.' Geordi: 'Worf, is this your idea of sex?' Worf: 'This *is* sex. But I have no place for it in my life now.'

Data: 'Sir, how is it that the Q can handle time and space so well, and us so badly?' Picard: 'Perhaps some day we will discover that time and space are simpler than the human equation.' Pass that sick bag now.

Notes: 'This is what humans call a truism.' 'You mean, hardly original.' 'You're the one who said it.' Forced surrealism (the pig soldiers and Q as Napoleon) cannot disguise the cheap sets, reminiscent of the original series, and the stilted dialogue. Perhaps it's unfair to say that everyone's out-of-character so early in the first season, but we'll say it anyway. (The dialogue quoted above is very uncharacteristic of Data, Picard and Worf.) Picard even calls Riker 'Riker' at one point. It's all very silly, and even the incidental music is rubbish. When the BBC showed this episode in 1990 they removed the shot of the spear protruding from Wesley's stomach (see also 'Conspiracy').

Troi has just been dropped off at Starbase G6 for a shuttle visit home. Picard has a *Globe Illustrated Shakespeare* in his Ready Room (Q quotes from *Hamlet*, *As You Like It* and *Macbeth*; Picard counters with a 'reinterpretation' of Hamlet's 'What a piece of work is a man!' speech). After 'Encounter at Farpoint', Q returned to the continuum, worried about the human compulsion to advance and develop. Wes wants to be ten years older, Data wants to be human ('This above all, to thine own self be true' – see season seven), and Geordi wants normal vision (he always imagined Tasha to be beautiful). Worf's 'wife' goes to attack Yar in a jealous rage (do they have a thing going? – see '11001001', 'Skin of Evil' and 'Legacy').

10: 'Haven'

US Transmission: 30 November 1987
UK Transmission: 14 November 1990
Writers: Tracy Tormé,
from a story by Tracy Tormé, Lan O'Kun
Director: Richard Compton
Cast: Rob Knepper, Nan Martin, Robert Ellenstein,

Carel Struycken, Anna Katarina, Raye Birk, Danitza Kingsley,

Michael Rider

When the *Enterprise* arrives at Haven, Troi hears that her mother, Lwaxana, has decided that it is time for Deanna's arranged marriage to take place. Her fiancé, Dr Wyatt Miller, and his parents come aboard with Lwaxana. Wyatt has been dreaming of the same girl for years, but it's not Deanna. Meanwhile, the *Enterprise* crew have to defend Haven from a ship containing plague-carrying Tarellians. One of them turns out to be Wyatt's dream woman, and he leaves to help them.

Stardate: 41294.5

Strange New Worlds: The class M planet Haven, or Beta Cassius, a famed paradise. It has a legendary reputation for healing the sick, and is ruled by an electorine.

New Life Forms: The chameleon rose, which changes colour with the holder's mood, and a mobile creeper plant, kept as a pet.

It was thought that the Tarellians were all killed in a biological war. The Alcyones destroyed their last but one ship eight years ago.

'Imzadi' means 'my beloved' to Betazoids. They still practise arranged marriages (genetic bonding), can communicate telepathically with each other, and give thanks for food by hitting a small gong. They hold weddings naked, give each other bonding gifts, and hold a pre-joining announcement ceremony.

Introducing: Lwaxana Troi, Deanna's sex-mad mother, and her tall, reserved valet, Mr Homn.

Technology: A Betazoid gift casket with a robotic face.

Riker's Conquests: He looks interested in two holographic musicians, and even seems quite keen on Lwaxana, but is still very attached to Deanna.

Data's Jokes: 'Could you please continue the petty bickering? I find it most intriguing.'

Notes: The kind of thing that makes you want to take up Crown Green Bowling.

It is Federation policy to assist life forms in need. They have agreed a treaty to protect Haven. Picard says that it's a tradition that disputes are not allowed at Federation functions (but he might be lying).

Deanna can read Riker's emotions and vice versa. Steven Miller was Deanna's father's best friend. Deanna's accent reminds Lwaxana of Deanna's father. She sacked her last valet, Mr Xelo, because he became attracted to her. Her full title is: Daughter of the fifth house, holder of the sacred chalice of Rixx, heir to the holy rings of Betazed.

11: 'The Big Goodbye'

US Transmission: 11 January 1988
UK Transmission: 12 December 1990
Writer: Tracy Tormé
Director: Joseph L. Scanlan
Cast: Lawrence Tierney, Harvey Jason, William Boyett, David Selburg, Gary Armagnal, Mark Genovese, Dick Miller, Carolyn Allport, Rhonda Aldrich, Erik Cord

Picard relaxes before an important diplomatic encounter by indulging in his passion for 1940s American detective stories. But an alien scan interferes with the holodeck fantasy, and Picard, Data and Beverly find themselves trapped in a deadly gangster scenario. Wesley and Geordi are able to right the damage, and Picard greets his pedantic guests perfectly.

Stardate: 41997.7

New Life Forms: The Jarada, a 'reclusive insect-like race known for their idiosyncratic attitude towards protocol'.

Technobabble: Picard ventures the opinion that 'the holodeck makes excellent use of finite space'.

Dialogue Triumphs: Beverly's reaction to the news that Picard is being interrogated by the police: 'Why should he have all the fun?'

Future History: Baseball: Joe DiMaggio's 56 game home run record lasts until 2026, when it is broken by a short-stop for the London Kings (see *DS9*'s 'If Wishes Were Horses').

Notes: 'I need your help, Mr Hill. Someone is trying to kill me.' A visually appealing switch of genre in tribute to the worlds of Chandler, Hammett and Cain, 'The Big Goodbye' works on most levels, although the end of the holodeck segment is very rushed. Lawrence Tierney and Harvey Jason do passable Sidney Greenstreet and Peter Lorre impressions.

The *Enterprise*'s 20th-century historian and 'fiction expert' is the likeable Mr Whalan. Picard says he has always had difficulty with spelling. He is a lover of the fictional detective Dixon Hill who Geordi describes as 'a 20th-century Sherlock Holmes'. Hill first appeared in 1934 in *Amazing Detective Stories*, reappearing in the novel 'The Long Dark Tunnel' in 1936, and other works. The story that Picard chooses to simulate takes place in San Francisco in 1941. Holodeck characters can only exist briefly outside the confines of the deck.

12: 'Datalore'

US Transmission: 18 January 1988
UK Transmission: 19 December 1990
Writers: Robert Lewin, Gene Roddenbury,
from a story by Robert Lewin, Maurice Hurley
Director: Rob Bowman

Cast: Bill Yeager

The *Enterprise* arrives at Omicron Theta, the planet on which
Data was found 26 years ago. In an underground bunker the
away team discovers an identical android, Data's 'brother' Lore.
Back on the *Enterprise*, Lore's twisted personality becomes
apparent when he deactivates Data and takes his place. He also
contacts the Crystal Entity with whom he collaborated to destroy the colony. Only Wesley notices the change in the android's
personality, but no one will listen to him except Dr Crusher
who is able to reactivate Data. The two androids battle and Lore
is transported into space.

Stardate: 41242.4

Strange New Worlds: Omicron Theta, former Federation outpost and the place of Data's 'birth'.

New Life Forms: The Crystal Entity, with whom Lore is able
to communicate.

Introducing: Lore, the first of Noonian Soong's androids (Data's older 'brother').

Technobabble: Geordi: 'Captain, I'm picking up a bogey coming in on a five o'clock tangent.' (Not babble, but it doesn't
half sound funny.)

Picard Manoeuvre: Wesley does it.

Deanna Underused?: Missing altogether.

Data's Jokes: Wesley: 'Have you got a cold?' Data: 'A cold
what?' As Lore notes, 'You also have trouble with their humour.'

Dialogue Triumphs: 'You make me wish I were an only child.'

Notes: 'Can this be another me?' Dark, imaginative and schizoid. There's a fight between Lore and Worf in a turbolift that is
terrifying. The story is heavily indebted to the original series

episode 'The Enemy Within'.

Data holds the memories of the 94 colonists of Omicron Theta. He was found by the Federation ship *Tripoli*. He has an 'off switch', the knowledge of which he entrusts to Dr Crusher (Riker switches Data off in 'The Measure of a Man'). Lore seems more 'human' than Data – his use of syntax and human contractions, for example. He's also as mad as toast. There are first references to Dr Noonian Soong, Data's 'father' (see 'The Schizoid Man', 'Brothers', 'Birthright, Part I' and 'Inheritance'). He was Earth's foremost robotics scientist until he tried to 'make Asimov's dream of a positronic brain come true' (Tasha certainly knows her SF). His nickname on the colony was 'Often Wrong'. The *Enterprise* chief engineer is Mr Argyle.

13: 'Angel One'

US Transmission: 25 January 1988
UK Transmission: 9 January 1991
Writer: Patrick Berry
Director: Michael Rhodes
Cast: Karen Montgomery, Sam Hennings,
Patricia McPherson, Leonard John Crofoot

Survivors from the freighter Odin crashed on Angel 1 seven years ago. The *Enterprise* arrives to rescue them but finds that the men are hunted as outcasts on a planet dominated by women. Meanwhile a 'flu-like virus created on the Holodeck is running rampant on the *Enterprise*. Whilst Riker uses his considerable skills to soften the frosty leader, Beata, Dr Crusher struggles to find the cure to the virus. Both succeed and the *Enterprise* leaves to investigate reported Romulan activity in the Neutral Zone.

Stardate: 41636.9

Strange New Worlds: Angel 1 (a class M planet with carbon-based fauna and flora) which the Federation last visited 62 years before.

Riker notes that on Kabatrus he donned furs to meet the leadership council and on Armus 9 he wore feathers (this doesn't prevent Deanna and Tasha cracking up upon seeing his ludicrous 'toy-boy' costume).

New Life Forms: Worf says Klingons appreciate strong women. Deanna implies that Betazed, like Angel 1, has a matriarchal oligarchy.

Riker's Conquests: Mistress Beata (actually, he is more *her* conquest).

Data's Jokes: On perfume: 'How does stimulation of the olfactory nerves affect the enjoyment of sex?'

Notes: 'Men are not objects to be possessed.' It's that old SF stand-by, 'The Planet of Women,' done, it must be said, pretty well, with a sub-plot involving a 'flu-like virus affecting the *Enterprise*. Good fun, if a little obvious (Beata forcing Riker to give her a good seeing-to is a nice subversion, though).

Geordi commands the ship in the absence of Picard, Riker, Data and Tasha (see also 'The Arsenal of Freedom'). Albeni meditation crystals are a prized gift.

14: '11001001'

US Transmission: 1 February 1988
UK Transmission: 16 January 1991
Writers: Maurice Hurley, Robert Lewin
Director: Paul Lynch
Cast: Carolyn McCormick, Gene Dynarksi, Katy Beyer, Alexandra Johnson, Iva Lane, Kelli Ann McNally, Jack Sheldon, Abdul Salaam el Rezzac, Ron Brown

Arriving at Starbase 74, orbiting Tarsas 3, the *Enterprise*'s computer system is to be upgraded by a race called the Bynars.

Most of the crew leave the ship, but Riker and Picard stay, and experience an extraordinary new holodeck program. This distraction enables the Bynars to take the ship out of dock and head for their home planet leaving the crew helplessly behind. Picard and Riker program the ship to self-destruct to avoid it falling into enemy hands, but on reaching the bridge find the Bynars dying. The aliens wish to use the *Enterprise* memory core as a store for their own master computer which is in danger from a pulse from a supernova. Picard and Riker complete the transfer and revive the aliens.

Stardate: 41365.9

Strange New Worlds: The *Enterprise* has been unexpectedly delayed at Omicron Pascal, and has a pressing engagement at Pelleus 5.

New Life Forms: The Bynars are an androgynous race of symbiotic midget mathematicians who complete each other's sentences and are linked in such a way to their central computer that they think and speak in near-binary. They come from Bynaus in the Beta Magellan system.

Riker's Conquests: Minuet. Pity she's a hologram! ('I'm as real as you need me to be.') Picard's Conquest, too.

Deanna Underused?: Absent without leave yet again.

Dialogue Triumphs: Riker's best line of the season: 'Keep notes, this project could turn out to be of interest to scholars in the future . . . A blind man teaching an android to paint. That's got to be worth a couple of pages in *somebody's* book.'

Notes: 'Gentlemen, if this is what you call enhancement you've got a gift for understatement.' Inventive and with remarkably confident characterisation despite holes in the plot big enough to pilot the *Enterprise* through – would Data really 'forget' to check if Picard and Riker had left the ship?

Worf and Tasha are partners in a sport called Parrises Squares (see 'Future Imperfect', 'Silicon Avatar', 'The First Duty', 'Timescapes'). Tasha notes that Worf is developing a sense of humour. Professor Terence Epstein is a leading Cybernetics expert who lectured at Beverly's medical academy. The *Enterprise* self-destruct requires authorisation from Captain and First Officer only. Riker's chosen holodeck program is a Jazz bar in New Orleans c.1958.

15: 'Too Short a Season'

US Transmission: 8 February 1988
UK Transmission: 5 December 1990
Writers: Michael Michaelian, D.C. Fontana,
from a story by Michael Michaelian
Director: Rob Bowman
Cast: Clayton Rohner, Marsha Hunt, Michael Pataki

Aging Admiral Mark Jameson returns to Mordan 4, where a group of terrorists have kidnapped the Ambassador and his staff. Many years ago Jameson successfully negotiated a similar hostage release on the planet, and he is obsessed by his new mission. The wheelchair-bound Jameson begins to get younger, the result of taking large amounts of an alien regenerative drug. The hostage situation is in fact a ruse to return Jameson to Mordan, where he covertly fuelled forty years of civil war by supplying arms to both sides. Karnas, the planet's leader, wants revenge, but he initially refuses to believe that the young man is actually Jameson. The Admiral manages to convince Karnas shortly before he dies, the result of the overdose of rejuvenating drugs.

Stardate: 41309.5

Strange New Worlds: The *Enterprise* begins the episode in orbit around Persephone 5. Mordan 4 has been at peace for five years. At the end of the story the *Enterprise* heads for Isis 3.

New Life Forms: The people of Cerebus 2 have developed a regenerative drug, although treatment is painful and often fatal. They have supplied Jameson with the drug in gratitude for an unspecified diplomatic success.

Notes: A very wordy and rather dull script, although the issues it deals with are interesting enough. The make-up for the old Admiral is less than convincing, leaving a gaping lack of credibility at the heart of the story.

Jameson suffers from Iverson's disease, which affects the body but not the mind, and has spent the last four years in a wheel-chair. Jameson was last in space on the *Gettysburg*.

16: 'When the Bough Breaks'

US Transmission: 15 February 1988
UK Transmission: 30 January 1991
Writer: Hannah Louise Shearer
Director: Kim Manners
Cast: Jerry Hardin, Brenda Strong, Jandi Swanson,
Paul Lambert, Ivy Bethune, Dierk Torsek, Michele Marsh,
Dan Mason, Philip N. Waller, Connie Danese, Jessica Bova,
Vanessa Bova

The planet Aldea uncloaks itself, and the infertile Aldeans propose an exchange of knowledge in return for the *Enterprise*'s children. Riker refuses, but the children are transported to Aldea anyway. The planet re-cloaks, although Geordi discovers a flaw in the shield. Picard and Beverly enter into new talks with the Aldeans, but the *Enterprise* is knocked three days' travel away. Wesley organises passive resistance amongst the children, and Beverly discovers the cause of the Aldeans' infertility: their planetary shield has weakened the ozone layer. Riker and Data beam down to neutralise the shield, and the Aldeans return the children.

Stardate: 41509.1 (at least 52 hours pass between 41509.1 and 41512.4).

Strange New Worlds: Aldea, cloaked subject of mythology in the Epsilon Mynos system, hidden for millennia. Zadar 4 is a colony with oceans. 'Neinman of Xerxes 7' is a mythical world.

New Life Forms: The pale, infertile, light-sensitive, chromosome-damaged, humanoid Aldeans.

Notes: This is as exciting as creosote.

There seem to be only seven children (including Wesley) on the *Enterprise*. The ship's schools teach basic calculus. Riker adopts a John Wayne limp. Something like a tribble is kept as a pet on board ship. Dolphins survive on Federation planets.

17: 'Home Soil'

US Transmission: 22 February 1988
UK Transmission: 23 January 1991
Writers: Robert Sabaroff,
from a story by Karl Guers, Ralph Sanchez, Robert Sabaroff
Director: Corey Allen
Cast: Walter Gottell, Elizabeth Lindsey, Gerard Prendergast,
Mario Rocuzzo, Carolyne Barry

The *Enterprise* checks the terraforming station on Velara 3, and encounters an apparent murder mystery when engineer Arthur Malencon is killed by a laser drill. While Geordi investigates Data is almost killed by the same drill. They come to a surprising conclusion: the planet is home to inorganic life. A microscopic sample is beamed to a medical lab, where it reproduces, breaks a quarantine field, and communicates with the ship. It is intelligent, and continues to reproduce, angry with the terraformers. Riker realises that it's photosensitive and, when the entity tries to control the ship's computer, he shuts off the lab lights. The alien begs for mercy and is beamed home, Velara 3 being placed under quarantine.

Stardate: 41463.9

Strange New Worlds: Velara 3 in the Pleiades Cluster.

New Life Forms: A tiny intelligent inorganic life form, made of mineral salts, capable of vast energy manipulation.

Riker's Conquests: He tries to pump Luisa Kim for information.

Dialogue Triumphs: The aliens' name for humans: 'Ugly bags of mostly water.'

Notes: Mario Roccuzzo gives a vastly OTT British luvvy performance.

18: 'Coming of Age'

US Transmission: 14 March 1988
UK Transmission: 6 February 1991
Writer: Sandy Fries
Director: Michael Vejar
Cast: Ward Costello, Robert Schenkkan, John Putch, Robert Ito, Stephen Gregory, Tasia Valenza, Estee Chandler, Brendan McKane, Wyatt Knight, Daniel Riordan

While Wesley takes his Starfleet exams on Relva 7, Picard is visited by his old friend Admiral Gregory Quinn. With Quinn is Lt Commander Dexter Remmick, who is ordered to find evidence of wrongdoing on the ship. Meanwhile, Wesley is being tested against the other candidates, including Mordock, a Benzite. Jake Kurland, who failed to become an Academy candidate, steals a shuttle, intending to run away. The shuttle plunges towards the planet, but Picard manages to save Jake. Remmick delivers his report: he can find no failings. Quinn ordered the investigation because he thinks there's something wrong with Starfleet, and he wants Picard to support him by becoming the admiral in charge of the Academy. Wesley meanwhile takes the final test, beating his fear of life or death decisions, but loses his place to his friend Mordock. Picard informs Quinn that he'll stay as captain of the *Enterprise*, and the Admiral leaves, still pondering the conspiracy.

Stardate: 41416.2

Strange New Worlds: Relva 7, a Starfleet exam centre. Beltane 9 is a world where one may sign on to a freighter. Ardron 4 is also mentioned.

New Life Forms: Benzites are blue creatures who breathe with the help of an artificial mouth device (see also 'A Matter of Honor').

Regulian rats are scary. Bulgallian sludge rats and melanoid slime worms are unpleasant. Zaldans are web-fingered humanoids who regard politeness as insincere.

Technology: The matter/antimatter ratio is always 1:1 in starship engines.

Deanna Underused?: She's in one scene.

Future History: The Federation is over two hundred years old (see 'The Outcast').

Notes: This is the first we hear of the alien conspiracy within the Federation, and the story has two plot-lines which compete with each other for maximum dullness. The conspiracy plot wins by being pointless as well as dull.

The Federation Academy is led by its Commandant, an Admiral. The Inspector General's Office conducts internal inquiries. Picard failed his Starfleet entrance exam the first time, but passed on the second attempt. Candidates can always re-apply. Part of the exam is the psyche test, which involves a candidate's deepest fear. Worf's is dependence, especially regarding his life. Wesley will be sixteen next month.

19: 'Heart of Glory'

US Transmission: 21 March 1988
UK Transmission: 27 February 1991
Writers: Maurice Hurley,
from a story by Maurice Hurley, Herbert Wright,
D.C. Fontana
Director: Rob Bowman
Cast: Vaughn Armstrong, Charles H. Hyman, David Froman,
Robert Bauer, Brad Zerbst, Dennis Madalone

Three Klingons are found on a damaged Talarian ship drifting in the Neutral Zone. They claim they were attacked by Ferengi, and are interested in Worf's position on the ship. He joins them in a death ritual when one of them dies of his injuries. They tell Worf what actually happened: they're opposed to the Klingon/Federation truce, and they destroyed a Klingon cruiser sent to apprehend them. Another Klingon ship arrives, demanding that the criminals be handed over. With Worf's help they're imprisoned, but manage to escape, one of them being killed in the process. The last Klingon, Korris, holds the *Enterprise* to ransom by pointing his weapon at the dilithium crystal chamber. After negotiations, Korris forces Worf to kill him, allowing him an honourable death.

Stardate: 41503.7

Strange New Worlds: Klingon outpost MZ5. The Halee system is a dangerous Klingon place. We hear of Starbase 84.

New Life Forms: The Talarians apparently live a long way

34

from the Neutral Zone.

The Klingon death ritual is seen by outsiders for the first time. Klingons howl at the death of a Klingon, a warning to the dead that a Klingon warrior is about to arrive. They do not respect corpses. Klingons use phasers, and carry the Federation symbol in their cruisers. Their homeworld, or culture, is known, by at least some Klingons, as Kling (compare with *DS9*'s 'The House of Quark').

Technology: Starship engines emit deuterium gas. Talarian ships carry Merculite rockets. A phaser aimed into the dilithium crystal chamber could destroy the *Enterprise*. Geordi's VISOR is connected to a visual acuity transmitter in this episode, transmitting pictures back to the ship.

Picard Manoeuvre: A rare two-handed variation after setting speed.

Deanna Underused?: Absent.

Notes: A great episode, but Riker's suggestion to go immediately to saucer separation, and the sudden appearance of a third Klingon on the ship, are very strange.

The Neutral Zone is 24 hours away from Earth for subspace communications. When the Romulans attacked Khitomer, Worf was taken to Gault, a farming colony, by a human. He had a foster brother who also went to the Academy, but failed (see 'Homeworld').

20: 'The Arsenal of Freedom'

US Transmission: 11 April 1988
UK Transmission: 20 February 1991
Writers: Richard Manning, Hans Beimler,
from a story by Maurice Hurley, Robert Lewin
Director: Les Landau
Cast: Vincent Schlavelli, Marco Rodriguez, Vyto Ruginis,

Julia Nickson, George de la Pena

Searching for the missing USS *Drake* in the Lorenze cluster, the *Enterprise* comes across the deserted world Minos, once famed for its arms sales. Riker is greeted by Rice, the *Drake*'s captain, but he realises that the man is a holographic illusion. Killer machines attack the away team: the drones are destroyed, but the next wave proves much more adaptable and quick. Crusher is hurt by a fall into a cavern, and is tended by Picard. Soon the *Enterprise*, commanded by Geordi, is attacked by the automated defences of Minos. Picard discovers that the cave is the control room for the weapons system, and switches it off. Geordi, having ordered saucer separation, is able to destroy the final attacking probe.

Stardate: 41798.2

Strange New Worlds: Minos, destroyed by its ultimate weapon system, the Echo Papa 607. 'We live by the motto: "Peace, through superior fire-power . . ." Remember: the early bird that hesitates, gets wormed.'

New Life Forms: The Minosians were notorious for selling arms to both sides in the Ersalope wars.

Dialogue Triumphs: Riker: 'No, the name of my ship is the *Lollipop* . . . It's just been commissioned, it's a good ship.'

Picard: 'Mr La Forge, when I left this ship it was in one piece. I would appreciate your returning it to me in the same condition.'

Notes: A story that hits its audience with a mallet in order to make a simple point (that weapons are bad news). A coach and horses can be driven through the holes in the plot: how can a civilisation be destroyed by a weapons system that can be shut down so easily? Why doesn't the machine that attacks the *Enterprise* also withdraw? Still, the beaming down of most of the *Enterprise*'s executive officers does give Geordi room to develop.

Riker was at the Academy with Paul Rice, who accepted command of the *Drake* after Riker turned it down to join the *Enterprise* (see 'The Pegasus'). Beverly Crusher's grandmother helped to colonise Arvada 3, the site of an unspecified tragedy, and cared for the colonists after regular medical supplies ran out (see 'Sub Rosa'). In this story the *Enterprise*'s chief engineer is Mr Logan.

21: 'Symbiosis'

US Transmission: 18 April 1988
UK Transmission: 13 February 1991
Writers: Robert Lewin, Richard Manning, Hans Beimler,
from a story by Robert Lewin
Director: Win Phelps
Cast: Judson Scott, Merritt[1] Butrick, Richard Lineback,
Kimberly Farr

The *Enterprise* picks up a distress call from the freighter *Sanction*. The freighter crew are more concerned by the fate of their cargo of the drug felicium than the threat to their own lives. Felicium – a substance refined from plants that only grow on Brekka – is the cure for a plague that is rife on the neighbouring planet of Ornara. The Ornaran and Brekkian survivors argue over who owns the cargo, but Crusher's analysis reveals that felicium is also a narcotic. The Ornarans are now immune to the plague but experience terrible withdrawal symptoms when deprived of felicium, a position the Brekkians have cynically exploited for almost 200 years. Picard, constrained by the Prime Directive, refuses to tell the Ornarans the truth – but also refuses to mend their freighters. After a painful period without felicium the Ornarans will eventually come to realise that they don't

[1] The actor's name is incorrectly spelt Merrit on screen.

need the drug.

Stardate: Not stated.

Strange New Worlds: Ornara and Brekka are in the Delos system.

New Life Forms: The Ornarans were on the verge of discovering space travel when they became infected by the plague. The Brekkians were less technologically advanced. Both peoples appear able to discharge electricity from their bodies at will.

Notes: Another tale that falls into the old *Star Trek* trap of confusing preached messages (Tasha on drugs, Picard on non-involvement) with strong drama. Thankfully, the ending is largely unresolved to give a hint of ambiguity to a very straight-forward episode.

Drugs and poverty are huge problems on Yar's planet (see 'Legacy').

22: 'Skin of Evil'

US Transmission: 25 April 1988
UK Transmission: 6 March 1991
Writers: Joseph Stefano, Hannah Louise Shearer,
from a story by Joseph Stefano
Director: Joseph L. Scanlan
Cast: Mart McChesney, Ron Gans, Walker Boone,
Brad Zerbst, Raymond Forchion

A shuttle containing Troi crashes on a planet, and the away team sent to investigate are prevented from approaching the wreckage by Armus, a huge, dark creature of limitless evil. Without any motive it kills Yar and sucks Riker into its tar-like body. On the *Enterprise* Wesley discovers fluctuations in the creature's powers, and the away team are eventually beamed back, leaving Armus alone once again. The crew are comforted by a holographic message that Yar recorded before her death.

Stardate: 41601.3

Strange New Worlds: Vagra 2, an uninhabited world in the Zed Lapis sector, where Deanna's shuttle crashes.

New Life Forms: Armus, the evil 'skin' of a civilisation of 'Titans', 'creatures whose beauty now dazzles all who see them'.

Deanna Underused?: She's in shuttle 13, returning from a conference. Marina Sirtis revels in a larger-than-usual role.

Dialogue Triumphs: Yar's holographic farewell: 'My friend Data, you see things with the wonder of a child, and that makes you more human than any of us.'

Notes: The memorable 'Tasha dies' episode is really rather good. Armus is intermittently convincing and grotesque, the imagery as Riker is swallowed-up proving especially disturbing. When Tasha's death comes it's as sickeningly arbitrary as death in the real world, leaving no time for a soliloquy or banal philosophising. When it comes, however, Tasha's farewell is excellent.

Yar asks Worf to help her with the Mishiama wristlock and break prior to a martial arts competition on the *Enterprise* in three days time. Worf is made acting chief of security on Natasha Yar's death.

Picard quotes from Shelley's *Prometheus Unbound* ('a great poet'): 'All spirits are enslaved that serve things evil.'

23: 'We'll Always Have Paris'

US Transmission: 2 May 1988
UK Transmission: 13 March 1991
Writers: Deborah Dean Davis, Hannah Louise Shearer
Director: Robert Becker

Cast: Michelle Phillips, Rod Loomis, Isabel Lorca, Dan Kern, Jean-Paul Vignon, Kelly Ashmore, Lance Spellerberg

Investigating a time-loop, the *Enterprise* rescues Jenice, an old flame of Picard's he never thought he'd see again, and her husband, Dr Paul Manheim. Manheim's experiments have caused the time disturbance and now threaten to rip open the very fabric of space. The scientist himself is dying, his body unable to cope with his experience of alternative dimensions, but Data is able to seal the space-time breach. Manheim is cured, and Picard is able to say farewell to Jenice – in a Paris created on the holodeck.

Stardate: 41697.9

Strange New Worlds: A research station on Vandor 4, a planet circling a B-class giant and a pulsar. The *Enterprise* is on its way to Sarona 8 for some shore leave. The Blue Parrot Café on Sarona 8 serves exotic blue drinks. Coltar 4, in the Ilecom system, is a farming colony which felt the effects of Manheim's experiments. Manheim's lab was alleged to be in the Pegos Minor system.

Picard Manoeuvre: As an expression of embarrassment after saying goodbye to Jenice.

Future History: The rules for Fencing have changed (most notably that fencers are allowed to change direction on the piste).

Notes: Stewart acts his socks off, but the *Casablanca* atmosphere is somewhat lacking.

Picard left Paris 22 years ago. He had a relationship with Jenice, but left her abruptly for Starfleet (certain details given here, including the timescale, do not quite tie in with information given in later stories, notably 'Family' and 'Tapestry'). He is an accomplished sabre fencer, although in the bout we see he is forced to make a 'desperate' *Prise de Fer* (envelopment) more usually associated with foil and épée. The transporter chief is Mr Herbert.

24: 'Conspiracy'

US Transmission: 9 May 1988
UK Transmission: 20 March 1991
Writers: Tracy Tormé,
from a story by Robert Sabaroff
Director: Cliff Bole
Cast: Henry Darrow, Ward Costello, Robert Schenkkan,
Ray Reinhardt, Jonathan Farwell, Michael Berryman,
Ursaline Bryant

A covert meeting is called by Captain Walker Keel, which Picard attends. Accidental deaths, changes in key personnel and mysterious orders lead to the suspicion amongst several captains that Starfleet has become the victim of a conspiracy. When Keel's ship is destroyed, Picard decides to return to Starfleet Command and put his suspicions to the test. Starfleet has, indeed, been infiltrated by a parasitic alien race. Picard walks into a trap, but Riker comes to his aid and together they eliminate the alien threat.

Stardate: 41775.5

Strange New Worlds: Dytallix B (one of seven uninhabited planets mined for the Federation by the Dytallix Mining Corporation), the fifth of six planets orbiting the red giant Mira. The *Enterprise* is *en route* to the ocean planet of Pacifica.

New Life Forms: The (nameless) insect parasites. Said to have been discovered by a survey team in a distant part of the galaxy, they attach themselves to the spinal column of the host body, breathing through a small gill in the neck.

Data's Jokes: Geordi tells Data a (seemingly risqué) joke with the punchline 'Now just try doing that in hyperspace'. Data analyses the joke and decides (straight-faced) that it is 'hilarious'.

Notes: 'Something is beginning. Don't trust anyone . . .' A semi-sequel to 'Coming of Age' – the Starfleet conspiracy being alien-influenced – and indebted to *Alien*, this dark and nefarious episode was hacked to pieces by the censors on transmission in Britain (notably scenes involving the mother alien).

Code 47 is a Starfleet emergency channel, 'Captain's Eyes Only'. Walker Keel, captain of the SS *Horatio*, is one of Picard's two most trusted friends (the other being Jack Crusher, whom Keel introduced to Beverly). Keel and Picard first met on Tau Ceti 3. Tryla Scott made captain faster than anybody in Starfleet (it is implied she broke a record set by Picard). The three most senior Starfleet officers involved in the conspiracy are Earth Admirals Quinn and Aaron, and Vulcan Admiral Savar. Commander Remmick is the host body for the mother parasite.

25: 'The Neutral Zone'

US Transmission: 16 May 1988
UK Transmission: 27 March 1991
Writers: Maurice Hurley,
from a television story by Maurice Hurley,
from a story by Deborah McIntyre, Mona Glee
Director: James L. Conway
Cast: Marc Alaimo, Anthony James, Leon Rippy,
Gracie Harrison, Peter Mark Richman

Data and Worf discover an ancient capsule, containing cryogenically frozen humans from the 20th century. Meanwhile, two Federation outposts in sector three-zero have been destroyed, so the *Enterprise* heads for the Neutral Zone. As Data and Troi deal with the revived humans and their problems in adjusting to life in the 24th century, Picard has the first human contact with the Romulans in over fifty years. Mutual concerns over the destruction of outposts on both sides lead to a tentative agreement on the pooling of information.

Stardate: 41986.0 (Data tells Ralph Offenhouse that the date is 2364 by the old calendar).

Deanna Underused?: 'The local shrink?' Actually, no, her assessment of the Romulans proves to be spot-on, and she helps Claire Raymond find her descendants.

Data's Jokes: 'Occupation: Homemaker. Must be some kind of construction work.'

Dialogue Triumphs: Picard: 'A lot has changed in the past 300 years. People are no longer obsessed with the acquisition of 'things'. We have eliminated hunger, want, the need for possessions. We've grown out of our infancy.'

Tebok on Worf: 'Silence your dog, Captain.'

'Data, they were already dead; what more could have happened to them?!'

Future History: The 'sleepers' were frozen 'about 370 years ago' (the 1990s seemingly). Cryogenics was a 'fad' in this era, although it didn't progress far into the 21st century. Similarly, television as an entertainment doesn't last much beyond 2040.

Notes: 'I think our lives just became a lot more complicated.' A game of two halves. The stuff with the sleepers is speed-written fan-fiction tat (three cypher examples of 20th century humanity wake up in the *Star Trek* universe, something done to death in the fanzines). However, the other aspect (the return of the Romulans) is marvellous.

Three pages into Claire Raymond's descendents are the names William Hartnell, Patrick Troughton, Jon Pertwee, Tom Baker, Peter Davison and Colin Baker.

The Romulans are 'intensely curious', fascinated by humans, although their belief in their own superiority is total. There has been no direct contact with the Romulans in 53 years, since the 'Tomed incident'. Geordi says this 'cost thousands of lives'. Worf hates the Romulans who killed his parents in an attack on Khitomer when they were supposed to be the Klingons' allies.

He thinks the Romulans are 'without honour'. There has been no contact with Starbases in sector three-one since Stardate 41903.2. The destruction of the Romulan and Federation colonies by unknown forces is the first reference to the Borg (see 'Q Who').

Second Season

22 45-minute episodes

Created by Gene Roddenberry

Executive Producer: Gene Roddenberry
Co-Executive Producers: Rick Berman, Maurice Hurley
Producers: Burton Armus (26–38), Mike Gray (26–38), John Mason (26–38), Robert L. McCullough (38–47)
Associate Producer: Peter Lauritson **Line Producer:** David Livingston **Executive Script Consultants:** Hans Beimler (40–47), Richard Manning (40–47) **Story Editors:** Leonard Mlodinow (29–37), Scott Rubenstein (29–37), Melinda M. Snodgrass (34–47) **Creative Consultant:** Tracy Tormé

Regular Cast: Patrick Stewart (Captain Jean-Luc Picard), Jonathan Frakes (Commander William Riker), LeVar Burton (Lt Geordi La Forge), Michael Dorn (Lt Worf), Marina Sirtis (Counselor Deanna Troi), Brent Spiner (Lt Commander Data), Wil Wheaton (Wesley Crusher), Diana Muldaur (Dr Pulaski, 26–32, 34–47), Colm Meaney (Transporter Chief O'Brien, 26–27[1], 30, 32–41, 43–45, 47), Whoopi Goldberg (Guinan, 26, 29, 34-35, 41, 47 (flashback only)), John de Lancie (Q, 41), Majel Barrett (Lwaxana Troi, 44), Gates McFadden (Dr Beverly Crusher, 47 (flashback only)), Denise Crosby (Tasha Yar, 47 (flashback only))

---

[1]Credited as Transporter Chief for these episodes.

26: 'The Child'

US Transmission: 21 November 1988
UK Transmission: 3 April 1991
Writers: Jaron Summers, Jon Povill, Maurice Hurley
Director: Rob Bowman
Cast: Seymour Cassel, R.J. Williams, Dawn Amemann, Zachary Benjamin, Dore Keller

The *Enterprise* is on an errand of mercy, carrying samples of a plasma plague, when Deanna seems to become history's second case of virgin birth. Her 'child' develops at a remarkable rate, growing a number of years in mere hours. At the same time one of the plague samples begins to mutate: if it breaks out of its containment field, it will infect the entire crew. Deanna's 'child' reveals itself to be a benign life force which wished to know more about mankind. Understanding that it is having a dangerous effect on the ship, it leaves.

Stardate: 42073.1

Strange New Worlds: Audet 9 and Epsilon Indi are mentioned. An outbreak of an unclassified plasma plague occurs in the Rachelis system.

New Life Forms: Deanna's child, 'a life force entity' largely composed of Eichner radiation. The (normal!) Betazoid gestation period is ten months.

Introducing: Dr Katherine (Kate) Pulaski, Crusher's replacement as ship's medical officer.
Guinan, alien hostess of the Ten-Forward lounge bar.

Technobabble: How can a 'life force entity' effect the growth of a virus on another part of the ship?

Riker's Conquests: Trying it on with Deanna two minutes after she's given birth is remarkable even by Will's standards.

Data's Jokes: Dr Pulaski's mispronunciation of his name is the episode's running gag.

Dialogue Triumphs: Pulaski, on Data's offer to help during the birth: 'Counselor Troi is going to need the human touch, not the cold hand of technology!'

Notes: 'I don't mean to be indelicate, but who's the father?' The kind of episode that makes the viewer think 'What the hell was *that* all about?' Not even Marina Sirtis' genuinely appealing performance and the sensational Guinan/Wesley scenes can save this. Drivel of the highest order.

Geordi has been promoted to chief engineer. Beverly has become head of Starfleet Medical. Wesley is due to join her but elects to stay on the *Enterprise*.

Deanna names her son after her father, Ian Andrew. According to Wesley, people say that Guinan is very old, that she's from Novocron, and that she knew Captain Picard on the *Stargazer* (she says this last piece of information is incorrect).

27: 'Where Silence Has Lease'

US Transmission: 28 November 1988
UK Transmission: 10 April 1991
Writer: Jack B. Sowards
Director: Winrich Kolbe
Cast: Earl Boam, Charles Douglass

On their way to the Morgana Quadrant, the *Enterprise* investigates a strange 'void in space'. Phantom images confuse the crew, until they realise they have become trapped like rats in a maze. The intelligence behind the trap, Nagilum, reveals itself, and explains that it wishes to understand more about human reactions to death. For this purpose it will require half of the crew to die in order to satisfy its curiosity. Picard and Riker set the ship to autodestruct, but with mere seconds to spare the entity releases the ship, saying it has learned enough.

Stardate: 42193.6

New Life Forms: Nagilum, a mega-powerful entity who wants to understand death by killing half the crew.

Technobabble: 'Our sensors are showing this to be the absence of everything. It is a void without matter or energy of any kind.' What??! As Picard notes, 'Hardly a scientific answer, Commander!'

Deanna Underused?: No, but the writer seems unwilling to give her and Pulaski lines in the same scene.

Data's Jokes: Pulaski continues to refer to Data as 'it'.

Dialogue Triumphs: 'Beyond this place there be dragons.' 'We should be seeing stars by now.'

Notes: 'Whatever it is, we seem to be inside it.' Very odd indeed. An episode of no great originality (*everybody's* done the 'throbbing-black-mass-in-space' plot before), but packed with many great little moments (Picard's discussion with Data on death, Geordi's reaction to the destruction of the phantom Romulan ship). The pre-title sequence (Riker and Worf in a holodeck nightmare) has nothing to do with the plot, but is fabulous anyway. The story is more ambitious than its lowly reputation suggests.

The *Enterprise* is in the unexplored Morgana Quadrant. Her sister ship is the *Yamato* (NCC 1305-E, see 'Contagion'). All Federation ships have walls made of tritanium. Worf indulges in holodeck calisthenics every day. He recalls an ancient Klingon legend concerning a gigantic space creature.

The O'Brien character still isn't named, but we know he's a lieutenant.

Picard listens to Eric Satie's *Trios Gymnopédies* (First Movement) as he awaits the ship's self-destruct.

28: 'Elementary, Dear Data'

US Transmission: 5 December 1988
UK Transmission: 10 April 1991
Writer: Brian Alan Lane
Director: Rob Bowman
Cast: Daniel Davis, Alan Shearman, Biff Manard, Diz White,
Anne Elizabeth Ramsay, Richard Merson

Data and Geordi play Holmes and Watson in the holodeck, but Geordi is annoyed that Data only goes through the motions of solving a mystery, knowing already the outcome of the stories. Pulaski is tempted into joining in when Geordi programmes in an original Holmes mystery, betting that it will be beyond Data, but it's nothing more than a feeble combination of old stories. Geordi tells the computer to create an adversary capable of beating Data, and a power surge occurs. Professor Moriarty appears, and abducts Pulaski. Data and Geordi find his hiding place, and discover that he's worked out the plans of the *Enterprise*. They leave the holodeck, but can't shut it off. The computer has given the villain consciousness, and he gains some control over the ship. Picard enters the holodeck and negotiates. Moriarty only wants continued existence outside of the holodeck, but Picard can't help, although he recognises that Moriarty has departed from his evil characterisation. He offers to save the program and work to recreate him. Moriarty agrees, and frees the ship.

Stardate: 42286.3

New Life Forms: Moriarty, an existentialist construct created by the holodeck.

Technology: The holodeck can write new stories in a particular style, and, as it turns out, create life! There's a mortality failsafe to stop people getting killed. The holodeck works on a similar basis to the transporter, being able to create solid matter.

Riker's Conquests: No, it's Pulaski's turn for a bit of crumpet.

Deanna Underused?: She gets one line.

Dialogue Triumphs: 'Merde' again.
 Pulaski to Moriarty: 'Lumps, Professor? What sort of lumps?'

Notes: Lestrade's English accent is a hoot, but Geordi prefers to impersonate James Mason. Data's research on Holmes fails to include the apocryphal nature of the deerstalker. Once we get past the holodeck's incredible ability to create consciousness, this is a great piece of real SF, a bit of a first for *ST:TNG*, meditating as it does on the nature of consciousness and free will, and with an unexpectedly humane Moriarty. It's a pity the character gets changed for 'Ship in a Bottle.'

Geordi served with Captain Zambada as an ensign. He's now captain of the USS *Victory*. Geordi's Starfleet speciality is anti-matter power and dilithium regulators.

29: 'The Outrageous Okona'

US Transmission: 12 December 1988
UK Transmission: 24 April 1991
Writers: Burton Armus,
from a story by Les Menchen, Lance Dickson,
David Landsberg
Director: Robert Becker
Cast: William O. Campbell, Joe Piscopo, Douglas Rowe,
Albert Stratton, Rosalind Ingledew, Kieran Mulroney

The *Enterprise* rescues Captain Okona and his faulty ship. He charms and romances the crew, befriending Data, who consults Guinan and a 20th century holodeck comedian on the nature of humour. Meanwhile, two small, harmless ships arrive from different planets, both wanting custody of Okona. One leader claims that Okona has made his daughter, Yanar, pregnant; the other that he stole a priceless jewel. Okona maintains his innocence, but refuses to elaborate. Wesley persuades him not to run off, and Okona opts to marry Yanar. However, the other leader's son, Benzan, objects: it turns out that Benzan gave his father's jewel to Okona to pass on to Yanar, who he loves. Benzan is the father of the child. The aliens leave, almost reconciled. Data performs to a holodeck audience, but realises that they're programmed to laugh. Feeling that he's failed, he's surprised when everyone laughs at his accidental joke.

Stardate: 42402.7

Strange New Worlds: The Omega Sagitta system, where the twin worlds coalition of Madena (Altec and Straleb) was colonised two hundred years ago.

New Life Forms: The glob fly is a Klingon buzzing insect, about half the size of a mosquito. It doesn't have a sting.

Technology: The bridge's main viewer can connect three ships at once in conference mode.

Riker's Conquests: Riker rolls his eyes at Okona a lot, like he wouldn't get up to that sort of thing himself.

Data's Jokes: Data's Jerry Lewis and Groucho Marx are the only funny things on display here. 'A monk, a clone and a Ferengi decide to go bowling together . . .'

Future History: 23rd century comedian Stano Riga told quantum maths jokes.

Notes: A horribly unfunny episode, with a sort of self-conscious roguery which becomes utter gittishness within five minutes. Is that 'You're a droid . . .' line supposed to be funny?

Data can't get cold, hot or drunk (with alcohol: see 'The Naked Now'). Regulations call for a yellow alert even when the *Enterprise* is attacked by lasers (which can't even penetrate the navigation shields).

30: 'Loud as a Whisper'

US Transmission: 9 January 1989
UK Transmission: 1 May 1991
Writer: Jacqueline Zambrano
Director: Larry Shaw
Cast: Howie Seago, Marnie Mosiman, Thomas Oglesby,
Leo Damian, Richard Lavin, Chip Heller, John Garrett

The *Enterprise* crew take deaf negotiator Riva, who communicates through his three-person 'chorus', to Solais 5, where two warring factions are seeking an end to hostilities. Riva arranges an initial meeting, but one of the delegates kills Riva's chorus, and the fighting resumes. Troi eventually persuades Riva not to give up, and Riva asks to be left alone on the planet with the two factions. Their attempts to learn his sign language will also be their first communication with each other.

Stardate: 42477.2

Strange New Worlds: Ramatis 3 (home of Riva), Solais 5 (home of the two factions of Solari, at war for 1500 years). The *Enterprise* has just left the Lima Sierra system, a three-planet system where one planet has a very odd orbit.

New Life Forms: The Solari, primitive humanoids with gnarled faces. Riva's three person 'chorus', each individual interpreting an aspect of his personality.

The leaders of Fendaus 5 are limbless. Stomps are blind. The Leyrons of Malkus 9 developed written language before gestural.

Introducing: Transporter Chief O'Brien: the Irishman is given a name at last.

Deanna Underused?: For once, no. Picard tells her: 'Thank you. Well done.'

Dialogue Triumphs: Picard's memorable shout to Riva: 'You are not alone, do you understand?'

Notes: Dull as something very dull indeed. And what's all that stuff with the planetary hologram at the start about?

Riva negotiated several Klingon/Federation treaties. Before his involvement the Klingons had no word for 'peacemaker'. He has never failed an assignment. M9 is a kind of sign language.

Optic nerve regeneration is possible (Pulaski's done it twice). Geordi is in constant pain, but he doesn't resent the VISOR or his blindness.

31: 'The Schizoid Man'

US Transmission: 23 January 1989
UK Transmission: 8 May 1991
Writers: Tracy Tormé,
from a story by Richard Manning, Hans Beimler
Director: Les Landau
Cast: W. Morgan Sheppard, Suzie Plakson,
Barbara Alyn Woods

Coming to the aid of the brilliant scientist Ira Graves, who is dying, Data befriends the man. Graves taught Noonian Soong everything he knew, and claims to have found a way to cheat death by transferring his consciousness into a computer. Graves' companion, Kareen, is evacuated when the scientist dies in Data's arms. Data begins to behave strangely, showing jealousy towards Picard when he is kind to Kareen. Troi examines the android and reports that there are two different personas in Data's mind – and the emotional one is becoming stronger. Data tells Kareen that he is now Graves, and that he loves her, but she spurns his offer of a similar existence as an android. He accidentally hurts her and attacks Picard. Guilt-stricken,

'Graves' downloads himself into the ship's computer, leaving his knowledge, but not his persona, intact. Data recovers.

Stardate: 42437.5

Strange New Worlds: Gravesworld, Starbase 6.

New Life Forms: Rigelian oxen are notoriously healthy.

Picard Manoeuvre: When sitting beside Data.

Data's Jokes: 'A fine, full, dignified beard . . .'

Notes: Dull and obvious, but creepy in places.

Ira Graves, the greatest human mind in the universe, studied molecular cybernetics. Darnay's disease affects the brain and nervous system, and is terminal. The USS *Constantinople* is a transport ship used to ferry colonists, carrying 2012 of them. Bodies are sent into space in coffins. Before qualifying from the Academy, Starfleet personnel have to pass a psychotronic stability exam (see 'Coming of Age').

32: 'Unnatural Selection'

US Transmission: 30 January 1989
UK Transmission: 15 May 1991
Writers: John Mason, Mike Gray
Director: Paul Lynch
Cast: Patricia Smith, J. Patrick McNamara, Scott Trost

The *Enterprise* is heading for Star Station *India* to liaise with a medical courier when it picks up a faint distress signal from the USS *Lantree* in the adjacent sector. The ship is discovered, its entire crew having died of old age. The *Lantree*'s last port of call, the Darwin Genetic Research Centre, is also stricken with an aging disease. The crew are desperate to save their genetically-engineered 'children', and Pulaski volunteers to examine a child to ascertain if they carry the virus. Pulaski begins to age, and quarantines herself on Darwin station, but is eventually cured by the *Enterprise*'s transporter biofilter, which rids her DNA of the disease. The children, however, must remain in isolation for ever.

Stardate: 42494.8

Strange New Worlds: The Darwin Genetic Research Centre is on Gagarin 4.

New Life Forms: The children are physically and mentally very advanced for their age, and are capable of telepathy and telekinesis. A side-effect of the children's active immune system is that antibodies released to fight the Thelusian 'flu have affected the DNA of their parents, leading to accelerated aging.

Technobabble: 'Well, I'll have to get into the biofilter bus and patch in a molecular matrix reader . . . But the waveform modulator will be overloaded without the regeneration limiter in the first stage circuit.'

Dialogue Triumphs: Picard to Pulaski: 'God knows, I'm not one to discourage input, but I would appreciate it if you would let me finish my sentences once in a while.'

Data does a medical check on Pulaski: 'All systems are functioning within normal specifications, doctor.' 'The manufacturer will be pleased to hear it.'

Notes: 'The quarantine of the Darwin station must be maintained for ever.' A rather enjoyable story, nearly ruined by a nasty justification of scientific experimentation at the end (Pulaski's voice-over implies that the crew of the *Lantree* were sacrificed to the cause of scientific advancement when they were in fact accidental victims of experiments with a dubious ethical premise). Rather oddly, this feels like *another* story to introduce the Pulaski character.

The *Lantree* is a class 6 Federation supply ship assigned to sector Gamma 7, captained by L. Isao Telaka. Its normal complement is 26 officers and crew, and the ship carries class three defensive armaments. The emergency access code Picard uses to enable the *Enterprise* to operate another ship remotely is 'omicron omicron alpha yellow daystar 27'.

Thelusian 'flu is an 'exotic but harmless renal virus'. Dr Katherine Pulaski is the author of *Linear Models of Viral Propagation*, a standard work. She has not used the *Enterprise* transporter before, and is frightened of molecular disintegration (cf. Reg Barclay's concerns in 'Realm of Fear'). Her last ship was the USS *Repulse*. It is stated that when the transporter is used a trace of the person is stored.

33: 'A Matter of Honor'

US Transmission: 6 February 1989
UK Transmission: 22 May 1991
Writers: Burton Armus,
from a story by Wanda M. Haight, Gregory Amos,
Burton Armus
Director: Rob Bowman
Cast: John Putch, Christopher Collins, Brian Thompson,
Peter Parros, Laura Drake

With the Federation exchange programme in full-swing, Riker volunteers to be the first Federation officer to serve on a Klingon ship. Mendon, a young Benzite ensign, joins the *Enterprise*, and reports the presence of a dangerous bacteria on the *Enterprise*'s hull – but only after a delay that nearly destroys the ship. A similar bacteria on the Klingon ship *Pagh* leads to Riker being branded a traitor by Kargan, its captain. However, Will tricks Kargan into teleporting on to the *Enterprise*, and then assumes command, proving his dedication to the Klingons by ordering the Federation ship to surrender. Mendon redeems himself by finding a way of destroying the bacteria.

Stardate: 42506.5

Strange New Worlds: The *Pagh* is on undesignated manoeuvres within the Pheben system. Tranome Sar was the site of a battle between the Romulans and the Klingons.

New Life Forms: The sub-micron bacteria that attacks the molecular bonds of the *Enterprise* hull's tritanium plating can be destroyed by a tunnelling neutrino beam.

Wes mistakes Mendon for Mordoc (see 'Coming of Age'), but Mendon explains that Benzites from the same geostructure look alike. Eagerness to please is described as being a Benzite trait, and they are very methodical.

The hierarchy on a Klingon ship works by (for example) a first officer assassinating a weak captain. Klingon delicacies include pipius claw, heart of targ (see 'Where No One Has Gone Before'), gagh (serpent worms, best served live: see 'Unification'), bregit lung and rokeg blood pie (see 'Family').

Riker's Conquests: He makes a joke which implies he'd be happy to bed Klingon women.

Deanna Underused?: She's AWOL.

Dialogue Triumphs: '*Enterprise*, this is Captain William Riker of the Klingon vessel *Pagh*. I order you to lower your shields and surrender.'

Notes: 'There will be a briefing and indoctrination session in 15 minutes.' A great little story, built around a credible premise, although the conclusion is a bit convenient (the Klingon captain holding on to Riker's device without question and being transported on to the *Enterprise*). Riker as a Klingon captain is way cool.

Ensign Mendon is picked up at Starbase 179. The phaser range is seen for the first time (see also 'Redemption'). The second officer on the *Pagh* is Klag.

34: 'The Measure of a Man'

US Transmission: 13 February 1989
UK Transmission: 29 May 1991
Writer: Melinda M. Snodgrass
Director: Robert Scheerer
Cast: Amanda McBroom, Clyde Kusatsu, Brian Brophy

Commander Bruce Maddox's plan to disassemble Data leads to the android resigning from Starfleet. However, Maddox claims that Data is not sentient and, therefore, Starfleet property. Picard protests, and wants a new legal precedent to be established. Overseeing the case is Captain Philipa Louvois, whom Picard has not seen for ten years. Her role as prosecutor at the *Stargazer* court-martial ended their relationship. Riker is ordered to act as prosecutor to the very best of his ability, and to the first officer's immense regret he seems to prove that Data is no more than a machine. Picard is on the verge of accepting defeat when Guinan suggests that numerous androids like Data, denied their freedom and legal rights, would be no more than slaves, and the captain is able to convince Louvois that Maddox's proposals are immoral.

Stardate: 42523.7

Strange New Worlds: The *Enterprise* is docked at the newly established Starbase 173 near the Neutral Zone.

Technobabble: 'Have you determined how the electron resistance across the neural filaments is to be resolved?'

Poker Game: The first seen, involving Pulaski, Geordi, Data, O'Brien and Riker (initial dealer). O'Brien says that his luck is lousy unless he sits to the right of the dealer. They play five-card stud, nothing wild, and Data loses because he doesn't understand bluffing. Pulaski deals, playing seven-card high-low with a bye on the last card and 'the man with the axe takes all'.

Dialogue Triumphs: Louvois to Picard: 'It brings a sense of order and stability to my universe to know that you're still a pompous ass.'

Picard: 'Your honour, Starfleet was founded to seek out new life. Well – there it sits!'

Notes: 'I am going to disassemble Data.' A well-crafted story that cleverly uses Guinan to twist the theme into an examination of black slavery in the Americas.

A court-martial is standard procedure when any Starfleet ship is lost. Although subsequently forced out of Starfleet after the *Stargazer* inquest, Louvois later rejoined as an officer of the Judge Advocate General. It is stated that there have been *Enterprise*s around for 500 years, each one becoming a legend. Riker's access code is theta alpha 2 737 blue.

Maddox evaluated Data when he first applied to Starfleet Academy, and he was the sole committee member to oppose Data's entry, on the grounds that Data is not a sentient being. He holds the assistant chair of robotics at the Daystrom Institute. The android has received the Starfleet Command Decoration for Valour and Gallantry, a Medal of Honour, with clusters, the Legion of Honour, and the Star Cross. His ultimate storage capacity is 800 quadrillion bits, and his 'mental' speed is rated at 60 trillion operations per second. Data has a small hologramatic 'statue' of Yar (presumably her goodbye message from 'Skin of Evil'). He packs this, along with his medals and a book from Picard, when he is preparing to leave the *Enterprise*. Worf's farewell present to Data is a copy of *The Dream of the Fire* by K'Ratak (Worf believes that it was the Klingons who gave the novel its stature, but Pulaski disagrees). The Acts of Cumberland, passed in the early 21st century, would seem to indicate that Data is the property of Starfleet. Webster's 24th-century dictionary, fifth edition, describes an android as 'an automaton, made to resemble a human being'. Data of course doesn't hold a grudge, and later corresponds with Maddox (see 'Data's Day').

35: 'The Dauphin'

US Transmission: 20 February 1989
UK Transmission: 5 June 1991
Writers: Scott Rubenstein, Leonard Mlodinow
Director: Rob Bowman
Cast: Paddi Edwards, Jamie Hubbard, Peter Neptune,
Mädchen Amick, Cindy Sorenson, Jennifer Barlow

The *Enterprise*'s mission is to deliver Salia, the young heir of Daled 4, but this is complicated by her sour guardian, Anya, and by the girl's attraction to Wesley Crusher. To avoid an incident, Picard orders Wesley to avoid Salia, but the boy finds himself unable to stay away from her. Then Wesley discovers that Salia and Anya are both shape-shifting allasomorphs. Wesley initially feels betrayed by Salia, but the pair remain friends as she leaves for her planet.

Stardate: 42568.8

Strange New Worlds: Klavdia 3, an inhospitable world housing a research establishment where Salia has been studying for sixteen years. Rousseau 5, famous for its singing neutronic clouds.

New Life Forms: The allasomorphs, a race listed in the Galactic Zoological Catalogue as shape-shifters. Whether all of the inhabitants of Daled 4, a planet with a centuries-old civil war and two cultures 'as different as day and night', are allasomorphs is never made clear.

Technobabble: Geordi is making adjustments to the 'deuterium control conduit'.

Riker's Conquests: Guinan, but they're only teaching Wesley how to pick up girls.

Notes: 'I don't know if she'll have time for you, Wes. She's destined to rule an entire planet.' Pretty insubstantial, although it does include a priceless moment as Worf demonstrates the Klingon female's mating scream. (They also throw things at their intended mate. The men read love poetry . . . and duck a lot!) Also includes the series' funniest acting credit: Cindy Sorenson playing 'furry animal'.

Wesley likes Talian chocolate mousse (from Thalos 7).

36: 'Contagion'

US Transmission: 20 March 1989
UK Transmission: 12 June 1991
Writers: Steve Gerber, Beth Woods
Director: Joseph L. Scanlan
Cast: Thalamus Rasulala, Carolyn Seymour, Dana Sparks, Folkert Schmidt

Answering a distress call from her sister ship, the *Enterprise* arrives to see the *Yamato* destroyed. The ship's log reveals that the *Yamato*'s captain had discovered the mythical planet of Iconia. The Iconians were a powerful ancient race and the presence of Romulans fuels suspicions that they are keen to find Iconian weapons. The computer virus that destroyed the *Yamato* also seems to affect the *Enterprise*. On Iconia, Picard finds a time gateway, which he decides to destroy to prevent it falling into Romulan hands. As Data rewrites the *Enterprise* programs, Picard uses the gateway one last time, but ends up on the Romulans' ship. Fortunately, the *Enterprise* transporters are operational again and he is hurriedly beamed back on board.

Stardate: 42609.1

New Life Forms: The Iconians, a mythical race of empire-builders. Thought to be have been warlike, 'demons of air and darkness', Picard discovers that the reality may have been somewhat different. Their language influenced Dinasian, Dewan and

Iccobar vocabulary.

Data's Jokes: Having 'died' and then recovered, his bewildered 'May I help?' is one of the highlights of the episode.

Dialogue Triumphs: Riker on luck: 'Fate protects fools, little children, and ships called *Enterprise!*'

Notes: 'Time is the one thing we do not have in abundance.' Heavily influenced by the original series episode 'The City on the Edge of Forever', but still rather good with lots of clever dialogue. The Romulans are a bit wasted, however. Picard's 'Not today I think' as he is transported out of an execution contains just the right degree of self-mockery.

The *Yamato*'s captain, Donald Varley, is an old friend of Picard, sharing his keen interest in archaeology, which has fascinated Picard since the Academy. Picard drinks hot Earl Grey tea. Denius 3 is a major archaeological dig. The Romulan ship is the *Haakona*. When examining Data, Geordi refers to Maddox (see 'The Measure of the Man') as 'an expert'. The *Yamato*'s number here (71807) is different to that given in 'Where Silence Has Lease'.

37: 'The Royale'

US Transmission: 27 March 1989
UK Transmission: 19 June 1991
Writer: Keith Mills (a pseudonym for Tracy Tormé)
Director: Cliff Bole
Cast: Sam Anderson, Jill Jacobson, Leo Garcia,
Noble Williamson, Geoffrey Beecroft

A Klingon cruiser has discovered traces of a vessel in the atmosphere of an unexplored planet. But when Riker, Data and Worf investigate, they find themselves trapped in what seems to be an Earth casino. Data's discovery of the book *The Hotel Royale* provides some of the explanations: the hotel was created by an unknown alien race who used the book as source material when creating a world for a marooned astronaut from the 21st century. By acting out aspects of the novel's *denouement*, the away team is able to leave.

Stardate: 42625.4

Strange New Worlds: The eighth planet in the Theta 116 system. The atmosphere includes nitrogen, methane and liquid neon. The surface temperature is minus 291 degrees.

New Life Forms: Unnamed alien weirdos who built the 'make-believe' world based on one (badly written) novel.

Poker Game: No, but blackjack and crap in the casino. Data is really good at both.

Picard Manoeuvre: Performed twice.

Riker's Conquests: He seems to be getting friendly with Vanessa, the dumb blonde in the Casino ('When the train comes to town, everybody rides!').

Dialogue Triumphs: 'We're from the United Federation of Planets.' 'Of course you are!'

Worf's reaction to being trapped: 'Permission to use phasers, sir.'

Picard reading *Hotel Royale*: ' "It was a dark and stormy night." Not a very promising beginning.' Deanna: 'It might get better.'

Future History: The NASA design and US flag containing 52 stars (if Britain's the 51st state, what's the 52nd?) places the ship's origin as being between 2033 and 2079. Colonel Steven Richey, the commander of the explorer ship *Charybdis*, left Earth on 23rd July 2037. It was the third manned attempt to go beyond the solar system. He has been dead for 283 years (which means he lived in the Royale for about 45 years).

Notes: 'I can't believe this dialogue!' Thoroughly bizarre with lots of unanswered questions (who were the aliens? How did Richey's ship travel so far from Earth?). The premise and surrealism are vaguely amusing in an episode with its tongue firmly in its cheek.

Picard quotes *Alice in Wonderland*, and discusses the lost theorem of Pierre de Fermat (1601-1665) (rediscovered in the early 1990s, and obviously lost again by the 23rd century!). The novel *Hotel Royale* was written by Todd Matthews and concerns a 20th century Las Vegas casino.

38: 'Time Squared'

US Transmission: 3 April 1989
UK Transmission: 3 July 1991
Writers: Maurice Hurley,
from a story by Kurt Michael Bensmiller
Director: Joseph L. Scanlan

Finding a drifting shuttle craft, the *Enterprise* crew are horrified to discover its sole occupant is Captain Picard. According to the log, this Picard is from six hours into the future, having witnessed the destruction of the *Enterprise* in an energy whirlpool. Picard is torn between following his instincts, and being tied by what he thinks may have happened to his future counterpart. Stopping his future self from leaving the *Enterprise*, Picard breaks the time-cycle by heading the ship into the heart of the whirlpool. The double Picard vanishes as time resumes its normal course.

Stardate: 42679.2

Strange New Worlds: The *Enterprise* is *en route* to the Endicor system.

New Life Forms: A seemingly sentient 'mass of energy' described by Deanna as an entity.

Notes: 'What we're facing is neither a person or a place. It's time.' A look at the complexity and paradoxes of time, with a great double performance by Patrick Stewart.

In theory, the only way to travel in time is to exceed warp factor 10, or use the gravitational pull of a star as a slingshot (as shown in the original *Star Trek* series on several occasions). Picard refers to the Traveler (see 'Where No One Has Gone Before'). Worf speaks of 'the Moebius', the theory about a twist in the space/time fabric.

Riker makes good omelettes (usually). (The one made of Owon eggs at Starbase 73 is a disaster, although Worf seems to like it.) Riker's father hated cooking so left the chores to him. Riker's mother died when he was very young (see 'The Icarus Factor').

The Stardate from which the 'future Picard' comes from is 42679.5. Shuttle 5 is named the *El-Baz*.

39: 'The Icarus Factor'

US Transmission: 24 April 1989
UK Transmission: 10 July 1991
Writers: David Assael, Robert L. McCulloch,
from a story by David Assael
Director: Richard Iscove
Cast: Michael Ryan, Lance Spellerberg

Riker is offered the captaincy of the *Aries*. The Starfleet advisor sent to brief him is his father, Kyle, whom he hasn't spoken to for fifteen years. Meanwhile the tenth anniversary of Worf's Age of Ascension is approaching, and he is depressed that he is unable to take part in a traditional ritual. The Rikers resolve their differences after a one-sided Anbo-jytsu game. Worf's fellow officers make a holodeck recreation of the Ascension rite. Riker decides to turn down the *Aries* posting and remain on the *Enterprise*.

Stardate: 42686.4

Technobabble: The cure for nazaldine 'flu is tryptophan-lysine distillate and a generous dose of Pulaski's chicken soup.

Riker's Conquests: He and Deanna have an emotional good-bye scene.

Data's Jokes: After Worf has snarled angrily at him: 'He seems quite sincere in his desire for solitude.'

Dialogue Triumphs: Worf: 'With all due respect, Begone! Sir!'

Notes: 'I came here to bury the hatchet with my son, only to find the ground was frozen solid.' Interesting to find that daddy Riker is even more of a rake than his son. It's all a bit obvious, though the Worf subplot is very good.

Flaherty, the first officer on the *Aries* (which is searching for new life in the Vega Omicron sector), speaks forty languages. Dilithium crystals are still an important part of engine design. Pulaski has been married three times. She is a former lover of Kyle Riker. They met twelve years before during the Tholian conflict (see the original series episode 'The Tholian Web'). Kyle Riker has been a civilian advisor to Starfleet for some time, helping to work out Fuurinkazan battle strategy at the Tokyo base moving to Starbase Montgomery as a technical advisor. Will is about thirty, having 'fended' for himself since he was fifteen. His mother died when he was a toddler and he barely remembers her. He has been practising Anbo-jytsu (a martial art) since he was eight. He could never beat his father (because he always cheated). This is the 10th anniversary of Worf's Age of Ascension which is accompanied by a ceremony involving sadomasochism in sight of his family. O'Brien once saw a Klingon 'painstik' used on a two-ton Rectyne monopod ('poor creature jumped five metres at the slightest touch').

40: 'Pen Pals'

US Transmission: 1 May 1989
UK Transmission: 17 July 1991
Writers: Melinda M. Snodgrass,
from a story by Hannah Louise Shearer
Director: Winrich Kolbe
Cast: Nicholas Cascone, Nikki Cox, Ann H.Gillespie,
Whitney Rydbeck

Wesley is put in charge of a mineral survey team, and Data picks up a faint signal from someone on a disintegrating world. The little girl calling Data is from a society unaware of alien cultures, and to save her would involve breaking the Prime Directive. Picard initially orders that communication cease, but changes his mind as the girl is really only asking for help. Data beams down to move her to a safer area while Wesley's team works on a geological solution. When Data realises that the girl, Sarjenka, is in immediate danger, he brings her back to the *Enterprise*. Wesley's solution is implemented, and Pulaski removes Sarjenka's memories of Data and the ship. The girl is returned to her now safe planet.

Stardate: 42696.3

Strange New Worlds: The Selcundi Drema sector, containing at least four systems, one of which contains the volcanically disturbed planet Drema 4.

New Life Forms: The red-haired, big-foreheaded, orange-skinned, long-fingered humanoid natives of Drema 4.

An Elanian singer stone sings a different song for each holder (but not for Data). The Andorian zabathu and Klingon sark are both mounts.

Technology: Memories can be erased medically by Pulaski (but see 'Who Watches the Watchers').

Riker's Conquests: He flirts in the bar with a woman in a science uniform.

Dialogue Triumphs: O'Brien ignores Riker breaking the Prime Directive: 'Right sir, I'll just be standing over here, dozing off.'

Notes: Some terrible out-of-character dialogue, and much dull angst over the ever-so-breakable Prime Directive.

Where there's traka, there's usually dilithium. An eidogram is a sort of geological survey. Dilithium crystals in a planet's crust can cause geological instability.

There are cats on Betazed: Troi's mother disliked her kitten. Picard is a skilled equestrian (see also 'Starship Mine'). Riker oversees Wesley's education.

41: 'Q Who'

US Transmission: 8 May 1989
UK Transmission: 24 July 1991
Writer: Maurice Hurley
Director: Rob Bowman
Cast: Lycia Naff

Q brings Picard to a shuttle, wanting a hearing for his latest proposal. When Picard agrees, he returns him to Ten-Forward, to the horror of Guinan, who has old scores to settle with Q. The entity has been banished from the Q Continuum, and seeks a position onboard the *Enterprise*, saying that the Federation is unprepared for the perils that await it. When Picard insists that it is, Q transports the ship 7000 light years into uncharted space – an area that Guinan knows and fears. The *Enterprise* finds destruction similar to that along the Neutral Zone boundaries, and then encounters a Borg ship. A Borg beams aboard, and taps into the computer. When it's killed, another appears, this time with a shield. It completes the downloading and leaves. The Borg ship seizes the *Enterprise* with a tractor beam and slices into the saucer, killing eighteen crew. A phaser burst releases the ship, and an away team board the Borg vessel. They find that the collective intelligence's efforts are going into completing the repairs. The *Enterprise* flees, pursued by the ever-faster Borg ship, and Picard has to appeal to Q to take them home. He does so, but now the Borg know of the Federation they will soon be coming after them.

Stardate: 42761.3

Strange New Worlds: System J25, the inhabited sixth planet of which was attacked by the Borg, 7000 light years from Starbase 185 (or two years and seven months at maximum warp, contradicting the one light year/hour speed given earlier in the series). Raynus 6 is a place where engineering work may be accomplished.

New Life Forms: The Borg, a collective bio-mechanical intelligence that grows bodies which are fitted with artificial devices from an early age. They have been developing for thousands of centuries, and see other cultures simply as raw materials. They dissolve their dead after removing three elements from their circuitry. Their personal shields learn how to react to a particular weapon after a couple of hits, and their ship can regenerate. No attention is paid to harmless intruders inside the ship, which carries a weapon designed to weaken shields, a tractor beam and a cutting device. It's immune to photon torpedoes.

Technology: Photon torpedoes can be fired from the rear of the *Enterprise*.

Dialogue Triumphs: Picard to Q: 'To learn about you is frankly provocative, but you're next of kin to chaos.'

Q to Worf: 'Growl for me, let me know you still care.'

Notes: A splendid, genuinely disturbing tale.

Guinan's people were scattered by the Borg 100 years ago.

She wasn't with them at the time. Guinan and Q met 200 years ago, when she went under another name. She has finger gestures which may have some practical value against Q's powers.

Food dispensers have intelligent circuitry. Officer's quarters are on deck 9 of the *Enterprise*, which carries at least six shuttlecraft.

42: 'Samaritan Snare'

US Transmission: 15 May 1989
UK Transmission: 7 August 1991
Writer: Robert L. McCullough
Director: Les Landau
Cast: Christopher Collins, Leslie Morris, Daniel Benzali,
Lycia Naff, Tzi Ma

Picard, on his way to a cardiac replacement operation, and Wesley, travelling to his Starfleet exams, share a shuttle to Starbase 515. Meanwhile the *Enterprise* answers the distress call of the Pakleds, a seemingly slow race who want Geordi to repair their engines. The Pakleds stun him with his phaser and take him hostage, demanding weapons and advanced technology. Picards's operation is going badly, and the only person who might save him is Pulaski – so the *Enterprise* crew come up with a ruse to rescue Geordi, pretending that their hydrogen exhaust is a 'crimson force field'. Geordi is transported out, and Pulaski arrives in time to save Picard.

Stardate: 42779.1

Strange New Worlds: Starbase 515, where major surgery may be performed. Mention is made of a pulsar cluster in the Epsilon 9 sector. The Pakled are encountered in the Rhomboid Dronegar sector.

New Life Forms: The Pakleds: slow, fat, and with big eyebrows. They want technology, but aren't advanced enough to cope with it (but can hold an entire starship in a standoff having fooled its officers . . .). They steal technology.

The Jarada are a very intelligent species.

Technology: A venturi chamber is part of a sub-light engine system. Replacement hearts can be transplanted with only a 2.4 per cent mortality rate. Surgery is done within a sterile field, the patient rendered unconscious by neural callipers.

Technobabble: 'Damn it, I can't stop the heterocyclic declination!' You can tell the surgeon's a bit out of his depth with his dialogue. 'Thoracic polygramatics', indeed.

Future History: In the late 22nd century, interplanetary journeys were slow.

Notes: *Trek*'s fondness for kicking its fans in the teeth continues, the Pakled being an unsubtle satire on them, which backfires since the creatures, like fandom, take what they need from the Federation and manage to outsmart them for considerable lengths of time, despite being constantly patronised.

Wesley's latest Starfleet exam results allow him to continue on board the *Enterprise*. Pulaski is highly qualified in cardiac surgery. Picard gave Wes a book of philosophy by William James. He never had time to marry, and was top of his Academy class. Before the Klingons joined the Federation he was involved in a brawl with three Nausicaans at the Bonestell Recreation Facility on Starbase Earhart. He got impaled through the back, which pierced his heart, and the swift medical action which followed left him with a faulty replacement. (See 'Tapestry'.)

43: 'Up the Long Ladder'

US Transmission: 22 May 1989
UK Transmission: 21 August 1991

Writer: Melinda M. Snodgrass
Director: Winrich Kolbe
Cast: Barrie Ingham, John de Vries, Rosalyn Landor

The *Enterprise* is called to evacuate the colony on Bringloid 5 which is threatened by a period of intense solar flare activity. The Bringloidi mention in passing a group of settlers on another planet in the system. The people of Mariposa prove to be clones threatened by replicative fading who spurn sexual intercourse. When the Mariposans' appeal for fresh DNA is rejected they resort to kidnapping, but the new generation of clones is destroyed by Riker and Pulaski. Picard suggests that the cerebral Mariposans will only survive into the future if they 'breed' with the sensual Bringloidi, and both groups are left on a new, safer world.

Stardate: 42823.2

New Life Forms: The tea used in a Klingon tea ceremony is deadly to humans, and not too pleasant for Klingons either. (The rituals surrounding it resemble those of Japan.) Klingons have written much great love poetry over the centuries (see 'The Dauphin').

Riker's Conquests: Brenna Odell (who has the gall to ask Riker if he likes girls).

Dialogue Triumphs: A rather nervous Danilo Odell, introduced to Worf: 'I don't suppose security is much of a problem for you.'

Odell: 'Sir, would you happen to be married?' Picard: 'No. Why?' Odell: 'Well, you see, sir, I have a daughter . . .' Picard: 'Felicitations.'

Riker: 'That isn't necessary. The ship will clean itself.' Brenna: 'Well – good for the bloody ship!'

An exasperated Worf to Brenna: 'Madam, have you ever considered a career in security?!'

Future History: Earth was just recovering from World War Three in the early 22nd century. The European Hegemony was a loose alliance that proved to be 'one of the first stirrings of world government'. (The distress beacon used by the Bringloidi dates from this period, c.2123-2190.) Spaceflight records during this period were somewhat chaotic. The SS *Mariposa* left on 27 November 2123 for the Ficus Sector, under Captain Walter Granger. Its cargo included 225 Yoshimitsu computers. A major philosopher of the era was Liam Dieghan, who founded Neo-transcendentalism and advocated a return to nature.

Notes: 'Send in the clones.' An awful story with a patronisingly presented bunch of Irish simpletons, padded beyond belief with Worf's illness and an obvious trap. And just what does the title mean anyway?

The *Enterprise* leaves Starbase 73 to investigate the distress signal. Worf is suffering from rop'ngor, a Klingon 'childhood ailment' similar to measles. The ship's (replicated) whisky has no bite, according to Danilo Odell, so Worf gives him some chech'tluth, which knocks his socks off. Geordi's VISOR allows him to see when humans are lying to him (he detects variations in blush response, pupil dilation, pulse, breath rate, etc.).

44: 'Manhunt'

US Transmission: 19 June 1989
UK Transmission: 28 August 1991
Writer: Terry Devereaux (a pseudonym for Tracy Tormé)
Director: Rob Bowman
Cast: Robert Constanzo, Carel Struycken, Rod Arrants,
Robert O'Reilly, Rhonda Aldrich, Mick Fleetwood,
Wren T. Brown

The *Enterprise* is instructed to carry two Antedian delegates and Federation ambassador Lwaxana Troi to a conference on Pacifica. Lwaxana has entered her mid-life 'phase' and is desperate to find someone to marry. She pursues Picard, who escapes to his Dixon Hill fantasy world, Riker, and finally the holographic film noir barman. Frustrated in her marital ambitions, she uses her telepathy to reveal that the Antedians are carrying ultritium explosives with which to destroy the conference.

Stardate: 42859.2

Strange New Worlds: The Antideans come from Antide 3.

New Life Forms: The Antideans have been given the chance to join the Federation. They are tall, cylindrical, with fish-like faces, and have rarely been seen by humans before (Worf thinks them a 'handsome race'). They go into suspended animation before space flights, and eat vermicula (fly-like creatures kept in a huge tub).

Betazoid use of the chime to give thanks for a meal is, according to Data, 'quite unique, but not at all dissimilar to the Ooolans of Marejaretus 6, who use two large stones which are continuously struck together during the meal.' Apparently, eating must continue until the stones are broken. Data is interrupted when he begins to talk of the oligarchy on Actos 4. Betazoid women only become fully sexually active during the mid-life 'phase', during which time their sex drive quadruples (or more). There is a suggestion that this can interfere with their telepathic abilities.

Dialogue Triumphs: Lwaxana, on seeing Picard in dress uniform: 'And you, Jean-Luc – I wasn't aware you had such handsome legs.'

In Dixon Hill's 1941 San Francisco: 'You a Private Dick?' 'That's what it says on my door.' 'That supposed to be funny? Because if it is you gotta know that I ain't in the mood for funny.'

Notes: 'Never assume anything where Lwaxana Troi is concerned. Betazed women are full of surprises.' This is a slight but very funny episode, although one does wonder how a woman as tactless as Lwaxana Troi became an ambassador.

Data's after-dinner anecdotes are the stuff of legend aboard the *Enterprise*, according to Picard. However, as he's desperate to break up his quiet meal with Lwaxana Troi – and one such story appears to involve using pi to calculate the distance between the Omicron system and the Crab Nebula, which makes even the normally stoic Mr Homn yawn – this appears to be somewhat untrue.

The Parrot's Claw was a Dixon Hill novel.

45: 'The Emissary'

US Transmission: 26 June 1989
UK Transmission: 4 September 1991
Writers: Richard Manning, Hans Beimler,
from a television story by Richard Manning, Hans Beimler,
based on an unpublished story by Thomas H. Calder
Director: Cliff Bole
Cast: Suzie Plakson, Lance le Gault, Georgann Johnson,
Anne Elizabeth Ramsey, Dietrich Bader

Starbase 336 has recently received an automated transmission from the Klingon ship *T'Ong*, which left the Homeworld 75 years ago with its crew in suspended animation. The Klingon ship *P'Rang* is two days behind the *Enterprise*, so the job of defusing a potentially explosive situation falls to Picard and the others. Worf is reunited with former lover K'Ehleyr, who is half-Klingon and half-human. She explains that the reawakened Klingons will think that they are still at war with the Federation, and advises that the ship be destroyed. Picard orders Worf and envoy K'Ehleyr to come up with other options, but the two argue about their past and their level of commitment to each other. They have sex after one of Worf's holodeck combat programs but K'Ehleyr refuses to marry Worf. Despite their differences they are able to reassure the reanimated Klingons by pretending to be the *Enterprise*'s commanding officers.

Stardate: 42901.3 (towards the end of the story).

Strange New Worlds: The Boradis system has been recently colonised. The first Federation outpost was established 34 years previously on Boradis 3.

New Life Forms: K'Ehleyr says that Klingon and human DNA is compatible 'with a fair amount of help'. Klingons are monogamous. Once intercourse has taken place the Klingon norm is to then solemnise the 'mating' with a wedding oath. (Despite refusing the ceremony, in a very real sense K'Ehleyr *is* Worf's wife.)

Poker Game: Between Pulaski, Geordi, Data, Worf and Riker. Worf wins with a full house, beating Pulaski's straight flush, who loses her last chip. Worf is doing rather well. Data then deals ('Seven card stud, after the Queen, one-eyed Jacks and low card in the hole are wild', to which Geordi responds 'Wait a minute, let me write this down'), but the ensuing game is interrupted by a class two emergency message from Starfleet. Geordi accuses Worf – nicknamed 'the Iceman' – of bluffing, but he says 'Klingons never bluff'.

Dialogue Triumphs: Riker: 'How did you like command?' Worf: 'Comfortable chair.'

Notes: A most enjoyable episode, balancing Worf's love-life with the dilemma of the old Klingons.

K'Ehleyr joins the *Enterprise* from Starbase 193, journeying in a class 8 probe just under two metres long which travels at warp nine. She met Worf six years ago.

46: 'Peak Performance'

US Transmission: 10 July 1989
UK Transmission: 18 September 1991
Writer: David Kemper
Director: Robert Scheerer
Cast: Roy Brocksmith, Armin Shimmerman,
David L. Lander, Leslie Neal, Glenn Morshower

As part of Starfleet preparations to meet the Borg threat the
Enterprise is to take part in a war game against the *Hathaway*,
a much older, almost derelict ship. Sirna Kolrami, a Zakdorn
strategist, is to oversee events. Riker is put in charge of the
Hathaway, the odds of success heavily stacked against him.
However, Worf's *Enterprise* security codes and the expertise
of Wesley and Geordi might give the ancient ship an edge.
Nearby Ferengi think the battle is for real, however, and their
attack on the *Enterprise* leaves its weapons stuck in the harmless mode used for the war game. The Ferengi demand the secret weapon that they believe the *Hathaway* to possess, but are
fooled by the apparent destruction of the older ship.

Stardate: 42923.4

Strange New Worlds: The war game takes place in the Braslota
system.

New Life Forms: For over 9000 years the Zakdorns have been
regarded as having the finest strategic minds in the galaxy.
Kolrami is a third-level Grand Master at the game of stratagema,
and like all his kind he has a very confident, if not indeed arrogant, air.

Dialogue Triumphs: Worf and Riker before the latter takes on
Kolrami in stratagema: 'I've wagered heavily in the ship's pool
that you will take him past the sixth plateau.' 'And if I don't?'
'I will be . . . irritated.' (In fact, Riker is beaten in 23 moves.)

Notes: An excellent and well-crafted story where for once the subplots and the main action are all pulling in the same direction.

Picard says that on his ship the leader of an away team has total control of the mission, implying that this is not standard procedure. He regards Starfleet as primarily an exploratory organisation, but with the Borg threat he has agreed to the war game. In the war game Riker is given a crew of forty. The Hathaway has old avidyne engines, and makes a naval-type whistling noise to contact the crew (as did the *Enterprise* in some first season stories).

At the Academy Riker calculated the sensory blind spot on a Tholian vessel and hid in it during a battle simulation. As a lieutenant on the *Potemkin* (see 'Second Chances') his solution to a crisis was to shut down all power and hang over a planet's magnetic poles, thus confusing his opponent's sensors. Standard Starfleet manoeuvres include the Kumeh and Telubian manoeuvres.

Worf is interrupted making what appears to be a wooden boat.

47: 'Shades of Grey'

US Transmission: 17 July 1989
UK Transmission: 25 September 1991
Writers: Maurice Hurley, Richard Manning, Hans Beimler,
from a story by Maurice Hurley
Director: Rob Bowman

During a planetary survey Riker is infected by an organism which swiftly attacks his nervous system. Pulaski is unable to save him until she and Troi realise that the invading microbe's growth is slowed when Riker experiences negative emotions. Pulaski forces Riker to remember his most painful memories from his first two years on the *Enterprise*, and the micro-organism is destroyed.

Stardate: 42976.1

Strange New Worlds: Surata 4, never previously visited.

New Life Forms: The micro-organism that invades Riker's nervous system on a molecular level has elements of both bacteria and virus but is neither. It enters Riker's body via a thorn on a moving vine that seeks out warm-blooded beings, but proves to be sensitive to brain endorphins.

Dialogue Triumphs: Riker says that his grandfather was bitten by a rattlesnake. 'After three days of intense pain, the snake died.'

Notes: The pits, although at least no one has ever tried to claim that this episode is anything more than a shoddy cost-cutting exercise.

Tricordrazine is used to treat Riker.

Third Season

26 45-minute episodes

Created by Gene Roddenberry

Executive Producers: Rick Berman (48-51, 58-67, 69-73),
Gene Roddenberry (48-51, 58-67, 69-73)
Co-Executive Producers[1]**:** Rick Berman (52-57, 68),
Gene Roddenberry (52-57, 68), Michael Piller (52-73)

[1]As becomes clear in this season, sometimes the credit 'Co-Executive Producer' or 'Co-Producer' implies a separate role (as in the second season), while on other occasions the terms seem to indicate little more than the fact that two or more people are sharing the same role.

Producer: Ira Steven Behr (58–67, 69–73)
Co-Producers: Ira Steven Behr (56–57, 68), Hans Beimler
(48–73), Peter Lauritson (48–69, 71–73), Richard Manning
(48–73) **Line Producer:** David Livingston (48–73)
Executive Script Consultant: Melinda M. Snodgrass
(49, 51–59, 68–70) **Executive Story Editors:** Richard Danus
(53–60), Melinda M. Snodgrass (48, 50, 60, 64–67, 71) **Story
Editor:** Ronald D. Moore (64–73) **Executive Script
Supervisor:** Melinda M. Snodgrass (61–63)

Regular Cast: Patrick Stewart (Captain Jean-Luc Picard),
Jonathan Frakes (Commander William Riker), Levar Burton
(Lt Commander Geordi La Forge), Michael Dorn (Lt Worf),
Gates McFadden (Dr Beverly Crusher), Marina Sirtis
(Counselor Deanna Troi), Brent Spiner (Lt Commander Data),
Wil Wheaton (Wesley Crusher) Whoopi Goldberg (Guinan, 48,
53, 60, 62-63, 68, 73), Colm Meaney (Lt O'Brien, 49[1], 52-55,
58, 61, 67-70, 72-73), John de Lancie (Q, 60), Denise Crosby
(Lt Tasha Yar, 62), Dwight Schultz (Lt Reg Barclay, 68), Majel
Barrett (Lwaxana Troi, 71)

48: 'Evolution'

US Transmission: 25 September 1989
UK Transmission: 9 October 1991
Writers: Michael Piller,
from a story by Michael Piller, Michael Wagner
Director: Winrich Kolbe
Cast: Ken Jenkins, Mary McCusker, Randal Patrick

During the observation of a stellar explosion of a neutron-
supergiant binary star, the *Enterprise*'s computer core malfunc-
tions, threatening the project and the life's work of Federation

---

[1]Credited simply as O'Brien for this episode.

scientist Paul Stubbs. Wesley's genetics project involving the interaction of microbiotic nanites appears to be the cause. When Stubbs attempts to destroy the machines using radiation, the evolving creatures shut down the ship's life- support. Data communicates with the nanites and a compromise is reached.

Stardate: 43125.8

Strange New Worlds: A spectacular binary star system in the Kavis-Alpha region. Kavis-Alpha 4 is the unoccupied planet where the Nanites are allowed to live.

New Life Forms: Nanites, tiny robots with gigabytes of mechanical computer memory. Evolved by Wesley, they are able to 'mechanically enhance themselves' and have a collective consciousness. They are made in a plant in Dacca, Senegal, according to Stubbs.

Dialogue Triumphs: 'Do you know baseball? Once, centuries ago, it was the beloved national pastime of the Americas. Abandoned by a society that prized fast food and faster games. Lost in impatience.'

'A brand new era in astrophysics postponed for 196 years because of rain!'

Notes: 'We're heading straight into the path of stellar matter.' A well-judged season opener, with lots of good characterisation, only spoiled by a somewhat preachey attitude to science-without-conscience.

Dr Paul Stubbs is a highly respected Starfleet astrophysicist, studying 'the decay of neutronium expelled at relativistic speeds from a massive stellar explosion', which happens once every 196 years. Beverly is back on the *Enterprise* after a year at Starfleet Medical. Wesley is now seventeen. His final project for Advanced Genetics is on nano-technology. His father taught him baseball (presumably at a *very* young age). Picard quotes *Gulliver's Travels*. The Borg are mentioned (see 'Q Who').

⌐ has been married more than once, and has 'a lot' of

children, only one of which she couldn't relate to (this took 'several hundred years' to resolve itself). Assuming she isn't being facetious, this is the first hint of Guinan's longevity. Data says there hasn't been a systems-wide technological breakdown on a starship for 79 years. Beth Delta 1 has a city called New Manhattan.

49: 'The Ensigns of Command'

US Transmission: 2 October 1989
UK Transmission: 16 October 1991
Writer: Melinda M. Snodgrass
Director: Cliff Bole
Cast: Eileen Seeley, Mark L. Taylor, Richard Allen,
Grainger Hines[1], Mart McChesney

The first contact with the Sheliak Corporate, a race of non-humanoid pedants, in over a hundred years calls on the *Enterprise* to clear a human colony from a disputed planet. But the colonists of Tau Cygna 5, led by the bullish Gosheven, refuse to leave. Whilst Picard tries to find a diplomatic solution, Data attempts to fulfil his mission to prepare the colony for evacuation. Ultimately he can only do this with a show of strength.

Stardate: 43133.3

Strange New Worlds: Tau Cygna 5 in the de Laure belt. Ceded by the Treaty of Armens to the Sheliak (under section 133, paragraph 77). The original human settlers were from the colony ship *Artemis* heading for Septimus Minor, which crashed 92 years ago when the guidance systems failed. There are now 15,253 colonists.

New Life Forms: The Sheliak ('non-human intelligent life form

---

[1]Not credited on screen.

classification R3'). The Grisella, suggested by Picard as third party adjudicators, are a race with a long hibernation cycle.

Technobabble: Phasers don't function in the presence of hyperonic radiation, which randomises the phaser beams. Data uses his own neural subprocessor to relocate the beam continuously.

Dialogue Triumphs: The Sheliak to Picard: 'You do not converse, you jibber!'

Notes: 'The colony has been here for ninety years. We've never seen a Sheliak. I'd say that makes Tau Cygna 5 our planet.' A story of various types of prejudice, well handled. Stupid, but fun.

Data is in a string ensemble playing violin (O'Brien plays the cello). His playing is a precise imitation of the styles of Yasha Hyphites and Trenka Bronkin. His peers think that he lacks 'soul' (see 'Sarek', 'In Theory').

Heavy concentrations of hyperonic radiation are fatal to humans, although the Tau Cygnians have found a way to survive. Beverly notes that Mylan's work with radiation suggests that this is possible with 'viro-therapy.'

The Treaty of Armens is a 500,000 word document between the Federation and the Sheliak. The level of complexity was at the insistence of the Sheliak who consider Federation languages irrational.

50: 'The Survivors'

US Transmission: 9 October 1989
UK Transmission: 20 November 1991
Writer: Michael Wagner
Director: Les Landau
Cast: John Anderson, Anne Haney

A distress call from the colony Delta Rana 4 brings the shocking discovery that the entire population is dead, with the exception of an aged pair of human botanists. The couple are vague about the exact circumstances of the tragedy. An apparently hostile alien ship approaches the *Enterprise* but its weapons lack the power of those responsible for the colony's demise. It is subsequently revealed that the male survivor is actually an immensely powerful alien. His wife also died in the attack and, enraged, the alien destroyed the entire race responsible.

Stardate: 43152.4

Strange New Worlds: Delta Rana 4 has three moons. The Federation colony once had 11,000 inhabitants.

New Life Forms: The Douwd, an immortal race who delight in 'disguise and false surroundings'. 'Kevin' has lived in this galaxy for many thousands of years.

The Husnock, a species of 'hideous intelligence'. They know only 'aggression and destruction'. They were destroyed by 'Kevin' after they killed his wife.

Deanna Underused?: Yes, she spends half the episode in a coma.

Dialogue Triumphs: Riker, on the Husnock's fire-power: 'If that's the best they can do this should last about five minutes.'

Worf's attempt at polite conversation: 'Good tea. Nice house.'

Future History: Fifty years before (i.e. the 2310s) Earth still had sailing ships.

Notes: 'My apologies if I interrupted a waltz.' Eerie, with good location filming, although the script is wordy and self-indulgent.

Picard remembers an occasion when an Andorian crew hid from Starfleet by dismantling their ship. Data notes Rishon and Kevin Uxbridge are botanists originally from the aquatic city New Martim Vaz in the Atlantic ocean. They have been married for 53 years.

51: 'Who Watches the Watchers?'

US Transmission: 16 October 1989
UK Transmission: 30 October 1991
Writers: Richard Manning, Hans Beimler
Director: Robert Wiemer
Cast: Kathryn Leigh Scott, Ray Wise, James Greene,
Pamela Segall, John McLiam, James McIntyre, Lois Hall

An anthropological team on the planet Mintaka 3 requires help
without their primitive observers discovering their existence.
But a catalogue of medical emergencies elevates Picard to
godhood. When attempts at containing the cultural contamination fail, Picard ignores the Prime Directive and allows the
Mintakans knowledge of space travel. He leaves them, telling
them that they should follow logic and ignore superstition.

Stardate: 43173.5

Strange New Worlds: Mintaka 3.

New Life Forms: The Mintakans, proto-Vulcan humanoids at
the Bronze Age level. 'Quite peaceful and highly rational,' according to Deanna.

Technobabble: Geordi calls a hologram generator a 'duck
blind'.

Picard Manoeuvre: Yes, once.

Riker's Conquests: Will and Deanna go undercover as
Mintakans with Deanna as Riker's 'woman'.

Dialogue Triumphs: 'The Mintakans are beginning to believe
in a god. And the one they've chosen is you!'
    'You have taught us there is nothing beyond our reach.' 'Not
even the stars.'
    'Remember my people.' 'Always.'

Notes: 'Each of us . . . took an oath that we would uphold the Prime Directive. If necessary with our lives.' Imaginative and beautiful. The sense of wonder in the scenes of Nuria wandering around the *Enterprise* and Patrick Stewart's brilliantly angry performance mark this out as an authentic masterpiece. Anti-religion, questioning ethics and with a moral dilemma, the themes first explored here would continue in 'First Contact'. A gem.

Pulaski's technique for erasing short-term memory (see 'Pen Pals') is mentioned, but here it doesn't work!

52: 'The Bonding'

US Transmission: 23 October 1989
UK Transmission: 6 November 1991
Writer: Ronald D. Moore
Director: Winrich Kolbe
Cast: Susan Powell, Gabriel Damon

When Worf leads an away team to the home of the extinct Koinonians, the *Enterprise*'s archaeologist Marla Aster is killed by a booby trap. Picard has to tell her young son, Jeremy, of her death. Worf wants to bond with Jeremy in the R'uustal, a Klingon ceremony, but Marla reappears. An energy field from the planet has entered the ship: she is one of the non-corporeal race who shared the world with the Koinonians, who vowed never to let anyone suffer from wars again. She wants to give the boy his mother back. Wesley talks to Jeremy about his feelings of anger and loss, and he has his substitute mother depart, opting to take the R'uustal with Worf.

Stardate: 43198.7

New Life Forms: Koinonians, who destroyed themselves in a generations-long war, and the energy beings that secretly shared their world.

Riker's Conquests: 'We spent some time together.' Riker's way of saying he bonked Lt Aster.

Notes: Gabriel Damon acquits himself well, but one wonders if Worf called on Jeremy's help during the Klingon Civil War. An episode where it's quite easy for the viewer to lose the will to live.

Rushton is a fatal kind of infection. The Klingon bonding ceremony of R'uustal which involves lighting candles and exchanging robes, and leaves the participants as brothers. Worf's parents were killed when he was six.

53: 'Booby Trap'

US Transmission: 30 October 1989
UK Transmission: 13 November 1991
Writers: Ron Roman, Michael Piller, Richard Danus,
from a story by Michael Wagner, Ron Roman
Director: Gabrielle Beaumont
Cast: Susan Gibney, Albert Hall, Julie Warner

When the *Enterprise* is caught in an energy-sucking trap at the site of the last battle between the Promellians and the Menthars, Geordi calls on the assistance of a holodeck-simulated Leah Brahms, the designer of the *Enterprise*'s engines. They get on very well, and come up with the idea of flying the ship out of the trap on just two thrusters. Picard pilots the ship in a slingshot round an asteroid to escape, and the booby trap is destroyed.

Stardate: 43205.6

Strange New Worlds: Orelious 9 was reduced to rubble in a battle between Menthars and Promellians that neither side expected to be decisive.

New Life Forms: Promellians, extinct green reptiles with skull ridges. They were building cruisers while mankind was perfecting the mechanical clock.

Technology: Aceton Assimilators are primitive energy-sucking devices. The isolinear optical chip is a Federation information storage device. Warp drive is only possible within a subspace field. The next class of starship will have an adjustment made to the direction of the dilithium crystal lattice structure to allow crystal re-orientation.

Deanna Underused?: Her role is tiny.

Data's Jokes: 'I was never a boy.'

Notes: This episode has some intrusively horrid music, a terrible ending, and a nonsensical coda. Not fun.

Menthar strategies included the Cavis Teke Elusive Manouevre (which they were the first to use), and the Passive Lure Strategem (which was like a move of Napoleon's). The holodeck ship design program was recorded at Stardate 40174 in Utopia Planitia, Mars Station, drafting room 5. The dilithium crystal chamber was designed on Seran T One in 40052. Leah Brahms had her personality profile copied during 40056, and attended inter-galactic caucuses on Chia 7.

Astral 5 Annex is an organisation that catalogues and retrieves historical objects. The Daystrom Institute has a Theoretical Propulsion Group.

Picard built model airships as a child. O'Brien built ships in bottles (see 'All Good Things . . .'). Guinan is attracted to bald men, because one took care of her once (possibly Picard: see 'Time's Arrow 2'). Geordi fails to get off with Christy in the holodeck, then snogs a hologram (with hilarious results).

54: 'The Enemy'

US Transmission: 6 November 1989
UK Transmission: 27 November 1991

Writers: David Kemper, Michael Piller
Director: David Carson
Cast: John Snyder, Andreas Katsulas, Steve Rankin

The *Enterprise* crew answer a distress call from Galorndon Core, and find a lone survivor of a Romulan ship. However, Geordi gets separated from the others, and is left stranded on the planet. Beverly concludes that the Romulan needs a cell transplant, but the only candidate for donation is Worf, and he refuses. Wesley sends down a beacon for Geordi to find, but the lost crewman chances upon another Romulan, Patahk. Patahk takes Geordi prisoner. Romulan Commander Tomalak has meanwhile arranged a rendezvous with the *Enterprise* in the Neutral Zone, and when the ship misses it he is angry enough to cross into Federation space. Geordi and Patahk agree to work together and activate the beacon. Tomalak is further incensed when he hears of the death of the first Romulan, and is ready to begin a battle that will lead to war. Picard drops the *Enterprise*'s shields to beam up the two survivors, and Patahk's assurances of good treatment calm Tomalak. The *Enterprise* escorts his Warbird back to the Neutral Zone.

Stardate: 43349.2

Strange New Worlds: Galorndon Core, a Federation world lashed with charged particle storms, half a light year away from the Neutral Zone.

New Life Forms: Ultritium is a Romulan explosive. Romulans have green blood. They let children with birth defects die. One of their ranks is centurion, which is beneath commander.

Deanna Underused?: Two lines.

Notes: This is wonderful, an ancient scenario given some added weight and urgency.

Station Salem One was the scene of the first action in a war.

55: 'The Price'

US Transmission: 13 November 1989
UK Transmission: 4 December 1991
Writer: Hannah Louise Shearer
Director: Robert Scheerer
Cast: Matt McCoy, Elizabeth Hoffman, Castulo Guerra,
Scott Thomson, Dan Shor, Kevin Peter Hall

The Barzan people are about to sell the only known stable wormhole, and assemble a number of delegates to bid for it on the *Enterprise*. Devinoni Ral, a hired negotiator, is one of these, and he romances Troi. The Ferengi delegate, DaiMon Goss, poisons the Federation delegate, and Riker has to take his place. Geordi and Data, accompanied by a Ferengi pod, go through the wormhole in a shuttle, and find that it's not as stable as they thought. The Ferengi are stranded. Troi discovers that Ral is one-quarter Betazoid, and therefore empathic, a fact he hasn't revealed to the other delegates. Goss tries to destroy the wormhole, claiming that the Barzan have already made a deal with the Federation, but Ral talks him out of it. As Troi reveals, this is all a deception: the wormhole, being unstable, is worthless. In the end, Ral is grateful to her for revealing his duplicity: perhaps he can change for the better.

Stardate: 43385.6

Strange New Worlds: Barzan 2, completely inhospitable to alien life. Mention is made of Hurkos 3. The Denkiri arm of the Gamma Quadrant, a century away at warp 9, and the Delta Quadrant, 200 light years away from the Gamma Quadrant, and 70,000 light years away from the Federation.

New Life Forms: The inhabitants of Barzan, humanoids with flaxen hair, mouth fixtures and no manned space flight. The Caldonians, tall, crease-headed creatures into pure research. The Chrysalians, who have always been neutral, and thus enjoyed ten generations of peace.

Poker Game: Negotiation as poker.

Data's Jokes: Data comforts LaForge as he looks forward to spending a lifetime in a shuttle: 'There is a bright side, Geordi. You will have me to talk to.'

Dialogue Triumphs: Deanna gets sarky: 'God forbid I should miss my first look at the wormhole.'
  Riker's bluff: 'Poker . . . Is that a game of some sort?'

Future History: The European Alliance includes Brussels.

Notes: A lovely script, with Troi solidly characterised.
  The Manitoba Journal of Interplanetary Psychology is a periodical. Deanna is fond of chocolate sundaes and oiled foot massages, but aren't we all? The Ferengi pod is their equivalent of the shuttle. Tyrillium 323 is a valuable mineral, found on Caldonia.

56: 'The Vengeance Factor'

US Transmission: 20 November 1989
UK Transmission: 11 December 1991
Writer: Sam Rolfe
Director: Timothy Bond
Cast: Lisa Wilcox, Joey Aresco, Nancy Parsons,
Stephen Lee, Marc Lawrence, Elkanah J. Burns

The Gatherers, a band of thieving nomads exiled from their ancestor race, the Acamarians, have been attacking Federation science outposts. Picard decides to try to bring peace between the two factions. Talks between the Gatherer and Acamarian leaders are almost destroyed by the work of an assassin attempting to revenge the massacre of her clansfolk. Riker is able to prevent her scheme, but only at the cost of her life.

Stardate: 43421.9

Strange New Worlds: Acamar 3, and the Hromi cluster where the Gatherers are based.

New Life Forms: The Gatherers, 'nomadic marauders'. Originally from Acamar 3, where 100 years ago the culmination of centuries of clan warfare led to their departure. The Acamarians meanwhile have developed into a civilised race.

Riker's Conquests: Yuta, the cook (and last of the Tralesta clan whose aging process has been slowed by the other members of her clan). She cooks Will a spicy Parthas dish (a green vegetable with fleshy roots) and is then killed by him. Surely the meal wasn't *that* bad?

Technology: Amongst the technology the Gatherers have stolen are Tonkian homing beacons, Artonian lasers and Regalian phaser rifles. Noranium alloy vaporises at 234 degrees.

Dialogue Triumphs: 'I steal to survive, not because I enjoy it!'

'Your ambush would be more successful if you bathed more often!'

Notes: 'Fifty-three years, and she hasn't aged a day.' Not bad, just dull. There are hints of a *Highlander* influence, and a very slow-moving script.

There is some discrepancy as to how long ago the Lornack clan massacred the Tralesta (eighty years according to Marouk, 'a century' to Yuta).

57: 'The Defector'

US Transmission: 1 January 1990
UK Transmission: 18 December 1991
Writer: Ronald D. Moore
Director: Robert Scheerer

Cast: James Sloyan, Andreas Katsulas, John Hancock,
S.A. Templeman

The dramatic defection of a Romulan strategic officer, Setal,
who warns of a forthcoming invasion, sends the *Enterprise* to
battle alert. But Setal is in reality Jarok, a notorious admiral,
and, although apparently sincere, discovery of this leads to even
greater suspicion about his motives. Travelling into the neutral
zone, the *Enterprise* finds itself in a Romulan trap, but with the
aid of three Klingon ships a confrontation is avoided. Jarok,
knowing he has been used by the Romulans, kills himself.

Stardate: 43462.5

Strange New Worlds: Nelvana 3, site of an alleged Romulan
battle fleet. Romulus itself, although not seen, is described in
detail. Geographical features include the Apnex sea, the valley
of Chula and the fire falls at Gal Gaththong.

New Life Forms: 'Pahtk' and 'Tohzah' are Klingon curses.
'Veruul' is a Romulan insult. An Onkian is a Romulan unit of
heat.

Picard Manoeuvre: Yes, as he faces Tomalak's threats (does
he adjust his underpants too?).

Dialogue Triumphs: 'What a fool I've been. To come looking
for courage amongst a lair of cowards.'

Jarok on Data: 'I know a lot of Romulan cyberneticists that
would love to be this close to you.'

'One world's butcher is another world's hero. Perhaps I am
neither?'

Notes: 'A Romulan defector is almost a contradiction in terms.'
A very good episode, more akin to a 'serious' spy series than
SF. Nice layers of characterisation are established for the regulars, and for the main Romulan characters (the nobel Jarok, the
bullish Tomalak). The pre-title sequence, Brent Spiner and (a

heavily disguised) Patrick Stewart in a holodeck performance of Henry V (Act 4, Scene 1), is breathtaking, despite the lack of an on-screen writing credit for Midlands newcomer Bill Shakespeare.

Data plans to study the acting performances of Olivier, Brannagh, Shapiro and Solnock, though Picard advises against merely copying one style.

Admiral Jarok was responsible for the massacre of the Norkan outposts. The battle of Cheron (mentioned in the *Star Trek* episode 'Balance of Terror') was regarded as a humiliating defeat by the Romulans. The treaty of Algeron prohibits Federation entry into the Neutral Zone.

58: 'The Hunted'

US Transmission: 8 January 1990
UK Transmission: 8 January 1992
Writer: Robin Bernheim
Director: Cliff Bole
Cast: Jeff McCarthy, James Cromwell, J. Michael Flynn, Andrew Bicknell

Angosia 3 has requested Federation membership, and the application seems to be going well until the *Enterprise* is involved in tracking down a convict who has escaped from the planet's military penal colony, Lunar 5. The prisoner is Roga Danar, and his 'crime' is to have been a soldier in the Tarsian war. Like many of his kind he was unable to adapt to civilian life, and was imprisoned. Picard is disgusted by the behaviour of the Angosian leaders, but is reminded by Prime Minister Nayrok that these are internal matters. Danar escapes and liberates a large number of his fellow veterans, threatening the government. Nayrok's plea for help is rejected by Picard: it is, after all, an internal matter. If Nayrok can solve the problem then Angosia will be worthy of joining the Federation.

Stardate: 43489.2

Strange New Worlds: Angosia 3.

New Life Forms: The Angosians are said to be intellectuals and thinkers. They used biomechanical techniques to create 'super-soldiers' during the Tarsian war.

Technobabble: 'They used a combination of cryptobiolin and triclenidil macrospentol and a few things even I can't recognise.'

Notes: 'You made them what they are. You asked them to defend your way of life, and then you discarded them.' In other words, *Rambo* in space. A good mixture of action and hearty ol' *Trek* moralising.

Anesthezine is a sedative gas. At the end of the story the *Enterprise* heads off to Starbase Lya 3.

59: 'The High Ground'

US Transmission: 29 January 1990
UK Transmission: 29 November 1992
Writer: Melinda M. Snodgrass
Director: Gabrielle Beaumont
Cast: Richard Cox, Kerrie Keane, Marc Buckland,
Fred G. Smith, Christopher Pettiet

While attending to the victims of a bomb attack on Rutia 4 Dr Crusher is kidnapped by terrorist leader Kyril Finn. The Ansata terrorists want to involve the Federation in their struggle for 'freedom', and Finn is also keen to exploit the doctor's medical skills. Finn leads a bombing raid against the *Enterprise*, which is foiled, although Picard is also taken hostage. Wesley finds a way of tracking the terrorists' dimensional shift technology, and the Federation officers are liberated, Finn being shot by police chief Alexana Devos.

Stardate: 43510.7

Strange New Worlds: Rutia 4 is a non-aligned planet with a long trading relationship with the Federation. A 'generation' of peace has been shattered by the attacks of Ansata terrorists, who want autonomy and self-determination for their land on the Western continent. The Western area is effectively ruled by the Eastern continent, and was denied its independence seventy years ago.

Technology: Federation transporters leave residual ionisation in the air when used, but the dimensional shift transportation used by Ansata is much more difficult to trace. A dimensional jump, however, does create subspace pressure modulation, which can be monitored by an adaptive subspace echogram. True to the Elway Theorem, an abandoned 23rd century approach to folded or adaptive space transport, inter-dimensional travel is fatal over time.

Picard Manoeuvre: Jean-Luc does it when talking to Devos; Riker does a quick one after decking one of the terrorists.

Dialogue Triumphs: 'In a world where children blow up children, everyone's a threat.'

'The difference between generals and terrorists, doctor, is only the difference between winners and losers.'

Future History: Ireland is unified in 2024.

Notes: An excellent insight into the terrorist mind. Pleasingly, there's no sudden resolution to the planet's conflict – but peace can only begin when a boy lays down his gun.

Crusher comes from North America.

60: 'Déjà Q'

US Transmission: 5 February 1990
UK Transmission: 15 January 1992

Writer: Richard Danus
Director: Les Landau
Cast: Richard Cansino, Betty Muramoto, Corbin Bernsen

The moon of Bre'el 4 is in a declining orbit, and will soon crash into the planet. But this is a minor cosmic detail compared to the problems that Q is having, exiled from the continuum and hunted by a previous foe. Attempts to change the moon's orbit seem doomed to failure, especially after the intervention of Q's old enemy, the Calamarain. Q is set to perform a selfless act and sacrifice himself to save the *Enterprise* when the continuum decide he has learned his lesson, and the grateful super-being, with his powers restored, rights the moon's orbit, and shows his gratitude to the *Enterprise* crew in a variety of bizarre ways.

Stardate: 43539.1

Strange New Worlds: Bre'el 4 and its moon.

New Life Forms: The Bre'elians. The Calamarain exist as 'swirls of ionised gas', a cloud of energetic plasma and tachyons. They use Berthold rays to scan other creatures and 'have no sense of humour'. Q refers to his 'brothers and sisters' in the Q continuum, so there must, presumably, be female Q.

Data's Jokes: Q: 'Who does he think he is, giving me orders?' Data: 'Geordi thinks he is in command here. And he is correct!'

He describes his first, and only, Q-inspired laugh as 'a wonderful feeling'.

Dialogue Triumphs: Q on his contested powerlessness: 'What must I do to convince you people?' Worf: 'Die!'

Guinan, on Data: 'You could learn a lot from this one.' Q: 'Sure, the robot who teaches a course in humanity.'

'It's difficult to work in a group when you're omnipotent!'

Second Q: 'I find these humans rather interesting. After all the things you've done, they're still intent on keeping you alive!'

Q on Riker: 'You're so staid. You weren't like that before the beard!'

Notes: 'My life as a human being has been a dismal failure. Perhaps my death will have a little dignity.' A blisteringly funny episode, played almost entirely for laughs, although quite touching when it wants to be. The great Corbin Bernsen appears as a second Q (the one who misplaced the entire Deltived asteroid belt) in one of the best scenes in the entire series, matched only by the brilliant closing bridge scene. *The Next Generation* goes sitcom.

The Q continuum have stripped Q of his powers for 'spreading chaos throughout the galaxy'. Q could have chosen to exist as a Markoffian sea lizard, or a Belzoidian flea. Anything, as long as it was mortal. He suggests Picard is the closest thing he has to a friend in the universe. He is claustrophobic, prone to back trauma, an 'expert on moons' and has an IQ of 2005. When Deanna is unhappy she usually eats chocolate. Data doesn't require food, but sometimes eats a 'semi-organic nutrient suspension in a silicon-based liquid medium to lubricate my biofunctions'.

61: 'A Matter of Perspective'

US Transmission: 12 February 1990
UK Transmission: 22 January 1992
Writer: Ed Zuckerman
Director: Cliff Bole
Cast: Craig Richard Nelson, Gina Hecht, Mark Margolis, Juli Donald

The explosion of a science station seconds after Riker has teleported back to the *Enterprise* leads to accusations of murder against the Commander. It is alleged Riker, amorous for the wife of Dr Apgar, killed the scientist before leaving. Under

Tanugan law, guilt is presumed, and innocence must be proved
– which is what Picard sets out to do using the holodeck to
recreate the vital moments. The subsequent hearing establishes
Riker's innocence and the sinister machinations of Dr Apgar, a
weapons developer ready to sell to the highest bidder.

Stardate: 43610.4

Strange New Worlds: Tanuga 4.

New Life Forms: The Tanugans, whose justice system is the
reverse of Earth's. Dr Apgar is 'one of the greatest scientific
minds in the universe', though he is actually attempting to turn
his Krieger Wave converter into a weapon to sell to the
Romulans or the Ferengi.

Picard Manoeuvre: Yes, once.

Riker's Conquests: Mrs Manua Apgar. Allegedly.

Notes: 'Commander Riker. I am here to take you into custody.'
'On what charge?' 'Suspicion of murder.' *Petrocelli* in space.
OK up to a point, but there's a dreadful 'here's what really happened' ending that would've been thrown out of any impartial
court (note, Picard is the defence council *and* the judge).

The *Enterprise* has been studying a proto-star cloud. They
are delivering a shipment of dicosilium to Apgar. The metal
duranium seems to be used in starship interior design (cf. 'Where
Silence Has Lease' and the original series episode 'The Menagerie'). Picard paints, according to Data, 'in a haphazard
mélange of clashing styles', seemingly influenced by proto-
Vulcan styles and the work of Picasso and other cubists.

62: 'Yesterday's Enterprise'

US Transmission: 19 February 1990
UK Transmission: 29 January 1992
Writers: Ira Steven Behr, Richard Manning, Hans Beimler,

Ronald D. Moore,
from a story by Trent Christopher Ganino, Eric A. Stillwell
Director: David Carson
Cast: Christopher McDonald, Tricia O'Neill

Encountering a temporal rift in space, the *Enterprise* is suddenly in a very different place, as the Federation wages war with the Klingon empire, and only Guinan seems aware of the changes. The arrival of another *Enterprise*, this one thought destroyed 22 years ago, through a 'rift in time' has disrupted the timelines. Guinan explains to Picard that time is 'wrong' and that the *Enterprise*-C must go back through the rift. Tasha Yar, who in this timeline is still the ship's security officer, goes with the *Enterprise*-C, sensing that she does not belong here. Once the *Enterprise*-C has entered the temporal rift, time resumes its normal course, with only Guinan realising what they have all been through.

Stardate: 'Military log, Combat date 43625.2.'

Technobabble: 'The formation of a curl-loop from superstring material. It would require high energy interaction in the vicinity for such a structure to be formed.'

Deanna Underused?: Missing completely. Hardly surprising on a battleship.

Dialogue Triumphs: 'Let's make sure history never forgets the name *Enterprise*.'

Future History: Twenty-two years ago (the mid 2340s), a treaty was in the process of being forged between the Klingons and the Federation. This seems to have been largely cemented by the heroic defence of a Klingon settlement at Narendra 3 from attack by the Romulans by the USS *Enterprise* (NCC 1701-C, Captain Rachel Garrett). This *Enterprise*'s disappearance into the temporal rift changed time. The Romulans' actions went undiscovered (note that in 'The Neutral Zone' the Federation have had no contact with the Romulans for fifty years), the Klingons went to war with the Federation (a war they are winning): thus other, smaller changes to history, like the presence of Tasha Yar.

Notes: 'I don't belong here. I'm supposed to be dead.' Complex, dark and brilliant; easily the best episode of the series when it was first shown, and one that has had few equals since. The audience is thrown in at the deep end, and expected to understand without great explanation the sudden changes they are presented with. Only the Tasha/Castillo love story subplot is awkward and disappointing.

Tasha joined the *Enterprise* straight from the academy.

Data thinks that Guinan's species may have an awareness outside of linear time.

Back in 'reality', Worf thinks prune juice is a 'Warrior's drink'.

63: 'The Offspring'

US Transmission: 12 March 1990
UK Transmission: 5 February 1992
Writer: Ren Echevarria
Director: Jonathan Frakes
Cast: Hallie Todd, Nicolas Coster, Judyanne Elder, Diane Moser, Hayne Boyle, Maria Leone, James G. Becker

Data has created an android child, Lal. When Starfleet learn of her, they require that Data hand over his project to the Daystrom Institute so that her development can be observed. Picard is prepared to take the matter to the highest authority to stop Admiral Haftel splitting up 'father' and 'daughter', but fate takes a hand when the stress of new-found sentience becomes too much for Lal, causing a systems failure despite Data and Haftel's efforts.

Stardate: 43657.0

Strange New Worlds: The *Enterprise* is en route to the Selebi asteroid belt in sector 396.

New Life Forms: Another Soong-class android, Lal.

Riker's Conquests: Data finds Lal embracing a rather stunned Riker. 'Commander, what are your intentions towards my daughter?'

Data's Jokes: Wesley: 'She could learn a lot from children of her own age.' Data: 'She is only two weeks old!'

Dialogue Triumphs: 'I fail to understand how a five foot android with heuristic learning systems and the strength of ten men can be called a child.'

'There are times when men of good conscience cannot blindly follow orders. To order a man to hand his child over to the state. No, not while I'm captain.'

Notes: 'I have not observed anyone else on board consulting you on their procreation, Captain.' Delightful, if unashamedly sentimental, and with a beautiful performance by Hallie Todd as Lal. Like Maddox ('The Measure of the Man'), Starfleet's 'official' face (Admiral Haftel) proves to be deeper than his initial two-dimensional façade suggests. His 'It just wasn't meant to be' is a perfect coda. Jonathan Frakes' direction probably explains why Riker is only present in one scene.

The four selections for appearance Lal chooses are an Andorian female, a human male and female, and a Klingon male. The Daystrom annex on Galor 4 is presumably a small section of the Daystrom Institute (see 'The Measure of the Man').

64: 'Sins of the Father'

US Transmission: 19 March 1990
UK Transmission: 26 February 1992

Writers: Ronald D. Moore, W. Reed Morgan,
based on a teleplay by Drew Deighan
Director: Les Landau
Cast: Charles Cooper, Tony Todd, Patrick Massett,
Thelma Lee, Teddy Davis

The Klingon High Council has judged Worf's father a traitor,
aiding the Romulan massacre at Khitomer. Worf, with Picard's
backing, returns to the Klingon Homeworld to face his accus-
ers, knowing that an unsuccessful appeal will mean his death.
Investigations into the Khitomer massacre reveal that the real
traitor was the father of High Council member Duras. Nevertheless these revelations could plunge the Empire into civil war,
so Worf accepts discommendation and is outcast from Klingon
society.

Stardate: 43685.2 (twenty years after Khitomer).

Strange New Worlds: Our first look at the Klingon Homeworld,
particularly its first city.

Dialogue Triumphs: Kurn on Federation niceties: 'I find the
constraints a bit difficult to conform to. Just a short while ago I
had to stop myself from killing Commander Riker!'

Worf on Duras: 'This ha'Dibah should have been fed to the
dogs!'

Notes: 'I am Worf, son of Mogh. I have come to challenge the
lies spoken about my father.' *Richard III* with aliens. The first
step on the long road to 'Redemption', this is an astonishing
piece of television, devoting almost an entire fifty minute episode to such a heavy subject as Klingon politics.

Klingons believe in obedience and a strict form of command.
Kurn is Worf's younger brother. He was a year old when his
parents went to Khitomer (where 4,000 Klingons died) and was
left with a family friend, Lorgh. He was raised as Lorgh's son
and only became aware of his true blood line at his Age of

Ascension.

Riker's experiences aboard the *Pagh* in 'A Matter of Honor' are mentioned. Picard likes caviar.

In Klingon, cha'Dich means a defender, or second during trial or combat, Mek'ba is an aspect of a trial during which evidence is heard, Kut'luch is a ceremonial weapon of an assassin and ghojmok is a nurse. Picard speaks reasonably fluent Klingon.

It was Duras' father, Ja'rod, who was really responsible for the treachery.

65: 'Allegiance'

US Transmission: 26 March 1990
UK Transmission: 4 March 1992
Writers: Richard Manning, Hans Beimler
Director: Winrich Kolbe
Cast: Stephen Markel, Reiner Schöne, Jocelyn O'Brian, Jerry Rector, Jeff Rector

Picard is kidnapped and replaced by an exact replica. He finds himself held in a small cell with three other abductees and begins to plot a way out. The replica Picard, meanwhile, is only moderately successful in integrating himself into the *Enterprise* way of life, leading some of his officers to become suspicious. The real Picard discovers one of his fellow hostages is a traitor when she mentions classified information. The aliens reveal themselves to be curious about other races, and wished to study reactions to confinement. Picard gives them a taste of their own medicine before throwing them off his ship.

Stardate: 43714.1

Strange New Worlds: Several mentioned including Cor Caroli 5 (where the Phyrox plague has been eradicated: Starfleet have classified this information), Browder 4 (where the *Hood* is engaged in terraforming the planet), Mizar 2, Bolarus 9 and

Chalna. The nearest Pulsar to the *Enterprise* is located in the Lonka Cluster.

New Life Forms: The Mizarians, a pacifist race. The Bolians, Federation members who maintain an uneasy truce with the Moropa. The Chalnoth, an anarchic race whom Picard met twelve years ago aboard the *Stargazer*. And the nameless alien kidnappers who have no morality and don't like prisons!

Poker Game: Riker, Data, Deanna, Geordi and Worf play, with Deanna winning, before they are interrupted by the fake Picard.

Picard Manoeuvre: The fake Picard knows enough about his duplicate to perform this twice.

Dialogue Triumphs: 'Get off my ship!'

Notes: 'Jean-Luc, you are full of surprises today.' Amusing, if insubstantial, though the fake Picard flirting with Beverly is amazing. Nevertheless there are many problems with this. The aliens' reading of Picard's mind gives their replica an intimate knowledge of the *Enterprise* crew, yet within minutes Riker knows something is afoot. How?

The examples of Picard's heroism given by Haro include mentions of Mintaka 3 (see 'Who Watches the Watchers?') and his protection of the Wogneer creatures in the Ordek Nebula.

The fake Picard buys a round of ales in Ten-Forward (maybe this is what alerts Riker?!), and sings the ancient drinking song 'Heart of Oak'. Picard's quarters are on deck 9.

66: 'Captain's Holiday'

US Transmission: 2 April 1990
UK Transmission: 11 March 1992
Writer: Ira Steven Behr
Director: Chip Calmers
Cast: Jennifer Hetrick, Karen Landry, Michael Champion,
Max Grodénchik, Dierdre Imershein

Forced to take shore leave, Picard meets Vash, a beautiful archaeologist, along with a scheming Ferengi, and two time travellers. All are searching for the Tox Uthat, a 27th century superweapon. Picard and Vash seek the Uthat together, and develop something of a relationship, but nobody is exactly who they seem. Finally discovering that Vash already possesses the Uthat, Picard has the *Enterprise* destroy the artifact.

Stardate: 43745.2

Strange New Worlds: Risa (a holiday paradise, see 'The Mind's Eye', 'The Game'), Gemaris 5 (where Picard has served as mediator between the Gemarians and the Dachlyds). Icor 9.

New Life Forms: The Vorgons, time travellers from the 27th century. The Sarthongians of Sarthong 5 are said to be merciless to trespassers.

Introducing: Vash.

Riker's Conquests: None specifically, but he seems to have a thing about Risian girls (see 'The Game').

Dialogue Triumphs: 'You told me your four days in Zytchin 3 were wonderful.' 'I lied.'
    'I prefer to be acquainted with the women I kiss.'
    'She's a greedy and unscrupulous woman. A perfect mate for a Ferengi.'

Notes: 'The last thing I need is a partner.' Witty and epic, an Indiana Jones-type story of lost treasure, double dealing and . . . er, time-travelling aliens. Vash is a brilliant creation and should have returned far more often than she did.

   Picard's light holiday reading includes Joyce's *Ulysses* and *Ethics, Sophistry and the Alternate Universe* by Ving Kuda. Riker and Deanna's ploy to get Jean-Luc on holiday include the threat of a visit by Lwaxana. Hoverball is a Risian game. Horga'hn is a Risian symbol of sexuality; to display it openly is to seek 'Jamaharon'.

Tox Uthat, a mythical archaeological relic, is actually a 27th-century quantum phase inhibitor invented by scientist Kal Dano and capable of halting all nuclear reaction within a star. It was brought to the 22nd century to avoid capture by the Vorgons. Vash has served for five years as the personal assistant of Professor Samuel Estragon, who spent half his life searching for the Uthat. She says she planned to sell the Uthat to the Daystrom Institute.

67: 'Tin Man'

US Transmission: 23 April 1990
UK Transmission: 18 March 1992
Writers: Dennis Putman Bailey, David Birschoff
Director: Robert Scheerer
Cast: Michael Cavanaugh, Peter Vogt, Harry Groener

In the Hayashi system, the Federation has discovered a new life form, codenamed 'Tin Man'. The *Enterprise* arrives with a Betazoid specialist, Tam Elbrun, but find the Romulans are also interested. Data and Elbrun attempt to establish contact with Tin Man by beaming inside. Elbrun is successful and gets the creature to produce a shock wave that throws both the *Enterprise* and the Romulans away from it. Later Data tells Picard that Elbrun and Tin Man, having found mental peace in each other's company, intend to roam the universe together.

Stardate: 43779.3

Strange New Worlds: Beta Stromgren, a star in the final stages of collapse, in an area claimed by the Romulans. Chandra 5.

New Life Forms: 'Tin Man', an organic ship-creature, probably the last of its race; known as Gomtuu in its own language.

The Chandrarians are beautiful creatures who have a three-day ritual for saying 'hello'.

Dialogue Triumphs: 'You want them to hate you. Why?' 'Because I'm not a nice man!'

'This intelligence that swims naked through space like a fish in the sea. Totally alien. Mysterious . . . Ancient and alone. Lonely.'

'Perhaps you're just different. It's not a sin, you know, though you may have heard otherwise.'

Notes: 'Tin Man hurts, and wants to die.' Featuring Romulans, an organic ship, and a stressed-out empath, the final scenes in which Data takes another step towards humanity are quite astonishing. There's a great performance by Harry Groener as the screwed-up Betazoid.

Riker's former ship *The Hood* and Captain Robert De Soto were mentioned in 'Encounter at Farpoint'. De Soto is an old friend of Picard's.

Tam Elbrun is a Betazoid who developed telepathy during childhood rather than at adolescence as most Betazoids do. He works for Starfleet mainly as a first contact expert. However, his 'gift' is unstable, and after being involved in the Ghorusda disaster he was a patient at the Betazoid University where Deanna was studying.

Forty-seven people from the ship *Adelphi* were killed on Ghorusda including two friends of Riker's from the academy. The Federation report blamed Captain Darson, though others considered Elbrun at least partly to blame for not briefing the captain well enough on Ghorusda cultural taboos.

Tam calls Riker 'Billy Boy' in anger (good for him!). Data has tried to sleep from time to time, although he does not require rest (see 'Birthright, Part I').

The Romulan ships encountered are D'deridex-class Warbirds.

68: 'Hollow Pursuits'

US Transmission: 30 April 1990

UK Transmission: 25 March 1992
Writer: Sally Caves
Director: Cliff Bole
Cast: Charley Lang

Reg Barclay is an imaginative but shy diagnostic engineer, with a huge crush on Deanna. But his inability to interact with other crew members causes him to spend most of his time on the holodeck, where his fantasies surround his 'heroism'. Geordi is irritated by Barclay but, on Picard's instructions, attempts to befriend him, and discovers his holodeck secrets. When Barclay provides a solution to a potentially disastrous series of acceleration bursts, he becomes more confident and agrees to give reality another try. He bids goodbye to all of his holodeck programs (except number nine).

Stardate: 43807.4

Strange New Worlds: Nahmi 4, where there is a Correllium fever outbreak.

New Life Forms: The Mikulaks, mentioned briefly.

Introducing: Timid engineer Reginald Barclay: the first of his five appearances on the show.

Technobabble: Nucleosynthesis is 'alteration of matter at the atomic level'. Only five substances are capable of producing the specific forms seen on the *Enterprise*; invidium, jakmanite, lucrovexitrin, selgninaem and saltzgadum.

Picard Manoeuvre: Barclay does it (a nervous reaction?).

Deanna Underused?: Only as the Goddess of Empathy (whom we'd all like to see a lot more of).

Data's Jokes: 'Why is Lieutenant Barclay being clandestinely referred to as a vegetable?'

Dialogue Triumphs: 'There's nothing wrong with a healthy fantasy life so long as you don't let it take over.'

Notes: 'He just doesn't fit in here.' Great comedy, this is delightfully silly. It's good to see, for once, a less-than-perfect member of Starfleet, and Dwight Schultz's hilariously bumbling performance contains just the right shade of pathos, making Barclay sympathetic rather than just foolish. It's hardly surprising that the character has become one of the most popular returning guests.

Reg's nickname, 'Broccoli', was coined by Wesley. Picard 'isn't accustomed to seeing an unsatisfactory rating' on a member of his crew. Barclay previously served on the *Zhukov*, where Captain Gleason spoke highly of him. He drinks warm milk in Ten-Forward. It is indicated that he has developed several holodeck fantasies, the one seen by Geordi, Riker and Troi being largely based on *The Three Musketeers*. 'Holodiction' is an addiction to the holodeck. Geordi, referring to 'Booby Trap', says that he once 'fell in love in there'.

There isn't actually a regulation to prevent crewmen from simulating other crewmembers on the holodeck, although Riker thinks there should be! He does, however, think it is a breach of protocol. Deanna is vaguely amused until she sees the 'Goddess of Empathy'!

Guinan's uncle Terkim was 'the family misfit' (the only member of her family with a sense of humour).

69: 'The Most Toys'

US Transmission: 7 May 1990
UK Transmission: 1 April 1992
Writer: Shari Goodhartz
Director: Timothy Bond
Cast: Saul Rubinek, Nehemiah Persoff, Jane Daly

Data's shuttle explodes while ferrying important supplies for a Federation colony, but all the events are a mere ruse to place

Data in a collection of the galaxy's great treasures. His new 'owner', Kivas Fajo, is outraged when Data won't do as he is told, and threatens the life of his assistant, Varria, in order to ensure Data's cooperation. Data and Varria collaborate on an escape plan, but Varria is killed by Fajo. Data shoots Fajo, but is beamed aboard the *Enterprise*, the crew having discovered the truth about Fajo and his 'beneficence'.

Stardate: 42872.2

Strange New Worlds: Thanks to Fajo the Federation colony on Beta Agni 2 has a contaminated water supply (Fajo also supplies the cure, hytritium). According to Fajo, the Sigma Erandi system might also have some hytritium.

New Life Forms: Kivas Fajo is a Zibalian.

The Andorians wish to make a bid for a shipment of Tellurian spices. Ferengi add pearls to Veltan sex idols to increase their value (or so they think).

Technology: The transporter can not only detect a discharged weapon (Data fires the disrupter just as he is energised) but render it harmless.

Dialogue Triumphs: Fajo on Data: 'A marvellous contradiction – a military pacifist. Tell me, whose dreadful idea was it to enlist you in Starfleet to begin with?'

Notes: 'For an android with no feelings he sure managed to evoke them in others.' A rather ordinary comedy episode, with Fajo being particularly over-the-top. The ending is great, however, with Data seeming on the verge of emotional understanding as he fires at Fajo and then lies to Riker.

Hytritium – as well as being a cure for the contaminated water – is too unstable to be transported, so Data shuttles the material to the *Enterprise*. Data is composed of (amongst other things?) 26.8 kilos of tripolymer composites, 11.8 kilos of molybdenum-cobalt alloy and 1.8 kilos of bioplast sheeting. He has not killed anyone before (and is narrowly prevented from doing so here). When Geordi and Wesley inspect Data's room they find his framed medals (which Wes describes as being some of Starfleet's highest), the 'statue' of Yar, the Shakespeare book that Picard gave him (all seen in 'The Measure of a Man') and some playing cards and poker chips. The book is open at *Hamlet* ('He was a man, take him for all in all, I shall not look upon his like again'). Worf is chosen to replace Data at Ops, the second time, he says, he has taken the position of a dead colleague (see 'Skin of Evil').

Fajo is a member of the Stacius Trade Guild, and was educated on Eratus 5. He carries a proximity-actuated field device that impedes Data's positron flow. Fajo's treasures include the first Basotile (an abstract sculpture), which is hundreds of years old, a priceless vase made by the late Mark Off-Zel of Sirrie 4, the *Mona Lisa*, Dali's *The Persistence of Memory*, Van Gogh's *The Starry Night*, the Rejac Crystal, the *Lawmim Galactopedia*, the Emoliamanda Tapestry, the only-known Roger Maris trading card from Earth c.1962 (which still smells of gum), four Veltan sex idols and the last surviving lapling. He also has four of the five prototype Varon-T disrupters, which were banned by the Federation.

The USS *Grissom* is said to be close to the Sigma Erandi system. Fajo has visited Station Lya 4.

70: 'Sarek'

US Transmission: 14 May 1990
UK Transmission: 8 April 1992
Writers: Peter S. Beagles,
from a television story by Peter S. Beagle,
from an unpublished story by Marc Cushman, Jake Jacobs
Director: Les Landau
Cast: Mark Lenard, Joanna Miles, William Denis,
Rocco Sisto, John H. Francis

The *Enterprise* is to host the first meeting between the Federation, represented by Ambassador Sarek, and the Legarans. However, Sarek seems less than well, and relationships on the ship almost immediately deteriorate. Wes and Geordi fight, Dr Crusher hits her son, and a mass brawl develops in Ten-Forward. It seems that the Vulcan is experiencing the trauma of Bendii's syndrome and projecting his repressed emotions on to others. Sarek is incapable of continuing the negotiations, but the Legarans will deal with no one else. Picard proposes a Vulcan mind-meld – exchanging his own self- control for Sarek's rage – and the ambassador is able to complete his mission.

Stardate: 43917.4

Strange New Worlds: The *Enterprise* is in orbit around Vulcan. The Legarans come from Legara 4.

New Life Forms: The Legarans are said to be very sensitive to matters of protocol (preferring to do their business in rooms with no furniture and bare walls). Although not seen in the episode, the Legarans required a special pool to be constructed for them.

Bendii's syndrome is a very rare condition that affects Vulcans over 200 years old, and involves a loss of emotional control.

Picard Manoeuvre: When deciding to confront Sarek.

Notes: A vague Alzheimer's allegory is brought to life by a superb and vulnerable performance from Patrick Stewart after the mind-meld sequence.

Sarek's wife Perrin, like his previous wife (see the original series episode 'Journey to Babel'), is from Earth. Riker remembers studying Sarek at school, his achievements including the treaty of Alpha Cygnus 9, the admission of Coridon to the Federation and the Klingon alliance. Sarek is 202 years old, and has been working towards this conference for 93 years. Picard met Sarek briefly 'at his son's wedding' (almost certainly a reference to Spock: see 'Unification'). The USS *Merrimac* will take Sarek back to Vulcan.

Wesley has a date with Ensign Suzanne Dumont. Data has been programmed to reproduce the musical styles of over 300 concert violinists, including Heifetz, Menuhin, Grak-tay and Tataglia.

71: 'Ménage à Troi'

US Transmission: 28 May 1990
UK Transmission: 15 April 1992
Writers: Fred Bronson, Susan Sackett
Director: Robert Legato
Cast: Frank Corsentino, Ethan Phillips, Peter Slutsker,
Rudolph Willrich, Carel Struycken

Will and Deanna's shore leave on Betazed is ruined when they, and Lwaxana, are kidnapped by Tog, a love-struck Ferengi. Wesley earns himself a field promotion with his successful decoding of Riker's distress call from the Ferengi ship and the *Enterprise* confronts Tog, with Picard playing the part of a jealous jilted lover. Terrified, Tog returns his hostages.

Stardate: 43930.7

Strange New Worlds: Betazed is seen for the first time. Zampras 3 is mentioned.

Technobabble: All warp engines emit Cochrane Distortion, 'a fluctuation in the phase of the subspace field'. (See *Star Trek*'s 'Metamorphosis'.)

Dialogue Triumphs: 'From the smell of things, I'd say we were aboard a Ferengi vessel.'

'My, what big ears you have!'

Notes: 'Let's get one thing straight, little man. I am not for sale!' Another comedy episode, but this one hasn't the wit or strangeness of 'Déjà Q'. The opening scenes echo 'Journey to Babel'. Nice to see Will and Deanna out of uniform and on location for once. Patrick Stewart's eye-rolling over-acting in the last scene is excellent.

The biannual trade agreements conference on Betazed include the Ferengi for the first time. Deanna describes the Sacred Chalice of Rixx (see 'Haven') as an old clay pot with mould growing in it. Lwaxana's first husband wasn't much of a conversationalist, but was good in bed. Ninety-one per cent of Starfleet graduates are not assigned to Galaxy-class starships. The 3D chess move Riker uses to beat his Ferengi opponent is 'the Queen's Gambit, finished off with the Aldabren Exchange'.

72: 'Transfigurations'

US Transmission: 4 June 1990
UK Transmission: 22 April 1992
Writer: René Echevarria
Director: Tom Benko
Cast: Mark LaMura, Charles Dennis, Julie Warner,
Patti Tippo

On a mission to the Zeta Gelis star cluster, the *Enterprise* finds an injured amnesiac alien. Christening him 'John Doe', the crew are pleased as he displays astonishing healing powers. The arrival of a Zalkonian ship provides some of the answers to his background: 'John' is a mutant evolutionary step, hunted on his homeworld by the government who are afraid of his powers. With the help of Picard, 'John' completes his metamorphosis into a beautiful new life form.

Stardate: 43957.2

New Life Forms: The Zalkonians, a quasi-fascist race. They fear the unalike and the regeneration of 'John' and others into a mutant avatar race is a capital offence on Zalkon.

Picard Manoeuvre: Picard and Geordi are both at it.

Dialogue Triumphs: 'It is our mission to seek out life in all forms. We are privileged to have been present at the emergence of a new species.'

Notes: 'I seem to be a mystery, doctor, to you and to myself.' A bit of an obvious storyline, although not without its charm. Geordi's lack of skill in the romantic department isn't a surprise, especially since he finally gets a date with Christy Henshaw (see 'Booby Trap'). His choice of Worf as a guide in this is surprising (not to say worrying).

O'Brien has dislocated a shoulder kayaking on the holodeck.

73: 'The Best of Both Worlds 1'

US Transmission: 18 June 1990
UK Transmission: 29 April 1992
Writer: Michael Piller
Director: Cliff Bole
Cast: Elizabeth Dennehy, George Murdock

The annihilation of a Federation colony bears the hallmarks of a Borg attack. Starfleet's Borg tactics specialist, Lt Commander Shelby, is seconded to the *Enterprise*, and quickly lets everyone know she is after Riker's job. The Borg now seem to have a specific target, Picard. He is kidnapped by the automatons during a lightning attack on the *Enterprise*. An away team mission to recapture the captain fails, Picard having been assimilated by the Borg, becoming Locutus. As he tells the *Enterprise* crew that they, too, will be assimilated, Riker orders the firing of all weapons.

Stardate: 43989.1 (probably a Tuesday, as it's Poker night: see 'Cause and Effect').

Strange New Worlds: Jouret 4, one of the Federation's outermost colonies. Main town, New Providence.

Poker Game: Riker, Troi, Wesley, Data, Geordi and Shelby play. Wesley is 'new to the game'. Shelby calls Riker's bluff, and wins.

Picard Manoeuvre: Definite shirt-pulling moments here.

Data's Jokes: Concerning 'the early bird catches the worm': 'There is no evidence of aviation or crawling vermical life forms on Jouret 4.'

Dialogue Triumphs: 'Maybe I'm just afraid of the big chair.'

Shelby on Riker: 'All you know how to do is play it safe. I suppose that's why someone like you sits in the shadow of a great man for as long as you have.'

Notes: 'I am Locutus of Borg. Resistance is futile.' From the startling pre-title sequence, through the Riker/Shelby power-games and the magical Picard/Guinan scenes to the extraordinary climax, this is as good as it gets. Almost flawless.

Riker is in the process of turning down his third offered commission (the *Melbourne*). USS *Lalo* has just been destroyed by the Borg close to Zeta Alpha 2 near the Paulson Nebula, a cloud composed of 82 per cent dilithium hydroxyls.

When the Borg destroyed Guinan's people, they were scattered throughout the galaxy but continued to survive.

The Federation has sent its battle fleet to Wolf 359. 'We'll make our stand there.'

Fourth Season

26 45-minute episodes

Created by Gene Roddenberry

Executive Producers: Rick Berman (74–84, 86–99),

Michael Piller (74–84, 86–99), Gene Roddenberry (74–84, 86–99) **Co-Executive Producers:** Rick Berman (85), Michael Piller (85), Gene Roddenberry (85) **Producers:** David Livingston, Lee Sheldon (74–81) **Co-Producer:** Peter Lauritson **Supervising Producer:** Jeri Taylor (75–99) **Associate Producer:** Wendy Neuss **Line Producer:** Merri Howard (97) **Executive Story Editors:** Joe Menosky, Ronald D. Moore **Story Editors:** David Bennett Carren (82–99), J. Larry Carroll (84–99)

Regular Cast: Patrick Stewart (Captain Jean-Luc Picard), Jonathan Frakes (Commander William Riker), LeVar Burton (Lt Commander Geordi La Forge), Michael Dorn (Lt Worf), Gates McFadden (Dr Beverly Crusher), Marina Sirtis (Counselor Deanna Troi), Brent Spiner (Lt Commander Data), Wil Wheaton (Wesley Crusher), Colm Meaney (Lt O'Brien, 74–76, 78–79, 84–85, 87, 90, 95, 97–98), Rosalind Chao (Keiko Ishikawa/O'Brien, 84–85, 90, 98), Whoopi Goldberg (Guinan, 74–75, 83, 87, 89–90, 98–99), Jon Steuer (Alexander, 80), Patti Yasutake (Nurse Ogawa, 81[1], 87, 91, 96), Dwight Schultz (Lt Reg Barclay, 92), John de Lancie (Q, 93), Majel Barrett (Lwaxana Troi, 95)

74: 'The Best of Both Worlds 2'

US Transmission: 24 September 1990
UK Transmission: 6 May 1992
Writer: Michael Piller
Director: Cliff Bole
Cast: Elizabeth Dennehy, George Murdock, Todd Merrill

---

[1]Not named in this story. 'Clues' gives her first name as Alyssa, 'Identity Crisis' indicates her surname.

The *Enterprise*'s weapons prove ineffectual against the Borg. Leaving the *Enterprise* behind, the Borg head for Earth, massacring the Federation battlefleet *en route* at Wolf 359. Another attempt is made to recapture Picard, this time successfully. Data attempts to tap into the Borg's collective consciousness through Locutus. Gradually Picard's humanity wins the struggle for his psyche, and he gives Data the clue to enable the android to shut down the Borg.

Stardate: 44001.4

Technobabble: 'Your submicron matrix activity is increasing exponentially.'

Picard Manoeuvre: Riker does it on assuming the captaincy, and several times afterwards.

Dialogue Triumphs: Guinan to Captain Riker: 'I've heard a lot of people talking down in Ten-Forward. They expect to be dead in the next day or so. They trust you. They like you. But they don't believe anyone can save them.'

Deanna: 'How do you feel?' Picard: 'Almost human.'

Notes: 'Preparation is irrelevant. Your people will be assimilated as easily as Picard has been.' Cries of 'cop-out' are unfair, as this is a fitting climax to the saga. Worf and Data's daring kidnapping of Locutus/Picard is one of the best action sequences in the series. Only in the final few minutes does the speed of events disappoint.

Locutus refers to the Borg's assimilation of humanity as 'the New Order'. The Borg collective consciousness is divided into sub-commands necessary to carry out all functions: defence, communication, navigation. They are all controlled by a root command. The Wolf 359 battle is a disaster for Starfleet (see *Deep Space Nine*: 'Emissary'): the ships destroyed include the *Melbourne* and the *Tolstoy*.

Picard was the only Federation cadet to win the Academy marathon on Danula 2 (passing four upper classmen on the last of the hills of a forty kilometre race). Guinan says her relationship with Picard is 'beyond friendship, beyond family'.

Lt Barclay is mentioned. Beverly suggests using Nanites to defeat the Borg (see 'Evolution').

75: 'Family'

US Transmission: 1 October 1990
UK Transmission: 3 May 1993
Writers: Ronald D. Moore,
based in part on a premise by Susanne Lambdin,
Bryan Stewart
Director: Les Landau
Cast: Jeremy Kemp, Samantha Eggar, Theodore Bikel,
Georgina Brown, Dennis Creaghan, David Tristin Birkin,
Doug Wert

The *Enterprise* returns to Earth to allow its crew a chance to recover from the horror of the Borg attack. For Picard, this means a return to his home in France for the first time in twenty years and an awkward reunion with his brother, Robert. Worf's foster-parents visit their son, helping him come to terms with his discommendation. Beverly gives Wesley a stored hologram that Jack Crusher made for him before he died. Picard resists the temptation to leave Starfleet behind for an exciting new oceanic project and makes his peace with his brother. His nephew, René, dreams of following his uncle and exploring the stars.

Stardate: 44012.3

Strange New Worlds: McKinley Space Station, orbiting Earth. Labarre in France.

Technobabble: Theta Matrix compositors mentioned.

Dialogue Triumphs: 'What does it mean anyway? "Arrogant

son-of-a . . ." ' 'Let's talk about that later.'

'Why did you come back, Jean-Luc? . . . Because you want me to look after you again?'

And the magical coda: 'Let him dream.'

Notes: 'You always search for the future, and your brother for the past.' 'There should be room enough for both.' Lovely, despite the lack of French accents! A charming piece of pure soap opera, showing the human face of the *Star Trek* universe.

There are many continuity references to the events of 'The Best of Both Worlds' and 'Sins of the Father'. The impression given here is that Jack R. Crusher died when Wesley was an infant, as opposed to a five-year-old as stated in 'Encounter at Farpoint'.

Picard was a schoolboy prodigy and a superb athlete. His childhood friend, Louis, is a supervisor in the Atlantis Project (attempting to create another subaquatic continent). Robert gives Jean-Luc a bottle of wine (the '47) and tells him not to drink it alone (he takes this advice, see 'First Contact'). He says harmonic resonators were used to relieve the tectonic pressures on Drema 4 (see 'Pen Pals').

O'Brien's Christian names are Miles Edward. The last time his father was aboard, he was found chasing Nurse Stanton around the bio-bed in sickbay. Worf's human foster father, Sergey Rozhenko, was chief petty officer aboard the Excelsior-class *Intrepid*, and was a warpfield specialist. Worf would never touch human food. His mother, Helena, learned to cook rokeg blood pie (Riker's favourite: see 'A Matter of Honor'). Guinan tells Helena of Worf's love for prune juice (see 'Yesterday's Enterprise').

Will and Deanna are considering 'going back' to Angel Falls in Venezuela on shore leave. Jack Crusher proposed to Beverly by sending her a book entitled *How to Advance Your Career Through Marriage*.

76: 'Brothers'

US Transmission: 8 October 1990
UK Transmission: 4 May 1993
Writer: Rick Berman
Director: Rob Bowman
Cast: Cory Danziger, Adam Ryen, James Lashly

A medical emergency involving two young brothers means that the *Enterprise* must travel to a medical facility. But Data takes control of the ship, isolates himself on the bridge and changes course. Data has, it transpires, been given a homing signal by his creator, Noonian Soong. The scientist is dying, and wishes to give Data his life's work, an 'emotions' chip. However, the homing signal has also been received by Lore who arrives, angry at having been betrayed by his 'father'. Tricking Soong into believing he is Data, Lore takes the emotions chip and kills Soong, leaving Data to continue his search for humanity.

Stardate: 44085.7

Strange New Worlds: Ogus 2 (shore leave here is interrupted by the medical emergency).

Technobabble: Geordi is performing dilithium vector calibrations.

Dialogue Triumphs: Riker on Data's effect on the ship: 'The only way we discovered we'd come out of warp was by looking out of the window!'

'You didn't fill Data with substandard parts, did you, old man?!'

Notes: 'This is your lucky day, Data. You've found your long-lost father. And he's alive!' An astonishing triple performance by Brent Spiner, though his Noonian Soong is almost unrecognisable under a smothering of latex.

The fruit of the cove palm on Ogus 2 contains a deadly parasite. Starbase 416's laboratories can isolate the toxin. Data can imitate Picard's voice print. Data and Lore are virtually identical 'except for a little programming'.

The Crystal Entity from 'Datalore' is mentioned (here, and in 'Silicon Avatar', it is referred to as the Crystal*line* Entity). Soong never felt comfortable living anywhere without a pre-arranged escape route ('I admit, I didn't think I'd be running from a giant snowflake!'). Data whistles 'Pop Goes the Weasel', echoing 'Encounter at Farpoint'.

Lore spent two years floating in space before a fortunate meeting with a Pakled tradeship (see 'Samaritan Snare'). He sings 'Abdul Abulbul Amir'.

77: 'Suddenly Human'

US Transmission: 15 October 1990
UK Transmission: 5 May 1993
Writers: John Whelpley, Jeri Taylor,
from a story by Ralph Phillips
Director: Gabrielle Beaumont
Cast: Sherman Howard, Chad Allen, Barbara Townsend

On board a Talarian ship, the *Enterprise* crew discover a human teenager. The boy, Jono, wishes to be returned to his father, the Talarian leader Endar. Investigation proves that he is the child of a Starfleet couple, kidnapped after his parents were killed. Picard develops a close relationship with the boy, and persuades Endar that the decision regarding his future should be Jono's. However, the pressure placed on Jono comes close to killing him, and Picard returns the boy to his adoptive father.

Stardate: 44143.7

Strange New Worlds: The *Enterprise* is travelling through Sector 21947. Castal 1 is where Endar lost his son. The Woden Sector is also mentioned.

New Life Forms: The Talarians, a rigidly patriarchal society. During the Galen border crisis it was a common tactic of the Talarians to abandon their observation craft and rig them to self-destruct. This resulted in 219 fatalities in three days.

B'Nar is a Talarian signal of distress (resembling a high-pitched wail). T'stayan is a six-hooved Talarian beast. In Talarian society, fourteen is the male 'Age of Decision'. Alba Ra is a contemporary Talarian musical form (sounding not unlike avant-garde rock).

Data's Jokes: Data doesn't understand slapstick, but takes Riker's word for it that it is funny.

Dialogue Triumphs: 'I'm not cringing, I'm just acknowledging my limitations.'

Notes: 'If he is to find his humanity, you are the only one who can help.' *Star Trek* does child abuse. Worthy and, therefore, immensely dull, though the scene in which Deanna asks Picard about his own (seemingly painful) childhood is priceless.

Picard and Jono play racketball (a squash-like game). Jono is really the grandson of a Starfleet admiral, born on Galen 4. His parents were killed when the colony was overrun by Talarians. Riker knew another member of the family (Jono's uncle, seemingly) who was killed at the Kratner outpost.

The Stockholm Syndrome (20th century hijacking/abuse theory) is mentioned. Wesley thinks that the Banana Split is 'very possibly the greatest thing in the universe'.

Talarian warships are limited to neutrino particle weapons, high energy x-ray lasers and Merculite rockets, all of which are inferior to the *Enterprise*'s defences.

78: 'Remember Me'

US Transmission: 22 October 1990
UK Transmission: 6 May 1993
Writer: Lee Sheldon

Director: Cliff Bole
Cast: Eric Menyuk, Bill Erwin

After welcoming a friend on board, Beverly visits Wesley, conducting warp-field experiments in engineering. Explaining the procedure, Wesley finds his mother has gone. Later, Beverly is concerned when people begin to go missing on the *Enterprise*, starting with her friend, Dr Quaice. The crew is steadily reduced until only Beverly remains on board. Checking with the computer, Beverly realises she is in a contracting micro-universe. Meanwhile Wesley and Geordi's attempts to recreate the accident are unsuccessful. The arrival of the Traveler helps Wesley to create a doorway and Beverly dives back into reality just as her bubble universe collapses.

Stardate: 44161.2

Strange New Worlds: Starbase 133, Keda 2 (Dalen Quaice's home planet), Durenia 4. The Traveler's planet Tau Alpha C is mentioned (see 'Where No One Has Gone Before').

Picard Manoeuvre: Picard two, Wesley one, Beverly one.

Dialogue Triumphs: Beverly's description of the disappeared Worf to her bewildered colleagues: 'The big guy who never smiles?'

And the best line in TV history: 'Computer, what is the nature of the universe?' 'The universe is a spheroid region 705 metres in diameter.'

Notes: 'You know what the worst part of growing old is? So many of the people you've known all your life are gone, and you realise you didn't take the time to appreciate them while you still could.' A very clever episode, with a great part for Gates McFadden, and intelligent manipulation of audience expectations. Nice to see the Traveler back, too.

Dalen Quaice was Beverly's mentor; she interned with him on Delos 4 about fifteen years ago (this would have been in the period between Wesley's birth and Jack's death). Quaice's wife has recently died. Beverly reported for duty on the *Enterprise* on Stardate 41154 (see 'Encounter at Farpoint').

Kosinski's warpfield variations are mentioned as a consequence of the creation of the static warp bubble (see 'Where No One Has Gone Before'). The *Wellington* is the only other Starfleet vessel in the area.

There are 1014 people aboard the *Enterprise* (including Quaice). Other members of Beverly's medical staff include doctors Hill and Selar. The connection between a docked spacecraft and a starbase is called the umbilical port.

Beverly seems about to tell Picard something very important about their relationship, but she is interrupted. She also quotes from *The Wizard of Oz*.

79: 'Legacy'

US Transmission: 29 October 1990
UK Transmission: 7 May 1993
Writer: Joe Menosky
Director: Robert Scheerer
Cast: Beth Toussaint, Don Mirault, Vladimir Velasco,
Christopher Michael

Two Federation engineers are held prisoner on Turkana 4, Tasha Yar's homeworld, by one of the planet's cadres. The *Enterprise* discovers a world in the midst of civil war. A rival cadre, the Coalition, offers to help the *Enterprise*, and reveals that Tasha's sister Ishara is one of their number. Ishara works closely with Data on a rescue plan, but Ishara's real interest is in gaining access to the Alliance's power centre to cripple their defence systems. Data is given a lesson in betrayal as Riker foils Ishara's plans.

Stardate: 44215.2

Strange New Worlds: Turkana 4, an Earth colony torn by civil war for thirty years. It severed relations with the Federation nearly fifteen years ago. Its two factions or cadres are the Alliance and the Coalition.

Camus 2, site of an archaeological dig, is mentioned.

Poker Game: Riker, Worf, Deanna and Data play. Data has 'the best poker face' Riker has ever seen. He wins, and spots an attempted piece of chicanery by Riker.

Dialogue Triumphs: 'The enemy of my enemy is my friend.'

Notes: 'I'm sorry you never knew the woman Tasha became. I think you would have been proud of her.' Obvious, and misogynistic. *Star Trek* does *Warriors*. Badly.

Ishara is Tasha Yar's younger sister. Their parents were killed just after Ishara was born. Tasha hated the cadres, whom she blamed for her parent's death, but Ishara joined the Coalition. (If Tasha's dating of her 'abandonment' in 'The Naked Now' is correct, Ishara is about five years younger than her. Since Tasha left Turkana when she was fifteen, Ishara would have been ten.) The rape gangs Tasha refers to in 'The Naked Now' are mentioned. Riker feels guilt about Tasha's death under his command. Data says Tasha was 'especially close' to Riker, Worf and himself.

The first time Picard saw Tasha, she was making her way through a Carnellian minefield to help an injured colonist. Her ship had answered a distress call, as had Picard's (probably not the *Stargazer*). When Picard took command of the *Enterprise* he requested Tasha's transfer from her captain, who owed him a favour (these events do not tie in with 'All Good Things . . .' where Tasha was already on the *Enterprise* when Picard arrives).

Two Federation ships are referred to: the *Arcos* and the *Potemkin* (one of Riker's old ships, see 'Peak Performance'), which was the last Federation vessel to visit Turkana 4 six years ago. They were warned that anyone transporting to the planet would be killed.

Worf has seen 'proximity detectors' used on Manu 3. Telluridian synthale is a Turkanian drink.

80: 'Reunion'

US Transmission: 5 November 1990
UK Transmission: 10 May 1993
Writers: Thomas Perry, Jo Perry, Ronald D. Moore,
Brannon Braga,
from a story by Drew Deighan, Thomas Perry, Jo Perry
Director: Jonathan Frakes
Cast: Suzie Plakson, Robert O'Reilly, Patrick Massett,
Charles Cooper, Michael Rider, April Grace, Basil Wallace,
Mirron E. Willis

Investigating radiation anomalies in the Gamma Arigulon system, the *Enterprise* is contacted by K'Ehleyr who tells Picard that K'mpec, the Klingon leader, is dying. She also brings with her Alexander, her son by Worf. K'mpec asks Picard to be the Arbiter of Succession as no Klingon can be trusted. The two rivals as the next leader are Duras, son of the Romulan collaborator, and Gowron. K'Ehleyr's attempts to discover the truth of Khitomer prompts Duras to kill her. Worf takes his revenge on Duras, and Gowron is named the Klingon's new leader.

Stardate: 44246.3

New Life Forms: The Tholians and the Ferengi are mentioned. Klingons and Romulans have been 'blood enemies' for 75 years according to Geordi (although at the time of the Khitomer massacre – approximately 25 years ago – a tentative alliance existed).

Deanna Underused?: Missing completely.

Dialogue Triumphs: 'Lieutenant, you are a member of this crew and will not go into hiding whenever a Klingon vessel uncloaks.'

'Not even a bite on the cheek for old times' sake?'

Notes: 'What shall I tell Alexander? That he has no father?' Following the themes established in 'Sins of the Father', this is a hugely important episode, setting the Klingon saga off in a completely new direction. Worf's duel with Duras is extraordinary.

Worf's bat'telh (a scythe-like weapon) has been in his family for ten generations. The ritual of Rite of Succession is called Qua jiH nagil, part of which is Ja'chug, an oratory in which candidates list their triumphs. 'Ha'Dibah' is an insult, and 'JlH Dok' a term for spouse.

The molecular-decay detonator of a triceron bomb is described as a Romulan weapon.

81: 'Future Imperfect'

US Transmission: 12 November 1990
UK Transmission: 11 May 1993
Writers: J. Larry Carroll, David Bennett Carren
Director: Les Landau
Cast: Andreas Katsulas, Chris Demetral,
Carolyn McCormick, Todd Merrill, April Grace,
George O'Hanlon jnr

On a security survey of the Onias sector, Riker succumbs to toxic gases and wakes up sixteen years later to find himself captain of a much changed *Enterprise*. As he attempts to come to terms with a peace conference with the Romulans, and a son he doesn't know, Riker senses that something is wrong. This is confirmed when his dead wife is revealed to be Minuet. At first Riker believes that he has been subjected to a Romulan trap, but a slip of the tongue by his fellow prisoner (the boy who 'played' his son) tells Riker that this is also an illusion. The boy is really a lonely alien, perhaps the last of his kind. He accompanies Riker back to the *Enterprise*.

Stardate: 44286.5 (and, approximately two years after 58416 – allegedly).

Strange New Worlds: Alpha Onias 3 (a class M planet, barren and inhospitable). Miridian 6, another planet near the Neutral Zone, is also mentioned.

New Life Forms: Barash, a child-alien, from a nameless race of powerful shape-shifters. He may be the last of his kind.

Riker's Conquests: Minuet. Again. Only this time they're married! (See '11001001'.)

Notes: 'I don't believe this. Is it a dream?' A very clever script, with a fascinating look into a complex alternative future – it's something of a pity that it all turns out to be a fiction (and then, a fiction within a fiction). The pre-title sequence is brilliant. The sight of an aged Picard (with beard) is really funny.

Outpost 23 is the key to all Federation defences in the Neutral Zone. Its location is a closely-guarded secret. Will's trombone playing is the cause of much good-natured ribbing from his crewmates. The Curtis Creek Program is Riker's holodeck fishing fantasy.

In the Barash-created future Will is captain of the *Enterprise*. He contracted Alterian encephalitis on Alpha Onias 3 (a retro-virus that incorporates its DNA into the host, causing delayed-action amnesia from the moment of infection). Will has been captain for nine years, Picard having become an admiral. Geordi has cloned eye implants. Data is the first officer. There is a Ferengi conn ensign. Picard arrives on the Romulan ship *Decius* along with Deanna who works with him at Starfleet. Her replacement as *Enterprise* counselor was Minuet whom Riker married and had a son, Jean-Luc. Minuet died two years ago in a shuttle accident. Four years ago, Riker, and the *Enterprise*, saved a Romulan battle cruiser in distress and helped to forge closer relations between the two Empires. Tomalak is an Ambassador. The Starfleet insignia has altered (see 'Parallels').

Parrises Squares is mentioned (see '11001001', 'Silicon Avatar', 'The First Duty', 'Timescape'). Riker says he was slightly younger than Jean-Luc when he began playing.

82: 'Final Mission'

US Transmission: 19 November 1990
UK Transmission: 12 May 1993
Writers: Kacey Arnold-Ince, Jeri Taylor,
from a story by Kacey Arnold-Ince
Director: Corey Allen
Cast: Nick Tate, Kim Hamilton, Mary Kohnert

Picard asks Wesley to accompany him on one last mission before leaving for Starfleet Academy. Unfortunately, the old shuttle piloted by Captain Dirgo crashes on an inhospitable desert moon. Picard is seriously injured, but the *Enterprise* is forced to deal with a radioactive ship orbiting another planet. Picard and the others come across a fountain in a cave protected by a 'sentry' of energy. Dirgo is killed and Picard is injured, but Wesley uncovers the fountain and looks after his captain until rescued by the *Enterprise* crew.

Stardate: 44307.3

Strange New Worlds: Pentarus 5, where Picard has been asked to settle a dispute with the Salenite miners under Rigalian law. Gamelan 5, a world under threat from an old radioactive ship in orbit. Picard, Wesley and Dirgo crash on Lambda Paz, an M-class moon around Pentarus 3. (Both Pentarus 2 and 5, and four nearby moons, are also class M.)

New Life Forms: Songi, whose distress message is picked up by the *Enterprise*, is the only inhabitant of Gamelan 5 that we see. Beyond their pacifism no further information is given about their civilisation. Dirgo is presumably from Pentarus 5, and carries some transparent alcohol called dresci in a concealed container.

Technology: Like his phaser, Dirgo's shuttle, *Nenebek*, is an old example of the type. It has a duranium hull (see 'A Matter of Perspective', 'Hollow Pursuits' and the original series episode 'The Menagerie'). Hyronalin is used to treat radiation sickness (see the original series episode 'The Deadly Years'). Sonodanite and ermanium are metal alloys used in Federation shuttlecraft.

Dialogue Triumphs: 'I envy you, Wesley Crusher. This is just the beginning of the adventure.'

Notes: Wesley's last story as a member of the *Enterprise* crew expands the relationship with Picard first explored in detail in 'Samaritan Snare', to which reference is made. This story falls just the right side of sentimentality, although Picard seems to have mellowed a bit too much. Perhaps being at death's door does that to you. Ultimately the story is hampered by the lack of explanation surrounding the fountain, but the acting performances are strong enough to make this almost unimportant.

Picard hums the French song from 'Family', and talks about the most important teacher at the Academy, Boothby, who is actually the groundskeeper (see 'The First Duty' and 'The Game').

83: 'The Loss'

US Transmission: 31 December 1990
UK Transmission: 13 May 1993
Writers: Hilary J. Bader, Alan J. Adler, Vanessa Greene,
from a story by Hilary J. Bader
Director: Chip Chalmers
Cast: Kim Braden, Mary Kohnert

Phantom images appear in the *Enterprise*'s flight path, and Troi loses her empathetic abilities, which leads her to resign as ship's counselor. Two-dimensional creatures begin to pull the *Enterprise* towards a fragment of cosmic string, which means 'home' for them and destruction for the *Enterprise*, inadvertently trapped in their wake. Data is able to confuse the creatures for long enough to allow the *Enterprise* to escape, which causes Troi's abilities to return, no longer swamped by the emotions of the benign creatures.

Stardate: 44356.9

Strange New Worlds: The *Enterprise* is heading for T'lli Beta when it encounters the phenomenon. Geordi once took a skin-diving holiday on Bracas 5.

New Life Forms: The mysterious two-dimensional creatures that have unwittingly entrapped the *Enterprise* in their dash towards 'home'.

It is revealed that the Breen and the Ferengi cannot be sensed empathically.

Technology: Cosmic string is a proton thick but has the gravitational pull of a black hole. Data is able to 'simulate' another fragment of string towards the rear of the two-dimensional creatures via the *Enterprise*'s parabolic dish.

Notes: 'Therapists are always the worst patients.' A story of the need for true grief: with Troi's help, Ensign Brooks is able to recognise that she has covered over her emotional reaction to the death of her husband, but Troi is unable to see her sudden 'disability' in the same terms. It is nice to see a hint of the everyday life of the rest of the *Enterprise* crew, and to watch Troi at work, but perhaps she becomes a bit too unlikable when she loses her empathetic abilities.

Another reference is made to Picard's love of equestrianism (see 'Pen Pals', 'Starship Mine').

84: 'Data's Day'

US Transmission: 7 January 1991
UK Transmission: 14 May 1993
Writers: Harold Apter, Ronald D. Moore,
from a story by Harold Apter
Director: Robert Wiemer
Cast: Sierra Pecheur, Alan Scarfe, Shelley Desai, April Grace

As Data prepares to perform his honorary function as father of the bride at the wedding of Miles O'Brien and Keiko Ishikawa, the *Enterprise* receives Vulcan delegate T'Pel. She is about to take part in historic peace negotiations with the Romulans, but is killed in a transporter accident. Data investigates further, and concludes that T'Pel is not in fact dead. The truth is revealed: T'Pel was actually Sub-Commander Selok, a Romulan. Later that day the O'Briens' wedding goes ahead as planned.

Stardate: 44390.1

Strange New Worlds: At the end of the story the *Enterprise* leaves the Neutral Zone for Adelphous 4.

New Life Forms: Data mentions that a marriage on Galvin 5 is considered a success if a child is produced in the first year. (He says that Andorian marriages require 'groups of four unless–' but is interrupted.)

Introducing: Keiko Ishikawa, who Data first introduced to O'Brien.

Riker's Conquests: None, although Data postulates that Riker's easy-going manner and sense of humour accounts for his 'success in matters of love'.

Future History: Hinduism still exists in the 24th century.

Notes: A charming day-in-the-life story, spiced with a little Romulan intrigue, 'Data's Day' uses the android's narrative and 'everyday' events to great effect. It's obvious how far *The Next Generation* has come from the original series when at the end Picard flees from overwhelming Romulan forces. Kirk would have blasted them to hell.

Among the facts noted by Data in his report to Commander Bruce Maddox at the Cybernetics Division of the Daystrom Institute (see 'The Measure of a Man') are that it is 1550 days since the *Enterprise* was commissioned, and that the ensuing 24 hours will see four birthdays, two personel transfers, a celebration of the Hindu Festival of Lights (Divali, late October/ November), two chess tournaments, one secondary school play, and four promotions. During the course of the story Lt Juarez gives birth to a boy, and Data participates in the wedding of the O'Briens. Worf reports that Lt Umbato broke two ribs during a holodeck exercise, and that scanning of the Murasaki Quasar (see the original series' 'The Galileo Seven'?) continues. Data thinks of Geordi as his best friend, and has a cat (see 'In Theory'). He has contemplated marriage. Crusher was awarded first prize in the Tap and Jazz competition at the St Louis Academy, where she was known as 'the dancing doctor'. Geordi has his hair cut by a Bolian barber called V'Sal. T'Pel travels to the *Enterprise* in the *Zhukov* (see 'Hollow Pursuits'). Admiral Mendak's ship is the *Devoras*.

85: 'The Wounded'

US Transmission: 28 January 1991
UK Transmission: 17 May 1993
Writers: Jeri Taylor,
from a story by Stuart Charno, Sara Charno, Cy Chermax
Director: Chip Chalmers
Cast: Bob Gunton, Marc Alaimo, Marco Rodriguez,
Time Winters, John Hancock

Ben Maxwell, a greatly decorated Federation captain, appears to have gone rogue with a personal vendetta against the Cardassians with whom a peace treaty has recently been signed. Picard is ordered to bring him in. With Cardassian observers on board, the *Enterprise* tracks Maxwell's ship as it destroys two Cardassian vessels. Picard seeks advice from O'Brien, who served under Maxwell, and after intercepting the *Phoenix*, brings Maxwell on board. Maxwell alleges that the Cardassians are preparing for war. Picard follows his orders to arrest Maxwell, but also believes that Maxwell's hunches were correct, and warns the Cardassians that the Federation will be watching them.

Stardate: 44429.6 (almost a year after the treaty with the Cardassians).

New Life Forms: The first appearance of the Cardassians.

Picard Manoeuvre: Yes, once.

Dialogue Triumphs: 'It's not you I hate, Cardassian. I hate what I became because of you.'

'History will look at you and say "This man was a fool".'

'Take this message to your leader, Gul Macet: "We'll be watching".'

Notes: 'You must preserve the peace, no matter what the cost.' An exceptional episode, full of twists and turns and with an intriguing finale that gives the series a whole new direction. This is a major building episode for Miles O'Brien, from the domesticated scenes with Keiko, to the information about his past. The scene in which he describes to the 'friendly' Cardassian the first time he killed, (a Cardassian raider at Setlik 3), is one of the series' most emotional moments.

O'Brien served under Maxwell on the *Rutledge* as tactical officer ('the best I ever had'). During this period the Cardassians attacked the Setlik 3 colony, killing 100 people, including Maxwell's wife and children (the Cardassians maintain it was 'a terrible mistake'). O'Brien fondly remembers his days on the *Rutledge*, particularly his friendship with Will Kayden who also died at Setlik. The Irish folksong 'The Minstrel Boy' holds special significance. His mother cooked, rather than using a replicator.

Maxwell, who was decorated twice with the Federation's highest wartime honours, now commands the *Phoenix*. He congratulates Riker on his 'good work' during the Borg crisis. He thinks the Cuellar system is tactically important, and destroys a Cardassian settlement and two ships there. The last time Picard was in this sector was during the Cardassian conflict, fleeing at warp speed in the *Stargazer*.

Kanar is a drink with an acquired taste.

86: 'Devil's Due'

US Transmission: 4 February 1991
UK Transmission: 18 May 1993
Writers: Philip Lazebnik,
from a story by Philip Lazebnik, William Douglas Lansford
Director: Tom Benko
Cast: Marta DuBois, Paul Lambert, Marcelo Tubert,
Thad Lamey, Tom Magee

The apparent return to Ventax 2 of a mythical diabolist entity, Ardra, is dismissed as a con-trick by Picard. However, the woman clearly has great powers, and is claiming not only the planet, but also the *Enterprise* which is in orbit. Whilst Geordi searches for the source of her power, Picard calls for a legal contest, with the neutral Data as magistrate. Finally Ardra's cloaked power source is confirmed, as is Picard's suspicion that she is just a clever opportunist.

Stardate: 44474.5

Strange New Worlds: Ventax 2, once a highly polluted technological world, now an agrarian society.

New Life Forms: The Ventaxians. They 'sold their souls' to Ardra a thousand years ago. Their first contact was with a Klingon vessel seventy years ago.

Ardra, a female alien who claims to be known as Mendora in the Berrusian cluster, Torak to the Drellians, Fek'lhr Guardian of Gre'thor (where dishonoured Klingons go in the afterlife), and, by implication, the Devil on Earth. Actually a galactic con-artist of unknown origin, but with 23 aliases in this sector alone.

Data's Jokes: As Judge: 'The Advocate will refrain from expressing personal affection for her opponent' and '. . . from making her opponent disappear.'

Dialogue Triumphs: 'I refuse to abandon this planet to that woman!'

Notes: 'These people are convinced that their world is coming to an end tomorrow.' A 'shaggy dog' story without a decent punchline, this displays all the worst excesses of the original *Star Trek* series (complete with *Scooby Doo Where Are You?* ending). Even Patrick Stewart seems resigned to camp his way through a thoroughly rotten script. The first *Next Generation* episode to use the term 'environmentally-sound'!

Data continues his acting studies (see 'The Defector'), staging the Marley's ghost scene from *A Christmas Carol*, and discussing method acting with Picard, who quotes P.T. Barnum ('There's a sucker born every minute').

Q is mentioned in passing by Beverly. The ruins of Ligillium and the hidden Zatari emerald are used by Picard as bait for Ardra's greed.

87: 'Clues'

US Transmission: 11 February 1991
UK Transmission: 19 May 1993
Writers: Bruce D. Arthurs, Joe Menosky,

from a story by Bruce D. Arthurs
Director: Les Landau
Cast: Pamela Winslow, Rhonda Aldrich,
Thomas Knickerbocker

The early completion of the mission to Harrakis 5 has allowed Picard to give the crew extra personal time. For him, this involves another Dixon Hill holodeck program. The discovery of a wormhole renders the crew briefly unconscious. Data, who seems to have been immune to the effect, states that only seconds have passed but other indications are that as much as a day has actually gone by. As Data seems to be lying, the *Enterprise* heads for a class M-planet which they passed at the time of the blackout. An entity from a race called the Paxan possesses Troi and threatens the crew. Data confesses that the *Enterprise* visited the planet during the 'lost' day, but that the violently isolationist Paxans wanted to destroy them and that Picard's solution was to wipe the crew's memories. A second attempt is made to 'forget' the events, leaving none of the clues that lead to the first attempt's discovery. This time it appears successful.

Stardate: 44507.7

Strange New Worlds: An unnamed class-M planet in the Ngame nebula, a T-tauri-type star system. The image of a hydrogen-helium composition with a frozen helium core is an illusion based on Tethys 3 programmed into the computer by Data. The ship is *en route* to Evadne 4.

New Life Forms: The Paxans, xenophobic and powerful aliens who terraformed this obscure planet to provide anonymity from the rest of the universe. Their true form isn't seen as they communicate via Deanna.

Introducing: Crusher's assistant, Alyssa. First seen in 'Future Imperfect', this is the first story to give her a name. Her surname – Ogawa – is given in 'Identity Crisis'.

Technobabble: The 22nd century physicist Pell Underhill theorised that a major disruption in time continuity could be compensated for by trillions of small counterreactions.

Notes: 'And *this* is what you do for fun?' With plot elements similar to *Red Dwarf*'s 'Thanks for the Memory', this is an intriguing episode with the startling possibility of Data going rogue. The only episode in which a female crew member's suspenders are seen! Picard's statement that Data may be 'stripped down to his wires' if he has disobeyed orders is somewhat fascist for a man who has always defended the android's rights. It's difficult to fathom exactly how the crew will 'get it right' second time round, if only because their next contact with Starfleet will indicate that they've 'lost' 48 hours!

Data states he has twice before passed through unstable wormholes, the first during his tour of duty on the *Trieste*. (The other seems to be a reference to 'The Price'.) Small and unstable wormholes have been mapped near 39 T-tauri systems in the last 100 years. The wormhole's exit is 154 parsecs from the entrance.

Beverly's hobby is ethnobiology, growing Diomedian scarlet moss. O'Brien injured himself hanging a pot-plant for his wife.

88: 'First Contact'

US Transmission: 18 February 1991
UK Transmission: 20 May 1993
Writers: Dennis Russell Bailey, David Bischoff,
Joe Menosky, Ronald D. Moore, Michael Piller,
from a story by Marc Scott Zicree
Director: Cliff Bole
Cast: George Coe, Carolyn Seymour, George Hearn,
Steven Anderson, Sachi Parker, Bebe Neuwirth

Rivas Jakara is injured in a disturbance in Malcor 3's capital city. But when he is admitted to hospital the medics discover he is missing seven costal struts, and that his cardial and renal organs are in the wrong place. Jakara is Riker, sent to Malcor as an advance to the Federation's official 'first contact' with the Malcorans. Now that the existence of aliens has been discovered, Picard and Troi contact Malcor's Chancellor, Durken. However, the Malcorans have a xenophobic streak and Durken feels that the time is not right for such knowledge, especially after his security chief, Krola, attempts to lay the blame for his own death on Riker. Although satisfied of the Federation's intentions, Durken puts a hold on the Malcoran space program. The *Enterprise* leaves with an extra passenger, the Malcoran scientist Mirasta.

Stardate: None given – presumably between 44474.5 and 44614.6.

Strange New Worlds: Malcor 32,000 light years from Earth.

New Life Forms: The Malcorans, technologically emerging and on the verge of space flight. Their culture encourages the belief that they are alone in the galaxy, and the centre of it.

Riker's Conquests: Lanel, who wants to have sex with an alien ('There are differences in how my people make love.' 'I can't wait to learn!'). Will seems to satisfy her desires.

Dialogue Triumphs: 'We've been monitoring your progress towards warp drive capability. When a society reaches your level of technology . . . we feel the time is right for first contact.'

'This new era of space exploration, it fires the imagination. People see unidentified objects in the sky that turn out to be weather balloons.'

'My world's history has recorded that conquerors often arrive with the words "We are your friends".'

'Will I ever see you again?' 'I'll call you the next time I pass through your star system!'

'The stories will be told for many years I have no doubt. Of the ship that made contact, the alien who was held prisoner in the medical facility. There will be charges of a government conspiracy. Some of the witnesses will tell their tales and most of the people will laugh at them, and go back and watch the more interesting fiction of the daily broadcasts. It will pass.'

Notes: 'What are you?' An amazing episode, seemingly a tribute to 50s SF invasion mania, told largely from the point of view of the aliens. This matches the view of the Federation shown in 'Who Watches the Watchers'. Possibly the series' best-ever pre-title sequence.

The Federation observe a planet and its culture before first contact, monitoring their broadcasts, journalism, music and humour to understand them better. They also send in specialist integrators. Centuries ago, a disastrous first contact with the Klingons led to decades of war.

Picard puts the wine from 'Family' to good use. Durken says Malcorans have 'something similar'. Mirastra Yale leaves with the *Enterprise* at the end, saying she has been ready for space travel since she was nine years old. Durken hopes that the Federation will return in his and Picard's lifetime.

89: 'Galaxy's Child'

US Transmission: 11 March 1991
UK Transmission: 21 May 1993
Writers: Maurice Hurley,
from a story by Thomas Kartozian
Director: Winrich Kolbe
Cast: Susan Gibney, Lanei Chapman, Jana Marie Hupp

Geordi is excited to meet the real Leah Brahms, but she seems to loathe him and what he's done to her engines. She's married, and is suspicious about how Geordi knows so much about her. The *Enterprise* encounters a space creature, which attacks the ship. The ship's phasers kill the alien, but a scan reveals that it was about to give birth. With the ship's help the 'baby' is delivered. It attaches itself to the *Enterprise*, thinking it to be its mother, and starts to drain it of energy. Leah has discovered her holographic double, and is disgusted with Geordi, but the two manage to work together to change the frequency of the ship's radiation, and 'sour the milk', causing the creature to leave.

Stardate: 44614.6

Strange New Worlds: The seventh planet of the Alpha Omicron System, Starbase 313, and we also hear of the Guernica system.

New Life Forms: A pregnant spaceborne life form, consisting of plasma in a shell of silicates, actonites and carbonacious condrites. It feeds on keffnium, attacks with radiation and communicates by radio.

Circasian Plague Cats are unfriendly.

Technology: Small speeds for the *Enterprise* are measured in kph (we presume this means km/h).

It is possible to crawl inside the power transfer conduits. Melkanite interferes with the scanners.

Technobabble: Everything in space vibrates in a 21cm wavelength radiation band! The radiation the ship gives off can be changed! (Hence Romulan cloaking?) In this episode, the radiation given off is taken below visual range, which would not only make it invisible, but would toast the entity with microwaves!

Dialogue Triumphs: 'It thinks the *Enterprise* is its mother!'

Future History: Leah Brahms designed the power transfer conduits of the *Enterprise*. The Alpha Omicron system is yet to be charted.

Notes: Bwah ha hah!

It's a year since Geordi met a holodeck image of Leah Brahms.

Geordi makes a great fungilli, but writing isn't a strong point for him (cf. 'All Good Things . . .', where he's a novelist).

90: 'Night Terrors'

US Transmission: 18 March 1991
UK Transmission: 24 May 1993
Writers: Pamela Douglas, Jeri Taylor,
from a story by Shari Goodhartz
Director: Les Landau
Cast: John Vickery, Duke Moosekian, Craig Hurley,
Brian Tochi, Lanei Chapman

The *Enterprise* finds all the crew of the USS *Brittain* dead, except Hagan, a catatonic Betazoid. It seems that the rest of the crew killed each other, and when Troi dreams, she hears the phrase 'one moon circles'. The *Enterprise* seems stuck in the area, caught in a Tychon's Rift. A large explosion is needed to break free. As the crew begin to lose their temper with each other, Beverly realises that they've all lost their ability to dream – with the exception of Deanna, who is receiving messages from creatures trapped on the other side of the rift. The messages are preventing everyone else from getting REM sleep. She and Data deduce that the 'one moon' line refers to projecting hydrogen, which the aliens' ship can ignite. They do so, and both ships escape the rift.

Stardate: 44631.2

Strange New Worlds: An uncharted binary system. Starbase 220 is mentioned.

New Life Forms: Telepathic humanoid aliens trapped by the rift.

REM sleep occurs at different frequencies in Betazoids and humans.

Technology: A cortical scanner maintains REM sleep. Bussard collectors on the *Enterprise* collect hydrogen. A phaser setting of six or seven leaves charred corpses. Calendium explodes when exposed to hydrogen. Anesium and urium are explosives. No technology can block telepathy.

Deanna Underused?: Listen, sweetie, don't do a flying sequence in that costume. You're not as svelte as Supergirl.

Future History: Bela Tyken was a Malthusian captain who discovered the Tyken's Rift, a spatial anomaly that sucks out energy.

Notes: Quite good, apart from the Supergirl bits.

Guinan has a gun from Magus 3 behind her bar. The *Brittain* is a science vessel with a crew of thirty-four. Keiko leads the plant biology lab. Picard's grandfather went senile when he was young. He hardly ever recalls his dreams. Deanna often uses directed dreaming techniques.

91: 'Identity Crisis'

US Transmission: 25 March 1991
UK Transmission: 25 May 1993
Writers: Brannon Braga,
from a story by Timothy De Haas
Director: Winrich Kolbe
Cast: Maryann Plunkett, Amick Byram, Dennis Madalone,
Mona Grudt

Of the five-person team which investigated the disappearance of a whole colony on Tarchannen 3, only two have now not fled back to the planet: Geordi and his old friend Lt Commander Susanna Leijten. One of the fleeing team's shuttles is intercepted, but it burns up in the planet's atmosphere. An away team beams down and finds another of the missing shuttles. Susanna sees footprints being made by an invisible creature, and is returned to the ship, where she begins to turn into a different species. Geordi finds an extra shadow in the footage from the original mission, and discovers the true form of the invisible creatures. He too begins to change. Beverly removes the parasite that was causing the changes in Susanna, but Geordi has already beamed down to the planet. Using UV light his shipmates find him, and Susanna appeals to the human part of a now completely alien creature. Geordi is rescued, the parasite removed, and warning beacons placed around the planet.

Stardate: 44664.5

Strange New Worlds: Tarchannen 3, site of 49 mysterious disappearances. We hear of Starbase 112, and Malaya 4, where one may go for a physical.

New Life Forms: A parasitic creature with a reproductive system that transforms the DNA of its host, turning them into a chameleon-like humanoid that acts on instinct alone and can't see ultraviolet.

Technology: Kayolane is a sedative.

Deanna Underused?: Unseen.

Notes: Maryann Plunkett puts in a great performance in a well-directed, dark episode.

Five years ago, at 40164.7, Geordi, who already had his VISOR, was serving on the USS *Victory* (NCC 9754). He had a fraternal relationship with Commander Susanna Leijten. We hear of the USS *Aries* (NCC 45167).

92: 'The Nth Degree'

US Transmission: 1 April 1991
UK Transmission: 26 May 1993
Writer: Joe Menosky
Director: Robert Legato

Cast: Jim Norton, Kay E. Kuter, Saxon Trainor, Page Leong, David Coburn

Reg Barclay is knocked unconscious when investigating a mysterious alien probe. He seems unharmed, but his intelligence begins to expand exponentially. Barclay taps into the *Enterprise*'s computer, and is able to send the ship thousands of light years across the galaxy – where it is observed by an inquisitive Cytherian. Once the alien has seen enough, the *Enterprise* is sent back to its initial position, and Reg returns to normal.

Stardate: 44704.2

New Life Forms: The Cytherians, super-intelligent beings that explore the galaxy from the comfort of their home planet.

Technology: The Cytherian probe was designed to instruct computers on how to reach their star system at the centre of the galaxy but proved to be incompatible with the array and shuttle computers – so it reprogrammed Barclay instead.

Technobabble: When Geordi and Barclay test the probe they mention a passive high-res series, a neutron densitometer, active scan and positron emission.

'It just occurred to me that I could set up a frequency harmonic between the deflector and the shield grid using the warp field generator as a power flow anti-attenuator and that of course naturally created an amplification of the inherent energy output.'

Picard Manoeuvre: Super-brain Reg does his own version after Troi declines his offer of a walk in the arboretum.

Notes: 'Lieutenant, you could very well be the most advanced human being who has ever lived.' Another great Barclay episode.

The Argus Array is an unmanned sub-space telescope on the edge of Federation space. The *Enterprise* was going to take the probe to science station 402 in the Calaan system. The xaenes should be in bloom in the arboretum.

93: 'Qpid'

US Transmission: 22 April 1991
UK Transmission: 27 May 1993
Writers: Ira Steven Behr,
from a story by Randee Russell, Ira Steven Behr
Director: Cliff Bole
Cast: Jennifer Hetrick, Clive Revill, Joi Staton

Vash is about to go on another dubious archaeological dig, and Picard seems embarrassed in her company. Q decides that a lover's tiff such as this is best sorted out in his re-creation of Sherwood Forest, where he casts Vash as Marian and Picard as Robin. Robin and his Merry Men eventually rescue Vash, who promptly decides to explore the universe with Q.

Stardate: 44741.9 (a year after 'Captain's Holiday').

Strange New Worlds: The *Enterprise* orbits Tagus 3. Tagans no longer allow outsiders to visit the famous ruins, which were sealed-off more than a century ago.

New Life Forms: Q threatens to turn Vash into a Klabnian eel.

Riker's Conquests: Picard's spoof of Riker's chat-up lines: 'Eternity never looked so lovely . . . Your eyes are as mysterious as the stars.'

Dialogue Triumphs: Worf, on Vash: 'Nice legs . . . For a human.'

Riker and Picard discuss Q's latest appearance: 'Any idea what he's up to?' 'He wants to do something nice for me.' 'I'll alert the crew.'

Worf: 'Sir, I protest. I am not a Merry Man!'

Notes: *Trek* jumps on the *Prince of Thieves* bandwagon to reasonable effect. However, beneath the good comedy scenes (Worf smashing Geordi's mandolin, Troi shooting Data with an arrow) there is little to sustain the viewer's interest.

Picard is to give the keynote address to the Federation Archeology Council's annual symposium, which has been given in the past by such great Federation minds as Switzer, Klarc-Tarn-Droth and McFarlan. Vash is 'more or less' a member of the council. Despite Picard's warnings, Vash brought back some very important artefacts from Sarathong 5. Picard and Crusher share morning tea together.

94: 'The Drumhead'

US Transmission: 29 April 1991
UK Transmission: 28 May 1993
Writer: Jeri Taylor
Director: Jonathan Frakes
Cast: Jean Simmons, Bruce French, Spencer Garrett, Henry Woronicz, Earl Billings, Ann Shea

After an explosion in the *Enterprise*'s dilithium chamber, a Klingon exobiologist is suspected of smuggling Federation secrets to the Romulans. Admiral Norah Satie heads an investigation, from which, it seems, no one is safe. Although the explosion is proved to be an accident, crewmember Simon Tarses is shown to have lied about his genealogy. The finger of suspicion points at Picard when he attempts to defend the man, but by quoting her father Jean-Luc is able to expose Satie's mental instability and overzealousness.

Stardate: 44769.2

Strange New Worlds: Satie's assistant, Nellen Tore, comes from Delb 2. The Tarkainean diplomat who carried top secret information was tracked as far as the Krusos system. Simon

Tarses comes from the Mars colony.

Deanna Underused?: She's absent.

Dialogue Triumphs: Picard: 'Oh yes. That's how it starts. But the road from legitimate suspicion to rampant paranoia is very much shorter than we think.'

'Villains who twirl their moustaches are easy to spot. Those who clothe themselves in good deeds are well-camouflaged.'

Notes: The script of this gripping courtroom drama ensures that its exact allusions cannot be pinned down too precisely. To any American viewer it's 'about' McCarthyism, but to a British viewer in the mid-1990s it is transformed into an insightful critique of the Criminal Justice Act.

Retired Admiral Norah Satie helped uncover the alien plot in 'Conspiracy', which took place three years ago. Her father was a famous judge and noted libertarian. The *Enterprise* was last inspected at McKinley station (see 'Family'). Jean-Luc Picard (he appears to have no middle names) has been captain of the *Enterprise* for over three years (since Stardate 41124, cf. 'Encounter at Farpoint'). He is accused of violating the Prime Directive on nine occasions. Reference is also made to the T'Pel saga in 'Data's Day' and to his assimilation by the Borg in 'The Best of Both Worlds'. (The battle with the Borg saw the destruction of thirty-nine ships: 11,000 lives were lost.) The Seventh Guarantee of the Federation Constitution would seem to ensure a right to silence and/or that any person is innocent until proved guilty. Chapter Four Article Twelve of the Uniform Code of Justice grants a person the right to make a statement before questioning.

95: 'Half a Life'

US Transmission: 6 May 1991
UK Transmission: 31 May 1993
Writers: Peter Allan Fields,

from a story by Ted Roberts, Peter Allan Fields
Director: Les Landau
Cast: David Ogden Stiers, Michelle Forbes,
Terence E. McNally, Carel Struychen

Lwaxana Troi falls in love with Dr Timicin, a quiet scientist from a dying planet. Timicin is on the *Enterprise* to conduct experiments aimed at rejuvenating Kaelon's sun, but they end in failure. Lwaxana is outraged when she hears that, because he is almost sixty, Timicin will be unable to complete his work: at that age Kaelons commit ritual suicide. Lwaxana persuades Timicin to request asylum, but his own people and family are offended by his decision. Timicin eventually decides that it is right for him to go through with the Resolution, and Lwaxana beams down with him.

Stardate: 44805.3

Strange New Worlds: Kaelon 2, a planet circling a dying sun. Life can only continue on the planet for another thirty-to-forty years.

New Life Forms: The Kaelons are very reclusive, contact with the Federation having only just been established. For generations they have looked for a way to revitalise their dying sun. Timicin believes he has found a solution, involving helium fusion enhancement. When they reach the age of sixty Kaelons kill themselves in a ceremony known as the Resolution. Fifteen-to-twenty centuries ago their society showed no concern for their elders, who were placed in 'deathwatch' facilities (that is, their equivalent of nursing homes). From Lwaxana Troi's comments it would seem that she finds it difficult to read Kaelons' minds.

Technobabble: The star is unstable because of 'neutron migration'.

Dialogue Triumphs: Lwaxana: 'My life has been full. Now

and then perhaps it's overflowed a little.'

Notes: Despite its subject matter, this is a story almost entirely devoid of emotion, Lwaxana Troi proving particularly grating. In addition there are the usual horrible telepathic sequences between mother and daughter, but the ending is at least pleasingly ambiguous: it's difficult to decide whether letting Timicin beam down to his home planet to die is the ultimate in *Trek* tolerance or the latest example of *Next Generation*'s narrative subversion.

It took even the Federation three years to find a match for the Kaelons' own sun: the giant red star at the heart of the lifeless Praxillus system. Lwaxana knew a young astronomer from Rigel 4 who named a star after her. The women of Betazed used to wear huge wigs with holes in the middle for caged animals. Oskoids are a Betazoid delicacy.

96: 'The Host'

US Transmission: 13 May 1991
UK Transmission: 1 June 1993
Writer: Michael Horvat
Director: Marvin V. Rush
Cast: Barbara Tarbukc, Nicole Orth-Pallavicini,
William Newman, Frank Luz

The *Enterprise* is transporting a Federation mediator, Odan, to Peliar to settle a dispute. En route, Odan and Beverly become attracted to each other. A shuttle accident reveals that Odan is a Trill, a symbiotic race of a parasitic slug-like creature and a host body. The host dies due to its injuries, but it will be some time before a new host can arrive, so Riker volunteers to act as temporary host. Odan is still attracted to Beverly, and she struggles to accept Odan in whatever body he may inhabit. The dispute is settled and Odan is successfully transplanted into a new host – a female, something Beverly is unable to cope with.

Stardate: 44821.3

Strange New Worlds: Peliar Zel and its two moons Alpha and Beta.

New Life Forms: The Peliarians, a 'reasonable people trapped in their own anger'.

The Trill, a 'joined species' of host and symbiont. The symbionts are very long-lived, being transplanted into new host bodies periodically. They cannot use transporters as this will damage the symbiont (this is flatly contradicted during various *Deep Space 9* episodes, where Dax encounters no problems with transporters).

Riker's Conquests: Beverly. Well, sort of, but only with an alien slug in his belly.

Dialogue Triumphs: 'Those who cannot hear an angry shout may strain to hear a whisper.'

'I look at Will and I see someone I've known for years. A kind of brother. But inside, is he really Odan?'

Notes: 'This body is just a host. I *am* that parasite.' A Beverly love story (poor Bev, falling for a slug!). There's a great Crusher/Troi 'girls' talk' comedy scene in the *Enterprise* barbershop and a good performance by Jonathan Frakes. But the ending is a cop-out of the worst possible kind. When Beverly says humanity isn't ready for bisexual love affairs, what she means is American television isn't.

Beverly is working on an analysis of the respiratory problems on the Beta moon. She notes Wesley is top of the academy class in exobiology, but struggling in ancient philosophies. Beverly's first love was an eleven-year-old football player called Stefan (she was eight).

The first man Troi loved was her father who 'sang to me and kept me safe. And then he went away.'

Metrazene is a cardiac antiarrhythmic drug. The shuttle Riker and Odan use is the *Hawking*.

97: 'The Mind's Eye'

US Transmission: 27 May 1991
UK Transmission: 2 June 1993
Writers: René Echevarria,
from a story by Ken Schafer, René Echevarria
Director: David Livingston
Cast: Larry Dobkin, John Fleck, Edward Wiley,
Majel Barrett

En route to an artificial intelligence seminar, Geordi is kidnapped by the Romulans and subjected to horrific programming. When Geordi returns to the *Enterprise* he has no memory of the Romulans. The *Enterprise* is sent to a Klingon colony to investigate charges of Federation aid being given to rebel forces. Ambassador Kell, a Romulan collaborator, is planning to use Geordi as an assassin to kill Governor Vagh and cause a split between the Federation and the Klingons. Data uncovers the plot and prevents Geordi just in time. Kell is taken into custody, as Deanna begins the delicate task of deprogramming Geordi.

Stardate: 44885.5

Strange New Worlds: Krios, a Klingon colony currently facing a rebellion. (Is this a different Krios from that mentioned in 'The Perfect Mate'?) The rebels have attacked neutral Ferengi and Cardassian freighters near the Ikalian asteroid belt.

Technobabble: 'List the resonances of the sub-quantum states associated with transitional relativity.'

'E-Band emissions are difficult to localise.' 'Collapsing proto-stars sometimes emit E-band bursts.'

Deanna Underused?: She's only in two short scenes, although one is her sympathetic de-programming of Geordi.

Data's Jokes: ' "Forced to endure Risa". Your actual intent was to emphasise that you *did* enjoy yourself. I see how that could be considered quite amusing.'

Dialogue Triumphs: 'You swear well, Picard. You must have Klingon blood in your veins.'

'We need more than speculation . . . We need to know who, what, when, where and why. Otherwise, we could be going to war.'

Notes: 'Your captain and I will bring him to the cargo bay. I want you to kill him there in front of many witnesses.' Visually-stunning, this is a great episode; a debt to *The Manchurian Candidate* is evident, but it's done with such dazzling hallucinatory pace that one doesn't mind the derivative nature of the script. LeVar Burton is chillingly brilliant, and it's a great Worf episode too, continuing the themes of 'Sins of the Father' and 'Reunion' as a virtual prologue to 'Redemption' (Denise Crosby appears, unbilled and hidden in shadow).

Geordi likes Spanish guitar music, and drinks rectorine. His trip to Risa is on board the shuttle *Onizuker*. Implanted memories include attending specific seminars, gaining second place in a chess tournament, swimming and walking, 'eating enough for twelve people' (including one occasion when an Andorian waiter had trouble with an order), and a liaison with a girl called Janik.

O'Brien has served with Geordi for nearly four years.

98: 'In Theory'

US Transmission: 3 June 1991
UK Transmission: 3 June 1993
Writers: Joe Menosky, Ronald D. Moore
Director: Patrick Stewart
Cast: Michele Scarabelli, Pamela Winslow

Data develops a close relationship with science officer Jenna D'Sora who has just ended a long-term affair with another officer. Data takes advice from his friends on how to pursue the relationship. However, his attempts to develop a program that will allow him to fall in love prove hopelessly inadequate. Data realises that he has caught Jenna on the rebound and they agree to break off seeing each other.

Stardate: 44932.3

Strange New Worlds: Mar Oscura, an unexplored dark-matter nebula containing several class-M planets.

Data's Jokes: 'The cat's out of the bag.' 'Spot?'
As Jenna notes 'That's what I love about you Data, you make me laugh!'

Dialogue Triumphs: Riker's inevitable advice: 'I think you should pursue it . . . She's a beautiful woman, and she's crazy about you.'
'Honey, I'm home!'
'It appears that my reach has exceeded my grasp... I am, perhaps, not nearly so human as I aspire to be.'
Jenna asks Data what he has been thinking about whilst kissing her: 'I was reconfiguring the warp field parameters, analysing the collected works of Charles Dickens, calculating the maximum pressure I could safely apply to your lips, considering a new food supplement for Spot . . .'

Notes: 'I'd be delighted to offer any advice I can on understanding women. When I have some, I'll let you know.' A strange episode, featuring one horrifying moment (the crew woman killed sinking into the floor) and some fine comedy (Worf and Picard's reactions to Data's quest for advice on dating).
In addition to his violin prowess, Data also plays flute in a woodwind section that includes Keiko and Jenna D'Sora.
Jenna's father died when she was young. She has a younger brother. She gives Data a Tyrinean sculpture. Data's gift to her is crystilia, a flower from Telemarius 3.

Data's cat (see 'Data's Day') is called Spot. (It is referred to as a 'he', later contradicted: see 'Force of Nature'.) O'Brien leaves his socks on the floor for his wife to pick up. Guinan's new drink (which she discovered on Prakal 2) is a mixture of 87 per cent Saurian brandy, with Targ milk and Denesian meat.

Picard in shuttle 3 steers the *Enterprise* out of the dark matter field in which they are trapped.

99: 'Redemption'

US Transmission: 17 June 1991
UK Transmission: 4 June 1993
Writer: Ronald D. Moore
Director: Cliff Bole
Cast: Robert O'Reilly, Tony Todd, Barbara March,
Gwynyth Walsh, Ben Slack, Nicholas Kepros, J.D. Cullum,
Tom Ormeny, Majel Barrett

The *Enterprise* travels to the Klingon Homeworld for Picard, as Arbiter, to confirm Gowron's succession. Worf, meanwhile, must right the wrong that has been done to his family. Duras' sisters have discovered a bastard son of the dead Klingon, and make a surprise challenge whilst secretly working with the Romulans. Worf publicly backs Gowron, who upon becoming leader restores Worf's family honour. The Federation is hesitant to take sides in the forthcoming Klingon civil war and Worf, honour-bound, resigns his commission. The Duras family plan their next move with a Romulan commander who is the double of Tasha Yar.

Stardate: 44995.3

Strange New Worlds: The Klingon Homeworld.

Deanna Underused?: Yes, she's reduced to a non-speaking extra (as is Beverly).

Dialogue Triumphs: Picard: 'You have manipulated the circumstances with the skill of a Romulan. My decision will be announced at high sun tomorrow. Excellent tea, ladies!'

Gowron: 'Your blood will paint the way to the future.'

'You come to me and demand the restoration of your family honour and now you hide behind human excuses. What are you, Worf? Do you tremble and quake with fear at the approach of combat, hoping to talk your way out of a fight like a human? Or do you hear the cry of the warrior, calling you to battle like a Klingon?'

Notes: 'Your discommendation is a façade to protect less honourable men. It is a lie. Lies must be challenged.' A Shakespearian revenge-saga of court intrigue of epic proportions made all the more remarkable by the fact that ninety per cent of the protagonists are aliens with amusingly-shaped heads. A savage climax to the plot lines of 'Sins of the Father', 'Reunion' and 'The Mind's Eye', told with no consideration for first-time viewers. And isn't that cliffhanger great?

Women are not allowed on the Klingon high council. Duras' sisters, Lursa and B'Etor, plan to use his bastard son, Toral, to usurp power from Gowron, allied with the Romulans. They have a large force assembled near Beta Thoridar.

Worf's brother Kurn is commanding the Klingon warship *Hegh'ta*. Gowron is the son of M'Rel. Kellicam is a Klingon distance measurement. 'BaH' means fire, and 'Yintagh' is a Klingon expletive.

Guinan says she had a bet with Picard that she could make Worf laugh before he made lieutenant commander.

'We should not discount Jean-Luc Picard yet. He is human, and humans have a way of showing up when you least expect them.'

Fifth Season

26 45-minute episodes

Created by Gene Roddenberry

Executive Producers: Rick Berman
(100–103, 106–125), Michael Piller (100–103, 106–125),
Gene Roddenberry (100–103, 106–125)
Co-Executive Producers: Rick Berman (104–105),
Michael Piller (104-105), Gene Roddenberry (104–105)
Producers: David Livingston, Herbert J. Wright (112–117)
Co-Producers: Peter Lauritson, Joe Menosky, Ronald D.
Moore **Supervising Producer:** Jeri Taylor **Associate
Producer:** Wendy Neuss **Line Producer:** Merri D. Howard
(114) **Executive Script Consultant:** Peter Allan Fields
(118–120, 122–125)

Regular Cast: Patrick Stewart (Captain Jean-Luc Picard),
Jonathan Frakes (Commander William Riker), LeVar Burton
(Lt Commander Geordi La Forge), Michael Dorn (Lt Worf),
Gates McFadden (Dr Beverly Crusher), Marina Sirtis
(Counselor Deanna Troi), Brent Spiner (Lt Commander Data)
Colm Meaney (Lt O'Brien, 100–101, 104–105, 114), Rosalind
Chao (Keiko O'Brien, 104, 111, 114), Whoopi Goldberg
(Guinan, 100, 102, 121–122, 125), Michelle Forbes (Ensign
Ro Laren, 102, 104, 113–114, 117, 123), Patti Yasutake (Nurse
Ogawa, 105, 115, 117, 121, 124), Wil Wheaton (Wesley Crusher,
105, 118), Brian Bonsall (Alexander, 109, 115, 119, 121), Majel
Barrett (Lwaxana Troi, 119)

100: 'Redemption 2'

US Transmission: 23 September 1991
UK Transmission: 7 June 1994
Writer: Ronald D. Moore

Director: David Carson
Cast: Denise Crosby, Tony Todd, Barbara March, Gwynyth Walsh, J.D. Cullum, Robert O'Reilly, Michael Hagarty, Fran Bennett, Nicholas Kepros, Timothy Carhart, Jordan Lund, Stephen James Carver

At Starbase 234 Picard proposes a blockade of the Romulan border and several members of the crew leave for other ships in the fleet. Meanwhile, the Klingon civil war begins. Worf is kidnapped by the Romulans, whilst Picard is visited by Commander Sela, who claims to be Tasha Yar's daughter. The blockade is successful and an attempt to breach it is foiled by Data commanding the *Sutherland*. The Romulans abandon their Klingon allies. As Gowron celebrates his victory, Worf decides his place is on board the *Enterprise*.

Stardate: 45020.4

Strange New Worlds: Gamma Eridon, the location of the Federation fleet.

Technobabble: A 'tachyon detection grid', Geordi's cunning plan to detect the Romulans when cloaked (why didn't Scotty think of this ninety years ago?).

Dialogue Triumphs: 'Do we fall upon ourselves like a pack of Ferengi?'

'The Duras family will one day rule the Empire.' 'Perhaps. But not today!'

Notes: 'The Klingon civil war is, by definition, an internal matter.' A little disappointing after such a set-up, there are some great moments here (the Picard/Guinan scene after the shock revelation of Tasha having a daughter), but the sub-plot of Data encountering prejudice on the *Sutherland* detracts from the main theme. The finale is outstanding, Worf refusing to kill Toral ('It is the Klingon way.' 'I know, but it is not *my* way.').

The reference to the Romulans trying to undermine the Federation/Klingon alliance for the past twenty years indicates the *Enterprise*-C successfully changed history in 'Yesterday's Enterprise', and the fifty year silence noted in 'The Neutral Zone' now never happened.

Sela is Tasha Yar's daughter. There were rumours of survivors at Narendra 3, captured and taken to Romulus. A Romulan general was much taken by Tasha and spared the lives of the other survivors on condition that she become his mate. Sela was born a year after (Picard dates these events as 23 years ago, Sela as 24). Tasha was executed trying to escape when Sela was four.

Among the ships in the Picard-assembled fleet are the *Excalibur* (commanded by Riker and Geordi), the *Sutherland* (commanded by Data), the *Tian An Men*, the *Hermes*, the *Akagi* and the *Hornet*.

101: 'Darmok'

US Transmission: 30 September 1991
UK Transmission: 8 June 1993
Writers: Joe Menosky,
from a story by Philip Lazebnik, Joe Menosky
Director: Winrich Kolbe
Cast: Richard James, Paul Winfield, Ashley Judd,
Majel Barrett

The Children of Tama are a benign race whose language has not been understood during several encounters with Federation vessels. Their captain takes direct action to get the message across, having himself and Picard beamed down to a nearby planet. Picard and the alien captain, Dathon, attempt to communicate but find the language barrier impossible. Data discovers that the Tamarian language is based on narrative imagery from their legends; Dathon is attempting to recreate the legend of Darmok, a mythical hero who joined together with another warrior to defeat a common foe. On the planet, a vicious electro-magnetic entity attacks the captains, seriously injuring Dathon. He subsequently dies of his wounds, but not before Picard has gained a grasp of the Tamarian language. The *Enterprise* manages to rescue Picard, who informs the Tamarians of their captain's sacrifice.

Stardate: 45047.2

Strange New Worlds: El-Adrel 4.

New Life Forms: The Children of Tama (or Tamarians), 'an enigmatic race' whom Federation vessels have encountered on seven occasions in the last 100 years. They were called 'incomprehensible' by Captain Silvestri of the *Shiku Maru*. Their 'strange ego-structure' does not allow self-identity. They communicate through narrative imagery with reference to their mytho-historical sagas, and seem to originate from the planet Shantil 3.

Dialogue Triumphs: 'Darmok and Jalad at Tanagra.'

Notes: 'In my experience, communication is a matter of patience and imagination. I would like to believe these are qualities we have in sufficient measure.' Quite beautiful, an almost parable-like restating of Gene Roddenberry's concept for *Star Trek*, with alien races overcoming barriers to find understanding. So what if the plot is similar to *Enemy Mine*? A little gem.

In the Tamarian language, 'Darmok and Jalad at Tanagra' means to achieve friendship by fighting a common enemy. Other phrases used include 'Shaka when the walls fell' (indicating a failure or inability), 'Sokath, his eyes uncovered' (to understand), 'Tembra, his arms wide' (to give or share a gift), 'Cinda, his face black, his eyes red' (extreme anger), 'Chinza at the court of silence' (seemingly 'shut up!') and 'Darmok on the ocean' (alone).

Data says he has encountered 1754 non-human races during his period with Starfleet. There are 47 entries for the word

'Darmok' in the universal translator; these include a seventh dynasty emperor on Conda 4 and a frozen desert on Tazna 5. 'Tanagra' is the ruling family on Galas 2 and a ceremonial drink of Larici 4.

Picard tells the Mesopotamian legend of Gilgamesh to Captain Dathon.

102: 'Ensign Ro'

US Transmission: 7 October 1991
UK Transmission: 9 June 1993
Writers: Michael Piller,
from a story by Rick Berman, Michael Piller
Director: Les Landau
Cast: Scott Marlowe, Frank Collison, Jeffrey Hayenga,
Harley Venton, Ken Thorley, Cliff Potts, Majel Barrett

Given a dangerous assignment in the Cardassian sector, Picard is also stuck with the notorious Ensign Ro, a Bajoran officer. Attacks on Federation outposts have been blamed on a Bajoran extremist group displaced by the occupation of their world by the Cardassians. Ro, given secret orders by Admiral Kennelly, clashes with Picard but Guinan persuades Picard to trust her. With Ro's help, Picard establishes contact with the group's leader, who denies knowledge of the attack. The apparent destruction of the Bajoran's ship by the Cardassians whilst under the *Enterprise*'s escort confirms to Picard that Kennelly had betrayed the ship's position. Picard reveals that the ship was empty, but also that the Cardassians themselves staged the Federation attacks. Ro is given the chance to remain with the *Enterprise*.

Stardate: 45076.3

Strange New Worlds: Lya Station Alpha, where Picard meets Admiral Kennelly. Solarion 4, a Cardassian outpost destroyed (seemingly) by Bajoran terrorists. Bajoran refugee settlements Valo 3 (Jaz Holza's colony) and Valo 2 (Keeve Falor's colony on the southern continent).

New Life Forms: The Bajorans, whose homeworld was annexed by the Cardassians forty years ago. The Bajorans are now spread across the galaxy, 'terrorist' groups having formed to resist the Cardassians. Picard notes that before humans were able to stand erect, Bajor produced 'architects, artists, builders and philosophers.'

Introducing: Ro Laren, in the first of eight appearances.

Dialogue Triumphs: 'How convenient it must be for you. To turn a deaf ear to those who suffer behind a line on a map.'
Ro on Bajorans: 'They're lost. Defeated. I will never be.'

Notes: 'You were innocent bystanders for decades as the Cardassians took our homes and violated our people.' Angry and brilliant, a virtual pilot script for what would become *Deep Space Nine,* introducing the Bajoran/Cardassian war.

Beverly met Jaz Holza at a symposium. She considers him moderate (and a great dancer). Ro describes him as a token 'acceptable' Bajoran with no political power.

The *Enterprise* barber, Mr Mot, gives both Picard and Riker tactical advice (he mentions the Romulans). They put up with this because, as Riker notes, he's the best barber in Starfleet.

Ro Laren (Bajoran custom has the family name first and the individual or 'given' name second) was a former ensign on the *Wellington.* On Garon 2 she didn't follow orders which resulted in the deaths of eight away team members. She was court martialled and sent to the Stockade on Jaros 2. As a child of seven, she saw her father tortured and killed by Cardassians.

A long time ago Guinan got into some form of trouble. It is implied that Picard helped her. Picard's Aunt Adele's cure for the common cold was hot ginger tea with honey.

Bajorans have Antares-class cruisers, Cardassians Galor-class warships. The Cardassian Gul Dolak mispronounces his race's name on one occasion ('Car-day-sian' instead of 'Card-ass-ian').

103: 'Silicon Avatar'

US Transmission: 14 October 1991
UK Transmission: 10 June 1993
Writers: Jeri Taylor,
from a story by Lawrence V. Conley
Director: Cliff Bole
Cast: Ellen Geer, Susan Diol

When the Crystalline Entity attacks a Federation colony, Dr Kila Marr, whose son was killed at Omicron Theta, is sent to help the *Enterprise* track it down. Marr is obsessed with revenge, and is highly suspicious of Data, whose brother was responsible for the creature's attack. When she discovers that Data holds memories of all the Omicron colonists, including her son, her attitude changes. The *Enterprise* tracks the entity and is on the verge of establishing communications when Dr Marr changes the frequency of the ship's energy pulse, destroying the creature.

Stardate: 45122.3

Strange New Worlds: Melona 4, a new colony ravaged by the Entity. The Brechtian cluster contains two inhabited planets. A ship from Boreal 3 (the *Kallisko*) seems also to be destroyed by the Entity. During an Entity attack on Forlat 3, the colonists hid in caves, but were still wiped out.

Riker's Conquests: The doomed Carmen, leader of the Melona 4 colony. She thinks Riker is a 'free spirit'. They plan a dinner of dried chicken curry and wine in her tent. Then she dies horribly. Lucky girl.

Dialogue Triumphs: 'Its "needs" are to slaughter people by the thousand. It is nothing but a killing machine.'

Notes: 'I did it for you.' A twitchy, slightly awkward look at obsession and revenge, done better elsewhere. Functional, though the pre-title sequence is great.

There has, Data says, been no predetermined limit placed on his existence. He can play Spanish guitar.

There have been no survivors of any of the Entity's eleven recorded attacks. Kila Marr is a xenologist. She has devoted her life to the study of the entity after the death of her sixteen-year-old son, Raymond ('Rennie'), one of the colonists on Omicron Theta. Another Omicron colonist, Dr Clendenning, used gamma radiation scans to detect decay by-products from the Entity's antiproton trail. The Entity also deposits bitrious filament traces.

Parisses squares are mentioned again (see '11000110', 'Future Imperfect', 'The First Duty', 'Timescapes'). The refractory metals kalbonite and fistrium are found in the rocks of Melona 4.

Note: As in 'Brothers', the Entity is referred to as '*Crystalline*' (cf. 'Datalore').

104: 'Disaster'

US Transmission: 21 October 1991
UK Transmission: 11 June 1993
Writers: Ronald D. Moore,
from a story by Ron Jarvis, Philip A. Scorza
Director: Gabrielle Beaumont
Cast: Erika Flores, John Christopher Graas, Max Supera,
Cameron Arnett, Jana Marie Hupp

Hit by a quantum filament, which causes a containment breach, the *Enterprise* is in serious trouble. Picard is trapped in a turbolift with three children; Riker, Data and Worf are stuck in Ten-Forward with a pregnant Keiko O'Brien; and Deanna is the only

Command officer on the bridge. As Riker and Data attempt to find a way to engineering, Worf helps to deliver Keiko's child. Geordi and Beverly have their own problems in a cargo bay with a radioactive fire. Troi switches power to engineering in the hope that someone will be at the other end, and Riker arrives just in time to avert the destruction of the ship.

Stardate: 45156.1

Technobabble: 'We've got a problem. The quantum resonance of the filament caused a polarity shift in the anti-matter containment field.'

Picard Manoeuvre: Everybody's at it: O'Brien, Ro, even Deanna.

Deanna Underused?: Yes – and she's in charge!

Dialogue Triumphs: 'I shall appoint you my executive officer in charge of radishes.'

'You want me to take off your head?'

Worf and Keiko discuss her entering labour: 'This is not a good time, Keiko.' 'It's not open to debate!'

Notes: 'Congratulations, you are fully dilated to ten centimetres. You may now give birth.' Dumb, but brilliant, a parody of the disaster movie with some great set pieces and a knowing, postmodern edge of self-mockery. The Worf/Keiko scenes are about as funny as *The Next Generation* gets.

Worf took the Starfleet emergency medical course. O'Brien's father was called Michael, Keiko's Hiro. Picard used to sing 'Frère Jacques' at school. These days they sing 'The Laughing Vulcan and His Dog', which he confesses he doesn't know.

Beverly is auditioning Geordi for a production of *The Pirates of Penzance*.

Emergency Procedure Alpha 2 concerns overriding the computer and taking manual control. Quantum is a chemical compound used in thruster packs. Normally stable, it becomes volatile when it comes into contact with radiation. Polyduranide is used in the construction of starships. Hyronalin is a radiation treatment drug. Much of Data's bodywork is made from tripolymers (see 'The Most Toys').

105: 'The Game'

US Transmission: 28 October 1991
UK Transmission: 14 June 1993
Writers: Brannon Braga,
from a story by Susan Sackett, Fred Bronson, Brannon Braga
Director: Corey Allen
Cast: Ashley Judd, Katherine Moffat, Diane M. Hurley

On Risa, Riker picks up an interactive game which proves hugely popular. Wesley Crusher, on a visit from the academy, becomes friends with ensign Robin Lefler. They are suspicious of the game, which appears to be addictive and to have harmful side-effects. Data, who would have been immune to the game, is subject to a systems failure caused by Riker. The crew are, in fact, being manipulated by an alien race who plan to conquer the Federation with the game. However, Wesley is able to correct the damage caused to Data, and the android devises a neuro-optic burst device which counteracts the game's effects. The aliens are captured.

Stardate: 45208.2

Strange New Worlds: The (uncharted) Phoenix cluster.

New Life Forms: The Ktarians, who use a psychotropically addictive game to infiltrate the Federation.

Riker's Conquests: Etana, his Ktarian bit of rough. A bad move, even by his standards.

Deanna Underused?: She spends one scene describing the orgasmic joys of chocolate!

Dialogue Triumphs: 'A conflict has arisen between the planetary evolution team and the stellar physicists!'

Notes: 'How far does this game go?' 'As far as you can take it!' An implausible runaround, with a ridiculous plot. Mindless trashy fun. The cute Robin Lefler (from 'Darmok') provides the love interest in a rather good double act with Wesley. There's a good running joke about Wesley's birthmark.

Walter Horne, who taught Picard creative writing at the Academy, is still there, and teaching Wesley, who also sought out Boothby (see 'The Final Mission', 'The First Duty'). The groundsman didn't remember Picard until Wesley found an old year book photo. He once caught Picard carving 'A.F.' into his prize elm tree. Picard notes that 'A.F.' was the reason he failed organic chemistry. Wesley's Latin has improved. He likes Tarvokian pound cake (a Klingon dessert that Worf makes).

The *Zhukov* (Barclay's old ship, see 'Hollow Pursuits') is mentioned. The O'Briens' daughter is called Molly. Data mentions Beverly teaching him to dance in 'Data's Day'. He was prey to practical jokes whilst at the Academy, as is Wesley (although, seemingly, he gives as good as he gets). The Sadie Hawkins Dance is still held annually at the Academy.

Robin Lefler was a child of two Starfleet plasma specialists. She travelled a lot as a child and says her first friend was a tricorder (Wesley's was a warp coil!). She has friends at the Academy. Every time she learns something, she creates a 'law' so that she doesn't forget the lessons learnt. She has reached 102 laws (the 103rd is created especially for Wesley).

106: 'Unification I'

US Transmission: 4 November 1991
UK Transmission: 7 March 1993
(as a 90 minute special with 'Unification II')
Writers: Jeri Taylor,
from a story by Rick Berman, Michael Piller

Director: Les Landau
Cast: Leonard Nimoy, Joanna Miles, Stephen Root, Graham Jarvis, Malachi Throne, Norman Large, Daniel Roebuck, Erick Avari, Karen Hensel, Mark Lenard

Picard is briefed on the disappearance of Ambassador Spock. Spock has been traced to Romulus, and the Federation suspect that he may have defected. Picard discusses events with Sarek, who is dying. Sarek believes that Spock may be working towards a reunification of the Romulan and Vulcan peoples, and suggests that the progressive Senator Pardek be sought. Picard and Data travel to Romulus in a cloaked ship. Meanwhile the *Enterprise* crew investigate stolen Vulcan ships and machinery, encountering a vessel that self-destructs before any questions can be asked. Picard and Data, disguised as Romulans, are captured by members of Pardek's underground movement, and taken to see Spock.

Stardate: 45233.1

Strange New Worlds: Vulcan, Romulus. The *Enterprise* has to cancel its terraforming mission to Doraf 1, and visits Qualor 2, a Federation surplus depot.

New Life Forms: The Zakdorn (see 'Peak Performance') operate Qualor 2.

Notes: A good introductory story that benefits from a slower than usual pace. There's some great interplay between Data and Picard on the Klingon ship, the latter trying hard not to show his irritation at the bed ('shelf') provided.

A year has passed since Picard shared a mind-meld with Spock's father (see 'Sarek'). Sarek is very ill, and dies during the story. Picard met Spock once before the events of this story (see 'Sarek'), although his knowledge of him comes largely through historical records. Spock publicly attacked Sarek over his position regarding the Cardassian war. Vulcan mint is not like the Earth equivalent. Vulcan ships are often made of dentarium alloy. Picard asks a favour of Gowron (see 'Reunion', 'Redemption'), who is re-writing Klingon history to gain personal credit. Pardek, a Romulan senator, attended the Khitomer Conference (see 'Heart of Glory'), and has entered into trading negotiations with the Barolians.

107: 'Unification II'

US Transmission: 11 November 1991
UK Transmission: 7 March 1993
(as a 90 minute special with 'Unification I')
Writers: Michael Piller,
from a story by Rick Berman, Michael Piller
Director: Cliff Bole
Cast: Leonard Nimoy, Stephen Root, Malachi Throne,
Norman Large, Daniel Roebuck, William Bastiani,
Susan Fallender, Denise Crosby

Picard tells Spock of his father's recent death, and warns the Ambassador to stop his acts of 'cowboy diplomacy'. Spock refuses, but is betrayed by Pardek, who has been working for Commander Sela. Spock's mission has been subverted by the Romulan leadership, who plan a very different kind of unification with Vulcan: a Trojan Horse invasion. The stolen spacecraft, containing large numbers of Romulan troops, will approach Vulcan with a (holographic) message of hope and reconciliation from Spock. Spock and Data alert the *Enterprise*, who intercept the ships, which are immediately destroyed by a cloaked Warbird. The invasion is thwarted, and Spock is determined to stay on Romulus to continue working for the reunification of the two peoples.

Stardate: 45245.8

Strange New Worlds: Galorndon Core (see 'The Enemy') is

mentioned.

New Life Forms: The bar is full of them, including a fat Ferengi. A Bardakian pronghorn moose is mentioned.

Technology: The Romulans plan to use a holographic version of Spock to aid their plans, the technology later being subverted by Data.

Riker's Conquests: Will charms a six-armed, fuzzy-headed, wire-nosed pianist. There is simply no stopping the man.

Dialogue Triumphs: Picard, disguised as a Romulan: 'I think I'll take this opportunity to remove my ears.'

Notes: Despite the epic build-up, 'Unification' proves to be a standard tale of Romulan shenanigans, spiced by Spock's involvement and a homage to the *Star Wars* cantina sequence. It's fascinating to compare Spock and his *Next Generation* equivalent Data (who uses a nerve grip at one point): the former has constantly tried to repress his human side, while the latter has always been interested in becoming *more* human.

Spock refers to James Kirk and his role in the beginnings of peace with the Klingons (see *Star Trek VI*). Klingon opera is strident and Wagnerian. 'Jolan true' is a Romulan farewell.

108: 'A Matter of Time'

US Transmission: 18 November 1991
UK Transmission: 17 June 1993
Writer: Rick Berman
Director: Paul Lynch
Cast: Matt Frewer, Stefan Gierasch, Sheila Franklin,
Shay Garner

Professor Berlinghoff Rasmussen materialises on the bridge, saying he has come from the 26th century to watch the *Enterprise* crew take part in a historic moment. Rasmussen seems particularly interested in developments made in the last two hundred years. The ship's attempts to aid Penthara 4 reverse the effects of a crashing asteroid go disastrously wrong. Fortunately, Geordi's plan succeeds. Picard's suspicions about Rasmussen are heightened when it is discovered that several minor pieces of equipment have gone missing. Rasmussen allows Data to accompany him into his time craft where he reveals that he is actually from the past, the craft having been stolen from a genuine time traveller. He plans to take back the artifacts and claim to have invented them. He now hopes to add Data to his cache. This backfires and the professor is stranded in the 24th century as his craft disappears.

Stardate: 45349.1

Strange New Worlds: Penthara 4, where a type-C asteroid has struck an unpopulated continent. One of their cities is called New Seattle.

Poker Game: Geordi asks if he completes his questionnaire Rasmussen will give him a glimpse of next week's poker game.

Picard Manoeuvre: Yes, twice.

Dialogue Triumphs: 'Some of my best friends are empaths!'

'What if one of those I saved is a child who grows up to be the next Adolf Hitler, or Khan Singh? Every first year philosophy student has been asked that question since the earliest wormholes were discovered, but this is not a class in temporal logic.'

'A person's life, their future, hinges on each of a thousand choices. Living is making choices. You ask me to believe if I make a choice other than the one in your history book then your past will be altered. Well, I don't give a damn about your past records. Your past is my future, and as far as I'm concerned it hasn't been written yet!'

Future History: The 21st century had 'nuclear winters'. By the 26th century, mankind has developed time travel. The Warp

Coil and Phasers were invented after the 22nd century.

Notes: 'How delightfully primitive!' Funny, and inventive until the final scene. Matt Frewer's conman is such a likeable git that the viewer really wants him to escape. His stranding in the future, and Picard's sarcastic 'Welcome to the 24th century', are one of the few occasions when Starfleet seems like a fascist organisation. Boo!

The time-ship's hull is made from plasticised tritanium mesh unknown in the 24th century. Telurian plague has no cure. Rasmussen's list of famous blind men: Homer, Milton, Bach, Monet, (Stevie) Wonder, and . . . Geordi. Data can listen to 150 pieces of music simultaneously; in order to analyse the aesthetics, he tends to keep it to ten or less.

109: 'New Ground'

US Transmission: 6 January 1992
UK Transmission: 18 June 1993
Writers: Grant Rosenberg,
from a story by Sara Chamo, Stuart Chamo
Director: Robert Scheerer
Cast: Georgia Brown, Richard McGonagle,
Jennifer Edwards, Sheila Franklin, Majel Barrett

Worf's son Alexander returns to the *Enterprise*. The boy has proved too much for his human grandparents, and Worf is horrified to find that his son lies and bullies other children. A new drive system, the Soliton Wave, is being installed on the *Enterprise*. However, an initial test run proves disastrous. In an attempt to slow down, the ship fires its photon torpedos, but a fire breaks out in the biolab where Alexander is trapped. Worf and Riker save the boy, and Worf decides that Alexander should stay on the *Enterprise* with him.

Stardate: 45376.3

Strange New Worlds: Bilana 3. Lemma 2 ('about three light years away').

New Life Forms: Gilvos are an endangered species of lizard-like creatures from the rainforests of Corvan 2, being transported to the protected zoo planet of Brentalia (see 'Imaginary Friend').

Introducing: Alexander, as played by Brian Bonsall (cf. last season's 'Reunion').

Technobabble: The Soliton Wave, a method of propulsion by creating a 'non-dispersing wavefront of subspace distortion' which a ship can 'ride' like a surfboard.

Dialogue Triumphs: 'Klingon children are often difficult to control!'

Future History: White rhinos became extinct on Earth in the 22nd century.

Notes: 'I find that I would rather fight ten Bladuk warriors than face one small child.' A dull study of Worf's human qualities in which nothing of significance happens, apart from Riker saving a couple of Gilvos!

Alexander was born on 43rd day of Maktag (or Stardate 43205). (This is approximately 300 Stardates after 'The Emissary' – so the Klingon gestation period is about thirty days?!) Zephram Cochrane, inventor of the Warp Drive (from the *Star Trek* episode 'Metamorphosis'), is mentioned.

Worf tells Alexander the Klingon legend of the brothers Kahless and Morath who fought for twelve days over family honour. (See 'Rightful Heir', 'Birthright', 'First Born'.)

110: 'Hero Worship'

US Transmission: 27 January 1992
UK Transmission: 21 June 1993

Writers: Joe Menosky,
from a story by Hilary J. Bader
Director: Patrick Stewart
Cast: Joshua Harris, Harley Venton, Sheila Franklin,
Steven Einspahr

Data rescues the only survivor of the USS *Vico*, a child called Timothy, who claims that the ship was attacked by ruthless raiders. The story can't be proved, and Timothy becomes increasingly close to Data, taking on the emotionless personality and appearance of the android. When the *Enterprise* heads back to the Black Cluster, where the 'attack' occurred, Timothy sticks to his story, but when Picard reminds him that androids don't lie he says that the destruction of the ship was his fault. Although that's not true, Timothy's account of the disaster does give Data the clue he needs to lower the shields at the crucial moment, thus saving the ship from going the same way as the *Vico*. Timothy drops his android guise, but still wants to be Data's friend.

Stardate: 45397.3

Strange New Worlds: The Black Cluster, formed of collapsed protostars nine billion years ago, one of the most ancient formations in the galaxy and a gravitational obstacle. We hear of Starbase 514.

New Life Forms: The Breen have been known to attack things, and have outposts near the Black Cluster. The Dokkaran culture was known for harmony, one of its temples was Kural Hanesh.

Technology: Computer link-up signals can't penetrate emergency bulkheads. It's hard to maintain a cloaking field in a gravitationally unstable area, and disruptors, warp fields, sensors and phasers go all over the place. Computer posts on ships are only operable by specific individuals.

Notes: Admirable content; boring execution.

Tamarian Frost is a soft drink. Tagas the Magnificent is a mythological figure. The *Vico* was a research vessel. Geordi, at five, was caught for a couple of minutes in a fire before his parents rescued him.

111: 'Violations'

US Transmission: 3 February 1992
UK Transmission: 22 June 1993
Writers: Pamela Gray, Jeri Taylor,
from a story by Shari Goodhartz, T. Michael Gray,
Pamela Gray
Director: Robert Wiemer
Cast: Ben Lemon, David Sage, Rick Fitts, Eve Brenner,
Doug Wert, Craig Benton, Majel Barrett

A group of gentle empathic historians arrive on the *Enterprise* to try their deep-memory techniques on the crew. When Deanna, Riker and Beverly fall into comas, the finger of suspicion is pointed at them. The Ullians protest their innocence but when Deanna awakens, and is mentally probed, her memories implicate the Ullian leader, Tarmin. A further attack on Deanna by Tarmin's son, Jev, reveals that he is the real culprit.

Stardate: 45429.3

Strange New Worlds: The *Enterprise* is heading for Kaldra 4. The Ullians have previously visited Melina 2, two planets in the Nel system and Hurada 3.

New Life Forms: The Ullians, 'telepathic historians'. Not all are empathic and their gift requires many years of study. Betazoids can't empathically 'read' Ullians.

Riker's Conquests: This story sees the first explanation for the cooling in the Riker/Troi relationship. One night after a poker game 'some years before' (post-season one as Riker is 'with beard') an attempt by the pair at, ahem, 'interaction' was halted by Deanna who felt that their responsibilities made such a relationship inadvisable. This doesn't quite fit in with much of what had previously been established (and certainly *doesn't* fit in with 'Second Chances', which states Riker broke off the affair long before they served together).

Deanna Underused?: No, despite being in a coma for half the episode!

Dialogue Triumphs: Geordi: 'Got any memories you feel like digging up?' Riker: 'None I'd care to share with an audience!'
  'Klingons do not allow themselves to be probed!'

Notes: 'You shouldn't remember him like this.' Really heavy subject matter (mental rape) handled with tact (perhaps a bit too much) but memorable for Beverly's horrific nightmare sequence (which is one of the most genuinely scary moments in the series).

Keiko's grandmother was a painter. Geordi got his first pet, a Carcassian cat (see 'Galaxy's Child'), when he was eight.

'Memory invasion' was abolished by the Ullians three centuries ago. It carries a 'severe punishment'. Riker refers to the events of 'Shades of Grey' and Dr Pulaski.

In addition to Troi's nightmare, Riker remembers an accident in engineering in which a female ensign, Keller, was killed, and Beverly recalls the occasion when Picard (with hair!) brought her to see Jack Crusher's body.

Iresine Syndrome is a very rare neurological disorder first diagnosed in the 23rd century, characterised by a severely decreased histamine count.

113: 'The Masterpiece Society'

US Transmission: 10 February 1992
UK Transmission: 23 June 1993

Writers: Adam Belanoff, Michael Piller,
from a story by James Kahn, Adam Belanoff
Director: Winrich Kolbe
Cast: John Synder, Dey Young, Ron Canada, Sheila Franklin

A runaway stellar core fragment is heading straight to the reclusive colony of Moab 4, where a group of genetically- and socially-engineered humans live in a sealed biosphere. As the colony refuses to evacuate, Geordi beams down to aid scientist Hannah Bates: the solution to their problem lies in the nature of Geordi's VISOR, an irony as a blind man would not be allowed to be born in the biosphere. Meanwhile, Troi falls for Aaron Conor, the colony leader. The fragment is deflected, but Hannah, interested in a freer life outside, fakes a breach in the biosphere to force an evacuation. When that fails she requests asylum, and others follow. Aaron makes an eloquent speech, urging those who want to leave to give the colony six months, but they go anyway. The loss may destabilise the colony enough to destroy it, a state of affairs that Picard sees only too well.

Stardate: 45470.1

Strange New Worlds: A biosphere on the southern continent of Moab 4.

New Life Forms: Humans bred to fill specific roles in life.

Technology: In the last century, lower frequencies were used for communication. The *Enterprise* has the most powerful matter/antimatter system in Starfleet. Its tractor beam could move a small moon. Geordi's VISOR scans frequencies between 1 Hz and 100,000 Teraherz. Transporters have been in use for over a century.

Notes: Makes ditchwater look exciting.

The Prime Directive doesn't apply to human colonies. Picard doesn't approve of genetic engineering. Geordi has never been embarrassed by his blindness. Troi knows 'Humpty Dumpty'.

113: 'Conundrum'

US Transmission: 17 February 1992
UK Transmission: 24 June 1993
Writers: Barry Schkolnick,
from a story by Paul Schiffer
Director: Les Landau
Cast: Erich Anderson, Liz Vassey, Erick Weiss, Majel Barrett

An encounter with a craft leaves the *Enterprise* crew with amnesia. All they have retained is the knowledge necessary to operate the ship. Eventually, they find a way into the computer and discover the crew manifest, which is correct in all major respects except for the inclusion of first officer Kieran MacDuff. The computer further states that the Federation is at war with the Lysians, on a secret mission to destroy their command centre. Having blown-up one Lysian vessel as they approach their target Picard refuses to carry out their 'mission'. MacDuff tries to take command of the ship but is stopped by Worf and Riker. Once Dr Crusher has restored the crew's memories, it becomes clear that 'MacDuff' is actually an alien, a Satarran, a race at war with the Lysians who were attempting to end the conflict with outside help.

Stardate: 45494.2

Strange New Worlds: The Epsilon Silar System, an unexplored sector of the galaxy. Universal beauty spots include the Cliffs of Heaven on Sumiko 4 and the Emerald Wading Pool on Cirrus 4.

New Life Forms: The Lysian alliance and the Satarrans, who have been at war for decades. Little more is revealed, except that both are technologically underdeveloped.

Poker Game: No. Data and Deanna play 3D chess and, despite Data's chess knowledge (he mentions the Kriskov gambit and the el-Mitra sacrifice), Troi wipes the floor with him, saying chess isn't just a game of ploys and gambits but also of intuition. Their bet on the outcome is a Samarian sunset (a drink) 'made in the traditional style'.

Riker's Conquests: When everyone loses their memories, Ro is attracted to Riker (even waiting in his bed with a 'come-and-get-it-big-boy' look on her face), whilst Troi's feelings also survive. Lucky swine!

Dialogue Triumphs: 'Contact the operations officer to assist you.' 'He's in Ten-Forward waiting tables!'

'I feel as if I've been handed a weapon, sent into a room and told to kill a stranger.'

Notes: 'I don't know who any of you are.' Suitably clever, with a brilliant premise and scenes in which characters we know back-to-front stumble around in the dark, trying to find themselves. However, it is let down by a preposterous ending when, after the Satarrans have been exposed, Picard expresses his 'deep regret' to the Lysians over their ship which was 'lost' (i.e. the one the *Enterprise blew up!*). Sorry for killing your people, guys, but we lost our memories and thought we were at war. Maybe this was where Hitler went wrong in 1939?

Riker discovers his 'surprising' musical abilities, that he likes exotic food, loves to rock-climb and takes his holidays on Risa. His copy of Keats' *Ode to Psyche* was given to him by Deanna ('with love').

Amongst the information briefly seen in the 'crew manifest,' data biogs are that Beverly's maiden name is Howard (see 'Sub Rosa'), she was born in 2324, her middle initial is 'C' and Wesley shares his father's middle initial 'R'. Picard was born in 2305, his parents were Maurice and Yvette and he attended the academy from 2333 to 2338. Deanna was born in 2336.

114: 'Power Play'

US Transmission: 24 February 1992

UK Transmission: 25 June 1993
Writers: Rene Balcer, Herbert J. Wright, Brannon Braga,
from a story by Paul Ruben, Maurice Hurley
Director: David Livingston
Cast: Ryan Reid, Majel Barrett

The *Enterprise* picks up a distress call from a ship lost over 200 years previously. During their investigation Troi, Data and O'Brien seem to be possessed by the ghosts of the crew, and on their return to the *Enterprise* they secure themselves in Ten-Forward with a large number of hostages. The 'ghosts' wish only to be laid to rest, but Picard discovers that they are actually incorporeal prisoners striving to escape their penal colony. When he and all the 'ghosts' are in the hold, he says that he will open the cargo bay doors, killing them all, unless the 'ghosts' return to their prison. Soon Troi, Data and O'Brien are back to normal.

Stardate: 45571.2

Strange New Worlds: The *Enterprise* is in orbit around an unexplored moon of Mab-Bu 6. It is supposed to be uninhabited, and electromagnetic whirlwinds move over the satellite's surface.

New Life Forms: The incorporeal prisoners were brought to the moon over 500 years ago from the Ux-Mal system. The penal colony contains hundreds of criminals, deprived of their bodies as a punishment. They previously tried to escape in the *Essex*.

Jat'yln are Klingon possession legends.

Picard Manoeuvre: When he is captured as a hostage.

Notes: A gripping suspense tale. Sirtis, Spiner and Meaney act their socks off when possessed by the aliens.

The Daedelus-class starships went out of service 172 years ago. The USS *Essex* was commanded by Captain Bryce Shumar:

the first officer was Stephen Mullen, and the security chief was Lt Morgan Kelly. The ship – NCC 173 – carried a crew of 229, and Shumar reported to Admiral Utan Narsu at Starbase 12 (see 'Conspiracy' and the original series episode 'Space Seed'). It was destroyed by the moon's storms.

Riker has broken his arm before.

115: 'Ethics'

US Transmission: 2 March 1992
UK Transmission: 28 June 1993
Writers: Ronald D. Moore,
from a story by Sara Charno, Stuart Charno
Director: Chip Chalmers
Cast: Caroline Kava

Worf's spinal cord is crushed in an accident. Paralysed and facing a dishonourable existence, the Klingon asks Riker to help him commit ritual suicide. Riker refuses, and discovers that the Klingon's son should assist in such a ceremony. Worf can barely bring himself to see Alexander, but neurospecialist Dr Russell offers him an untried operation that will either cure the Klingon or kill him. Russell's cavalier approach to experimentation has already prompted Crusher to relieve her of all medical duties on the *Enterprise*, but eventually the operation goes ahead. Worf dies, but moments later his redundant systems kick in. Alexander can now help his father recuperate.

Stardate: 45587.3

Strange New Worlds: The transport ship *Denver* has struck a gravitic mine left over from the Cardassian war and crash-landed on a planet in the Mericor system.

Poker Game: Worf and Geordi discuss a Poker game in which Troi (pair of sixes) bluffed Worf (Jacks and eights). Geordi says that he uses the infrared-seeing properties of his VISOR to peep at the cards once the game is over.

Dialogue Triumphs: Alexander: 'This is part of that Klingon stuff, isn't it? My mother always said Klingons had a lot of dumb ideas about honour.'

'You scare me, doctor. You risk your patients' lives and justify it in the name of research . . . You take short-cuts – right through living tissue.'

Notes: 'I may have to respect your beliefs, but I don't have to like them.' A classic *Trek* morality play: how much experimental research is justified if it comes under the guise of possibly saving a patient's life? The 'death' of Worf is well-handled, his earlier interaction with his son and the others providing the story with the emotional impact needed to balance the delicate ethical debate.

The *Potemkin* (see 'Peak Performance', 'Legacy') brings Dr Russell, a neurospecialist, to the *Enterprise*. Crusher has recently written a paper on cybernetic regeneration. Klingons have done little research into neurological trauma as they would usually let a patient in Worf's condition die. Russell considers the Klingons to be 'over-designed', their bodies featuring twenty-three ribs, two livers, an eight-chambered heart and a double-lined neural pia mater. Almost every vital function has a built-in redundancy in case of failure: the Klingons refer to this as the Brak'lul. (Crusher speculates that they have backup synaptic functions, too.) The Hegh'bat ceremony is the Klingon's equivalent of Seppuku. A family member should attend, preferably the oldest son. Alexander is better at multiplication than anyone in his class.

Riker says he's lost count of the friends he's seen die, and mentions Sandoval (hit by a disrupter blast two years previously: s/he lived for two weeks), Fang-lee, Marla Aster ('The Bonding') and Tasha Yar ('Skin of Evil').

116: 'The Outcast'

US Transmission: 16 March 1992
UK Transmission: 29 June 1993
Writer: Jeri Taylor
Director: Robert Scheerer
Cast: Melinda Cilea, Callan White, Megan Cole

The J'naii, an androgynous species, seek the *Enterprise*'s assistance. Riker is assigned to work with Soren, and they become attracted to each other. The J'naii strictly forbid any form of sexual preference and, once Soren has begun to openly display 'her' feelings (considering 'herself' female), the J'naii take action to 'cure' these dangerous tendencies. Riker risks his career in an attempt to rescue Soren, but the cure has already been administered and 'it' renounces any former feelings for Riker.

Stardate: 45614.6

Strange New Worlds: The *Enterprise* leaves for the Phelan system.

New Life Forms: The J'naii, a single gender race who consider male or female qualities as primitive and abnormal.

Technobabble: 'Null space': during the creation of a star system, gravitational fields can condense into 'abnormal pockets'.

Poker Game: Worf, Beverly, Deanna and Data play 'Federation Day' in which twos, sixes and aces are wild. Worf considers it 'a woman's game'.

Riker's Conquests: Sorin, who asks Riker about his ideal woman. Riker requires intelligence, self-confidence, someone whom he can talk to 'and get something back'. Most important, she has to laugh at his jokes. (Tall order . . .)

(Offensive) Dialogue Triumphs: 'On this world, everybody wants to be normal.'

'I am female. I was born that way.'

Future History: The Federation was founded in 2161.

Notes: 'Commander, tell me about your sexual organs!' Prepare to have your intelligences insulted . . . Plus points first, 'The Outcast' tries hard to be radical and earnest. But with a sledgehammer message, offensively bland liberalism, and patronising view of bisexuality (the only 'happiness' for this poor creature is to give herself to Will Riker . . .), the episode is a hollow mess. Of course, we could be accused of missing the point here, but if you're going to tackle a subject as controversial as this, sitting on the fence isn't the best way to go about it. Deanna is nicely characterised throughout. Geordi sports a beard for the episode (as he does in 'The Quality of Life').

Riker has programmed his father's recipe for split pea soup into the *Enterprise* replicators. 'Helps keep you warm on the cold Alaskan nights.'

Federation shuttle craft feature two 1250 millicochrane warp engines, micron fusion thrusters and are not normally armed.

117: 'Cause and Effect'

US Transmission: 23 March 1992
UK Transmission: 30 June 1993
Writer: Brannon Braga
Director: Jonathan Frakes
Cast: Kelsey Grammer

The officers' poker night is interrupted by an emergency which results in the collision with another ship, and the destruction of the *Enterprise*. They next find themselves back in the poker game with no memory of the preceding events. However, Beverly suffers from a sense of *déjà vu* and, hearing a babble of conversation in her cabin, records it. To their horror, the crew discover that they appear to be locked in a circle of time in which they are acting out the same events over and over again, the babble of voices being echoes from a previous loop. Data thinks that he may be able to plant a memory to carry forward into the next loop. Again, the ship is destroyed, but when the circle begins next time subtle changes occur, particularly involving the number three. Data guesses that three refers to a suggestion made by Riker (his uniform has three pips), and the circle is broken when the collision is avoided. The *Enterprise* discovers it has been trapped for seventeen days, unlike the other ship, the *Bozeman*, which has been trapped for nearly ninety years.

Stardate: 45652.1 (several times).

Strange New Worlds: The Typhon expanse.

Technobabble: Geordi calls for a Gravitron Polarimeter at one point. And a 'temporal causality loop'.

Poker Game: Yes, and for once it has a major part to play in the plot. Riker, Worf, Beverly and Data play, Beverly winning after calling Riker's bluff.

Dialogue Triumphs: 'It's possible we've tried this a thousand times, and it's never worked.'

Notes: 'All hands, abandon ship!' A one-act play in four acts that works precisely because of the *déjà vu* that effects not only the crew but the viewer as well. The pre-title sequence of the ship's destruction is amazing. But why is it Beverly who suffers *déjà vu* and not the more likely Data or Deanna? And did the producers of *Groundhog Day* watch this episode at all?

Geordi has been treated several times for headaches related to his VISOR. Picard's Aunt Adele's cure for insomnia was a glass of steamed milk. The Klingon term for *déjà vu* is 'nlb poh'.

The *Enterprise* has spent 17.4 days within the causality loop when they break free. The USS *Bozeman*, a Soyuz-class starship under the command of Captain Bateson, has been stuck since 2278 (around ninety years).

118: 'The First Duty'

US Transmission: 30 March 1992
UK Transmission: 1 July 1993
Writers: Ronald D. Moore, Naren Shankar
Director: Paul Lynch
Cast: Jacqueline Brooks, Ray Walston, Robert Duncan McNeill, Ed Lauter, Richard Fancy, Walker Brandt, Shannon Fill

A member of Wesley's elite Academy squadron dies during practice manoeuvres. Picard, preparing to deliver the year's Starfleet Academy commencement address, is shocked by discrepancies between Wesley's testimony and the available evidence. Picard talks to Boothby and discovers that the Nova squadron were planning to perform a highly dangerous and banned flight manoeuvre as part of the celebrations. Picard confronts Wesley, saying that, whatever his commitment to the group and to the charismatic leader Locarno, his first duty is to the truth. On the final day of the inquiry, knowing that Picard will say what really happened if he doesn't, Wesley states that, at Locarno's insistence, they were practising to perform the Kolvoord Starburst manoeuvre, which claimed the life of Cadet Albert. Locarno is expelled from Starfleet; Wesley and the others are formally reprimanded, their academic work for the last year being rendered void.

Stardate: 45703.9

Picard Manoeuvre: When trying to express his gratitude to Boothby.

Dialogue Triumphs: Boothby, to Picard: 'What happened to your hair?'

Notes: A nice change of mood and tempo, leaving the *Enterprise* behind for Starfleet Academy and a none-too-flattering glimpse into Wesley's new life. It's good to know that swots don't always have it easy.

Picard is to deliver this year's Starfleet Academy commencement address. Wes's flight team were due to perform a demonstration near Saturn, the pictures of which would have been relayed back to the watching dignitaries at the Academy. Picard's superintendent at the Academy was a Betazoid (Jean-Luc was called into his office on a number of occasions); Riker's was a Vulcan. Picard hails from the class of '27 (as mentioned in 'Final Mission'), and displays a sudden interest in horticulture (although he says this has been acquired 'over the years'). Picard fought a (wrestling?) bout against a Legonian. Boothby also remembers the Academy's unexpected Parisses Squares tournament victory over Minsk in the final, and says that the Nova Squadron have received similar adoration for recently winning the Rigel cup.

Wes is allergic to metorapan treatments, having to have a bicaridine substitute. The single-seater spacecraft travel at 80,000 'kph', carry flight-recorders, and have emergency transport devices (with a comparable function to ejector seats). The Kolvoord Starburst manoeuvre involves five ships crossing within 10 metres of each other, igniting their plasma trails. It is spectacularly difficult, and hasn't been performed at the Academy for over a hundred years as it was banned following a training accident which killed all five cadet pilots.

Wesley's squadron includes Cadet Sito (see 'Lower Decks').

119: 'Cost of Living'

US Transmission: 20 April 1992
UK Transmission: 2 July 1993
Writer: Peter Allan Fields

Director: Winrich Kolbe
Cast: Tony Jay, Carel Struycken, David Oliver, Albie
Selznick, Patrick Cronin, Tracy D'Arcy, George Ede,
Christopher Halsted, Majel Barrett

Lwaxana Troi beams aboard, astounding her daughter with the
revelation that she is getting married to someone she's never
met. Even worse, Lwaxana won't be getting married in the nude,
as Betazoid custom dictates: her husband-to-be, Minister
Campio, comes from a very authoritarian, orderly and prudish
culture. Alexander is becoming increasingly rebellious, and
seems to recognise in Lwaxana a kindred spirit, much to Worf
and Deanna's horror. Meanwhile the ship's systems start to de-
generate, eaten away by parasites contained within a rogue asteroid recently destroyed by the *Enterprise*. As life support
breaks down only Data is left to cure the problem. The wedding is therefore able to go ahead – but Lwaxana turns up naked, having decided that a life of conformity is not for her.

Stardate: 45733.6 (towards the end).

Strange New Worlds: The *Enterprise* is *en route* to the
Moselina system. Minister Campio hails from the bureaucratic
world of Kostolain. As third minister of the conference of judges
he's close to royalty.

The parasites originated on an asteroid from the Pelloris Field
near Tessen 3. Mrs Troi and Alexander spend a lot of time in
the holodeck simulation of the Parallax Colony on Shiralea 6.

New Life Forms: The anarchic inhabitants of the Parallax
Colony include a fire sculptor, a juggler, a poet and a couple
who spend all their time arguing. The Wind Dancer is a head in
a bubble that stands guard so that 'only those whose hearts are
joyous may enter' (Worf pops the creature irritably). The Parallax Colony has a Laughing Hour and some famous mud baths.

The *Enterprise* is 'attacked' by the organic parasitic 'dust',
which consumes nitrium and exudes a gelatinous residue.

Dialogue Triumphs: Weird stuff from the Colony, including 'If you ever have a world – plan ahead. Don't eat it.'

Notes: 'Permission for an on board wedding is granted, Number One. Nothing will please me more than to give away Mrs Troi.' The clash of anarchy with order (Lwaxana, about to enter into a rule-bound marriage, encouraging Alexander to break a contract with his father) allows new depths to be revealed in her character. All the stuff in the *Wizard of Oz*-like Colony is well-weird, and the episode is worth watching just to see Worf in a mud bath.

   Nitrium is an intrinsic part of much of the *Enterprise*. Lwaxana Troi gets a petrokian sausage from the replicator instead of tea.

120: 'The Perfect Mate'

US Transmission: 27 April 1992
UK Transmission: 5 July 1993
Writers: Gary Perconte (a pseudonym for Reuben Leder),
Michael Piller,
from a story by René Echevarria,
Gary Perconte (Reuben Leder)
Director: Cliff Bole
Cast: Famke Janssen, Tim O'Connor, Max Grodenchik,
Mickey Cottrell, Michael Snyder, David Paul Needles,
Roger Rignak, Charles Gunning, April Grace, Majel Barrett

Plans for a ceremony of reconciliation between the warring planets of Krios and Valt Minor are disturbed when the Kriosian 'peace offering' proves to be an empathic mesomorph, who can become the perfect partner for any man. Released from stasis prematurely by meddling Ferengi, the Kriosian mesomorph Kamala is due to marry the Valtese leader Alrik, which Crusher states is no more than prostitution. Picard, wary of the effect the woman is having on his crew, confines her to quarters, but is forced to go to her for help when the Kriosian ambassador Briam is injured. He struggles against Kamala's charms, trying to show her that as a person she can have intrinsic value apart from her special abilities. Alrik arrives, committed to peace and the symbolism of the wedding, but not especially interested in Kamala. Just before the marriage Kamala tells Picard that she has chosen to 'bond' with him rather than Alrik, although Alrik will never notice: she will perform all duties required of her for the good of her people.

Stardate: 45761.3

Strange New Worlds: Krios (a different planet from the Klingon colony seen in 'The Mind's Eye'?) and Valt Minor have been at war for centuries, but once oversaw a vast empire, ruled by two brothers (also named Krios and Valt) from the Temple of Akadar. They both loved the 'extraordinary woman' Garuth, and the war started when Krios kidnapped her from Valt.

The *Enterprise* has just rescued some miners from Harod 4.

New Life Forms: The female empathic mesomorph Kamala. While male mesomorphs are common, a female empathic mesomorph is only born once every seven generations on Krios (Kamala is the first in a hundred years). If Briam is anything to go by, the Kriosians have long life-spans (the ambassador is 200 years old). The Ferengi are very interested in Kamala.

Valtese horns are said to sound like braying Targhee moon beasts.

Riker's Conquests: Riker snogs Kamala, but then says, rather bravely, 'This has been very educational, but I make it a policy never to open another man's gift.' (He then proceeds to a holodeck, although a cold shower might have been more helpful.)

Deanna Underused?: She doesn't appear.

Dialogue Triumphs: Qol, the Ferengi, when apprehended in the cargo bay: 'This is a misunderstanding. I was looking for the barber's shop.'

Notes: Some nice touches – the central idea of releasing a sensual woman on to the sterile *Enterprise* is a good one – but the end result is, like most Picard love stories, just a tiny bit dull.

We see Picard and Crusher's breakfast together (as mentioned in 'Qpid'). Picard's taste in women would seem to be 'independent, forceful, brilliant and adventurous'. He is interested in ancient Ventanen woven art, loves Shakespeare's sonnets, and remembers the gardens of Lesarée, near the village where he grew up. His mother made him learn the piano, which he hated.

121: 'Imaginary Friend'

US Transmission: 4 May 1992
UK Transmission: 6 July 1993
Writers: Edithe Swenson, Brannon Braga,
from a story by Lousie Matthias, Ronald Wilkerson,
Richard Fliegel
Director: Gabrielle Beaumont
Cast: Noley Thomton, Shay Astar, Jeff Allin, Sheila Kranlkin

Clara Sutter, the daughter of a crewman, has an imaginary friend, Isabella. When the *Enterprise* explores a new nebula, Isabella appears to Clara in the flesh. At the same time an inexplicable power drain begins. Gradually, Isabella becomes visible to more people and the crew discover that 'she' is responsible for the draining of energy, being an entity that feeds on this. Clara persuades her friend to leave the ship.

Stardate: 45852.1

Strange New Worlds: FGC-47, a nebula formed around a neutron star.

New Life Forms: 'Isabella', an alien entity manifested as a little girl. Her kind live on energy plasma.

Guinan had an imaginary friend, a Tarcassian razorbeast with golden eyes. Worf once took Alexander to the zoo on Brentalia (see 'New Ground') to see Kryonian tigers.

Dialogue Triumphs: 'Most grown ups have a hard time with things they can't see!'

Notes: 'There's no such thing as invisible people.' A bit twee and insubstantial, although it is nice for once to see the regulars from a child's perspective (Worf is particularly stern and frightening).

Geordi's parents are both in Starfleet, his father is an exobiologist, his mother a command officer (see 'Interface'). Geordi's childhood was spent travelling around with one or both of them, and although some aspects weren't perfect, he considered it 'one long holiday'(see 'Aquiel').

122: 'I, Borg'

US Transmission: 11 May 1992
UK Transmission: 7 July 1993
Writer: René Echevarria
Director: Robert Lederman
Cast: Jonathan Del Arco

The *Enterprise* discovers a crashed Borg ship with one survivor. The crew face their nightmare made flesh, and learn that blind hatred isn't always easy as they humanise the Borg and give him a name, Hugh. Picard plans to use Hugh by implanting a sabotage program in him and returning him to the collective, but he too has second thoughts about the ethics of this. Hugh, having befriended Geordi, wishes to stay with the *Enterprise* and is offered asylum, but Hugh knows that the Borg will not give up searching for him and so elects to return to the collective.

Stardate: 45854.1

Strange New Worlds: The Argolis cluster, six star systems being considered for colonisation. The Borg ship is found on a small moon orbiting the fourth planet of one of these.

Dialogue Triumphs: 'If you are going to use this person to destroy his race, you should at least look him in the eye once before you do it.'

Hugh: 'I think you are lonely.'

Notes: 'Resistance is . . . not futile.' An astonishing episode, doing the seemingly impossible in humanising the Borg, the series' most chilling bogeymen. A few aspects of the episode are troublesome (particularly some of the liberal nonsense that Beverly spouts) but the sight of both Guinan and Picard, who have good reason to hate the Borg, coming to terms with Hugh is life-affirming. A strange 'feel good' episode.

Picard and Guinan fence with foils (cf. 'We'll Always Have Paris'). Picard is 'much better' but Guinan is more cunning, feigning injury to win.

The Borg's designation is 'third of five', Geordi christens him Hugh. Picard initially compares him to a laboratory animal in an experiment (from 'centuries ago').

123: 'The Next Phase'

US Transmission: 18 May 1992
UK Transmission: 8 July 1993
Writer: Ronald D. Moore
Director: David Carson
Cast: Thomas Kopache, Susanna Thompson, Shelby Leverington, Brian Cousins, Kenneth Messerole

A Romulan vessel experiencing reactor core failure asks the *Enterprise* for help. A transporter failure apparently vaporises Geordi and Ro. Then they wake up on the *Enterprise*. As their friends prepare to hold a memorial in their honour, the pair discover that they are 'out of phase' with the rest of the ship, this having been caused by an experimental new cloaking device on the Romulan ship. The Romulans have also set a trap for the *Enterprise* so that when the ship goes to warp speed it will be destroyed. Geordi and Ro discover that anyon beams will make them visible again and so pursue Data creating chroniton fields. Finally Data understands their attempts and floods the ship with anyons, forcing the pair back into phase.

Stardate: 45892.4 (given on Ro's death certificate).

Strange New Worlds: The *Enterprise* is heading for the Garadius system.

New Life Forms: The Bajoran 'death chant' is over two hours long. 'Borhyas' is Bajoran for ghost or spirit. Bajoran religion teaches that the dead should make peace with their former life before passing on to whatever afterlife awaits.

Technology: The Klingons were reported to have experimented with a combination of a phase inverter and a cloaking device with little success.

Dialogue Triumphs: 'What about my uniform? My VISOR? Are you saying I'm a blind ghost with clothes?'

Ro to Picard: 'I don't believe this. I'm dead, you can't hear me, and I'm still intimidated by you.'

'They think we're dead, and they're having a party?!'

'Maybe we should develop our own interface. If it can teach Ro Laren humility, it can do anything.'

Notes: 'It's like I'm here, but I'm not here!' *Star Trek* does *Randall and Hopkirk (Deceased)*! The phased Romulan chasing Ro through the *Enterprise* (walls and all) is great. There's lots of good character-building, too.

Picard thinks if Ro hadn't lost her rank due to the incident at Garron 2 (not Garron 4, see 'Ensign Ro') she'd have made lieutenant commander by now. He first met Geordi when he was assigned to pilot Picard on an inspection tour: an offhand remark by Picard about the shuttle's engines caused Geordi to stay up all night refitting the fusion initiators.

Melakol is a Romulan measure of pressure, and kolam a unit of power flow. Chronitron particles are subatomic particles that transmit temporal quanta and are generated by an interphase generator. Data uses the anyon emitter to clear them.

The transporter chief is Lt Brossmer (O'Brien seems to be on leave).

124: 'The Inner Light'

US Transmission: 1 June 1992
UK Transmission: 9 July 1993
Writers: Morgan Gendel, Peter Allan Fields,
from a story by Morgan Gendel
Director: Peter Lauritson
Cast: Margot Rose, Richard Riehle, Scott Jaeck,
Jennifer Nash, Daniel Stewart

During a survey of the Parvenium system, the *Enterprise* encounters a probe. Picard collapses, and wakes up in another man's body. He is now Kamin, an iron-weaver on the planet Kataan. Although initially anxious to return to the *Enterprise*, he soon comes to believe that his life as Picard was a fever-induced illusion and, helped by his wife Eline, settles down, having a family, growing older, and discovering that the planet is dying through drought. The Kataans, knowing that their world is doomed, launch a probe containing their history so that those from the future will know about them. They chose Kamin as the eyes through which the future historians will see Kataan. Picard realises that this is the probe the *Enterprise* will encounter in thousands of years time, just as he reawakens on the bridge having, literally, lived another lifetime.

Stardate: 45944.1 (and a thousand years before the 24th century).

Strange New Worlds: Kataan (Ressik, in the Northern Province), an unmapped system with six planets, destroyed when its star went nova.

Deanna Underused?: On shore leave again?

Dialogue Triumphs: 'You've been dreaming about that starship of yours again, haven't you?'

'Seize the time, Meribor. Make "now" always the most precious time. "Now" will never come again.'

'The rest of us have been gone a thousand years. If you remember what we were and how we lived then we'll have found life again.'

Notes: 'This is not my life, I know that much.' *Star Trek* does *Quantum Leap*! Truly beautiful and life-affirming, one of the best scripts in the series' history. An award-winning episode. Picard lives another lifetime, marrying, having children and grandchildren, growing old on a dying world all in the space of twenty to twenty-five minutes real time. Difficult to watch without a lump in the throat and a prickly sensation behind the eyes. A masterpiece.

Kamin is a keen flautist (a trait he keeps when returning to Picard). His first stumbling attempts on the instrument result in a version of 'Frère Jacques' (see 'Disaster', 'Lessons').

125: 'Time's Arrow'

US Transmission: 15 June 1992
UK Transmission: 12 July 1993
Writers: Joe Menosky, Michael Piller,
from a story by Joe Menosky
Director: Les Landau
Cast: Jerry Hardin, Michael Aron, Barry Kivel, Ken Thorley,

Sheldon-Peters Wilfchild, Jack Murdock, Marc Alaimo, Milt Tarver, Michael Hungerford

Data's head is discovered in a 500-year-old cavern in San Francisco. Specific wave particles point to Devidia 2 as the origin of the mystery. On Devidia, an away team find a time vortex, and Data passes through it, finding himself in 19th century San Francisco, where he meets a younger Guinan. A pair of aliens are also in the past, seemingly stealing the life energy from innocent humans. Picard decides to follow Data into the past and leads an away team into the vortex.

Stardate: 45959.1

Strange New Worlds: Devidia 2, in the Marrab sector. Home of a single-cell microscopic life form LB10445.

New Life Forms: The Devidians, shape-shifters with microcentrum cell membranes. An Ophidian, a snake-like energy creature.

Technobabble: Triolic waves, the by-products of which have a deleterious effect on most living tissue.

Poker Game: Data plays in the 19th century (his opponents include Frederick La Rouque and the Indian Falling Hawk). He uses his communicator as a stake and wins heavily.

Dialogue Triumphs: Falling Hawk sees Data: 'Pale face!'
    'A man walks into town in his pyjamas, wins a grub-stake in a poker game, turns it into a horseless carriage and makes a million. That's America!'

Notes: 'At some future date I will be transported back to the 19th century where I will die. It has occurred. It will occur.' Some very good scenes with Geordi, Deanna and Riker concerning the foreknowledge of Data's death and a startling 'to be continued' climax. Also, the first major use of 'real' historical figures in *The Next Generation* (although neither Jack London nor Mark Twain are actually referred to by name until part two).

The 19th-century segments begin on 11 August 1893. Data and Geordi seem to play chess together. Data's positronic brain has an 'R-type phase discriminating amplifier' (Lore's is an L-type). The Starfleet communicator is a crystalline composite of silicon, berilium, carbon 70 and gold.

Guinan, on Earth in the 19th century, asks Data if her father sent him to find her.

Sixth Season

26 45-minute episodes

Created by Gene Roddenberry

Executive Producers:
Rick Berman (126–132, 134–136, 138–151),
Michael Piller (127–129, 134–136, 138–145, 147–151)
Co-Executive Producers: Rick Berman (133, 137),
Michael Piller (126, 130–133, 137, 146), Jeri Taylor (126–150) **Producer:** Peter Lauritson **Co-Producers:** Ronald D. Moore, Wendy Neuss, Jeri Taylor (151) **Supervising Producers:** David Livingston, Frank Abatemarco (126–138)
Line Producer: Merri D. Howard
Story Editors: Brannon Braga, René Echevarria

Regular Cast: Patrick Stewart (Captain Jean-Luc Picard), Jonathan Frakes (Commander William Riker), LeVar Burton (Lt Commander Geordi La Forge), Michael Dorn (Lt Worf), Gates McFadden (Dr Beverly Crusher), Marina Sirtis (Counselor Deanna Troi), Brent Spiner (Lt Commander Data) Colm Meaney (Lt O'Brien, 127, 132), Rosalind Chao (Keiko O'Brien, 132), Hana Hatae (Molly O'Brien, 132), Whoopi

Goldberg (Guinan, 126, 132, 147), Michelle Forbes (Ensign Ro Laren, 132), Patti Yasutake (Nurse Ogawa, 127-128, 147), Dwight Schultz (Lt Reg Barclay, 127, 137), Brian Bonsall (Alexander, 132-133), John de Lancie (Q, 131, 140), Siddig el Fadil (Dr Julian Bashir, 141)

126: 'Time's Arrow 2'

US Transmission: 19 September 1992
UK Transmission: 13 July 1993
Writers: Jeri Taylor, from a story by Joe Menosky
Director: Les Landau
Cast: Jerry Hardin, Pamela Kosh, William Bovett,
Michael Aron, James Gleason, Mary Stein,
Alexander Enberg, Bill Cho Lee, Majel Barrett

Samuel Clemens overhears a conversation between Data and Guinan and believes that they are aliens come to pollute Earth with destructive technology. Picard and the others discover the Devidians draining electro-chemical energy from humans using a cholera epidemic as cover. During a battle in the cavern, Data is decapitated and Guinan injured. Picard remains behind when the vortex closes, but the curious Clemens is taken to the future and, after having been convinced of the integrity of the *Enterprise* crew, returns to the 19th century and opens the vortex for Picard. Geordi manages to reattach Data's head.

Stardate: 46001.3

Dialogue Triumphs: Mrs Carmichael: 'I've heard you silver-tongued divvils before!'

Riker about to punch a Police officer: 'I want you to know I have the utmost respect for the law!'

Clemens: 'All this technology only serves to take away life's simple pleasures.'

Future History: Deanna tells Clemens that poverty was eliminated on Earth 'a long time ago'.

Notes: 'I keep telling you, there is no plot!' An accurate summing up, this is a mess with so many unanswered questions we'd need another book to list them. Where did the away team's 19th-century clothes come from? Who were the aliens? Why did they need human energy? What was their 'snake' and why did it manifest itself as a walking stick? Etcetera.

Great Picard/Guinan scenes (in both time zones). Jerry Hardin is good as Mark Twain, mentioning his 'recent' novel A *Connecticut Yankee in King Arthur's Court* (1888). The Jack London sub-plot also seems historically feasible.

Picard and the away team pretend to be a band of strolling players rehearsing *A Midsummer Night's Dream*. O'Brien is mentioned but not seen.

127: 'Realm of Fear'

US Transmission: 26 September 1992
UK Transmission: 14 July 1993
Writer: Brannon Braga
Director: Cliff Bole
Cast: Renata Scott, Thomas Belgrey, Majel Barrett

Barclay's fears about transporters are said by Crusher to be wholly without foundation, but when he transports to the aid of a stricken Starfleet science vessel he sees a creature inside the beam. The *Yosemite* strayed too close to a plasma streamer, and its crew have vanished. Barclay, bitten by one of the creatures, comes to the conclusion that the crew are trapped within the transporter beam. Conquering his fear, he pulls the first of the crewmembers free.

Stardate: 46041.1

New Life Forms: Quasi-energy microbes exist within the distortion field of the plasma streamer.

O'Brien encountered Talarian hook spiders whilst re-routing an emitter array at a starbase on Zayra 4. The spiders' legs are about half a metre in length.

Technobabble: 'It looks like he pushed molecular dispersion past the integrity point. Your patterns got caught in the beam.' 'The residual energy from the plasma streamer must have amplified the charge in the buffer enough to keep your patterns from degrading.'

Notes: Despite a few similarities to 'Relics' and 'Second Chances' later on this season (people kept alive in transporter beams), this is a very enjoyable story. It's always nice to see Reg Barclay, and there are some interesting point-of-view transporting sequences. A clever parallel is established between futuristic worries about the transporter and our own fears of flying.

The Cardassians are attacking Ferengi ships. The science vessel USS *Yosemite* was sent to the Igo sector to observe a remote plasma streamer. Barclay is terrified of the transporter (cf. Dr Pulaski's attitude in the second season): he thinks he might be suffering from transporter psychosis. This was diagnosed in 2209 by researchers on Delinia 2. However, Crusher reminds him that there hasn't been a reported case for over fifty years, and warns him against accessing Starfleet medical information (see 'Genesis'). O'Brien on the other hand suffered from arachnophobia, but now keeps a pet tarantula called Christina which he found on Titus 4.

128: 'Man of the People'

US Transmission: 3 October 1992
UK Transmission: 15 July 1993

Writer: Frank Abatemarco
Director: Winrich Kolbe
Cast: Chip Lucia, George D. Wallace, Lucy Boryer,
Susan French, Rick Scarry, Stephanie Erb, J.P. Hubbell,
Majel Barrett

Lumerian Ambassador Ves Alkar is on the *Enterprise* prior to
mediating in a dispute on the war-torn planet of Rekag-Seronia.
His aged mother dies after giving Troi a sinister warning. Troi
helps Alkar overcome his grief by joining in the Lumerian funeral meditation, but thereafter her behaviour changes almost
beyond recognition. She begins to age, and the *Enterprise* crew
discover that Alkar's success as a mediator involves him projecting all his negative emotions into one other person, who
eventually dies. His aged 'mother' was no more than his young
former companion, and the same fate awaits Deanna. Crusher
places Troi in a death-like coma, which kills Alkar when he
attempts the transfer process again.

Stardate: 46071.6

Strange New Worlds: The repercussions of the conflict on
Rekag-Bironi are beginning to be felt by the Federation. The
high-level meeting takes place in the neutral city of Darthan.

New Life Forms: According to Ves Alkar, Lumerians are empathetic only with their own species. Whilst the funeral meditation appears to be a genuine Lumerian ritual, abused by Alkar
for his own purposes, it is not clear if his statement that Lumerian
custom forbids autopsy is true or simply an attempt to cover
his tracks.

Technobabble: 'I did find abnormally high levels of neurotransmitter residue in her cerebral cortex.'

Riker's Conquests: Riker finds an embarrassed ensign in Troi's
room and, despite her revealing dress, resists her advances. She
claws his cheek angrily.

Deanna Underused?: This is very much a Troi story, allowing Sirtis to be sensual, crudely erotic, jealous and hideously aged all in one story.

Notes: An interesting examination of ends justifying the means is marred by the story's implausible resolution ('killing' Troi, but only for a few minutes) and an odd morality that directly equates evil with sex. Also the plot is very similar to 'Sarek'.

We see Worf's 't'ai chi' lesson (the following day's class will be at 07:00, suggesting that this one is not): the discipline is named as Mok'bara in 'Birthright, Part II'.

129: 'Relics'

US Transmission: 10 October 1992
UK Transmission: 16 July 1993
Writer: Ronald D. Moore
Director: Alexander Singer
Cast: James Doohan, Lanei Chapman, Erick Weiss,
Stacie Foster, Ernie Mirich, Majel Barrett

The *Enterprise* has picked up the distress signal of the USS *Jenolen*, which was reported missing 75 years previously. The ship crashed on the surface of a huge constructed sphere, and Geordi discovers that there is a survivor, locked inside a transporter buffer. Captain Montgomery Scott greets his successor on the *Enterprise*, but feels very out of place on the new ship. Only when the *Enterprise* is about to be trapped within the sphere are Scotty's talents and experience appreciated: he and Geordi use his old ship to force open the 'door' of the globe to allow the *Enterprise* to make good its escape.

Stardate: 46125.3 (stated towards the end of the story).

Strange New Worlds: The Dyson sphere (named after 20th century scientist Freeman Dyson), an enormous hollow globe constructed around a G-type star. The interior surface area is equivalent to 250 million class M planets.

New Life Forms: The unseen and unspecified race who built the sphere.

Technology: The Dyson Sphere is composed of carbon neutronium.

Data explains the nature of synthehol, synthetic alcohol which lacks intoxicating side effects. Scotty can immediately tell that his 'scotch' is synthetic, and much prefers the Aldebaran whisky that Picard gave to Guinan.

Technobabble: What do you expect from a Scotty/Geordi story? 'The phase inducers are connected to the emitter arrays . . . The pattern buffer's been locked into a continuous diagnostic cycle.'

Deanna Underused?: She only appears in Scotty's leaving scene, getting one whole word of dialogue ('Goodbye'). Instead of saying 'Who are you?', Scotty kisses her on the cheek. Dirty old man.

Data's Jokes: Data, asked to identify an alcoholic drink, examines the bottle, sniffs the substance, pauses, and authoritatively pronounces 'It is green' (an acknowledgement of Scotty's similar line in the original series episode 'By Any Other Name').

Dialogue Triumphs: Scotty, telling the computer to recreate the old *Enterprise* on the holodeck: 'N – C – C – 1 – 7 – 0 – 1. No bloody A, B, C or D.'

Notes: 'The plasma intercooler's gone. The engines are overheating!' A whimsical piece of nostalgia, reasonably free of over-sentimentality. It's a shame that they had to give 'Relics' a thrilling adventure sub-plot at all. Scotty's scene on the old *Enterprise* is beautiful, a snatch of the original theme playing gently over the suddenly evocative bridge sound effects. It's a little odd, though, that he 'wakes up' 75 years into his future and does not appear to feel the loss of any of his contemporaries.

Scotty was a passenger on the *Jenolan*, heading towards Norpin 2 for his retirement. He alludes to past adventures involving the planets Elas ('Elaan of Troyius'), Argelius ('Wolf in the Fold') and Psi 2000 ('The Naked Time'), even repeating the legendary 'Ye cannae change the laws of physics' line. Scotty mentions Jim Kirk as though he's alive (but in the film *Star Trek: Generations* he knows he's dead). He spent 52 years working as a Starfleet engineer, although he rose to the rank of captain. He worked on eleven ships, ranging from freighters to cruisers and starships, but it's only the (original) *Enterprise* that he misses. Similarly, Picard talks of the *Stargazer*, which he sometimes yearns for, despite the technological sophistication of the *Enterprise*. Geordi says that impulse engine design hasn't changed for about two hundred years, and tells Scotty about the alien baby in 'Galaxy's Child'.

130: 'Schisms'

US Transmission: 17 October 1992
UK Transmission: 19 July 1993
Writers: Brannon Braga,
from a story by Jean Louise Matthias, Ron Wilkinson
Director: Ron Wiemer
Cast: Lanei Chapman, Ken Thornley, Angelina Fiordellisi, Scott T. Trost, Angelo McCabe, John Nelson, Majel Barrett

Investigating the Amargosa Diaspora, several crew members (including Riker, Worf and Geordi) experience persistent tiredness, subconscious revulsion of smooth objects and memory loss. Troi uses the holodeck to investigate the images that so disturb them and they conclude that aliens are experimenting on them. Riker disappears from the ship during his sleep and awakens on an other-dimensional ship being observed by robed figures. Riker and another kidnapped crewman return to the *Enterprise* using a small pocket of Solonagen subspace as their escape route. A coherent gravitron pulse is used to close the subspace rupture.

Stardate: 46154.2

New Life Forms: The hooded other-dimensional aliens. Almost nothing is revealed about them except that they have a solanagen-based molecular structure.

Technobabble: 'The metal itself is in a state of quasi-molecular flux.'

'Spatially inverted tetryon particles.' As Geordi notes, 'Something from that deep within subspace shouldn't exist in our universe.'

Not to mention an 'anapestic tetrameter' and a 'tertiary subspace manifold'. This is a Brannon Braga script, right?

Picard Manoeuvre: Riker does it whilst on the bridge.

Data's Jokes: His poetry recital, and in particular his 'Ode to Spot', are downright hilarious.

Dialogue Triumphs: 'If you want to touch people don't concentrate so much on rhyme and meter, think more about what you want to say instead of how you say it.'

'Your arm has been amputated, and surgically re-attached.'

Notes: 'Like it was something I dreamed.' *Star Trek* does *Fire in the Sky* (only better!). Great direction, with good use of the aliens and of weird camera angles. Picard's line 'We're still left with some unanswered questions' sums up the episode perfectly.

Beverly recommends Picard's Aunt Adele's hot milk toddy for Riker's insomnia.

Mr Mot mentions his colleague in the barber shop is Mr Setti (it is unclear whether he is also a Bolian).

131: 'True Q'

US Transmission: 24 October 1992
UK Transmission: 20 July 1993
Writer: René Echevarria
Director: Robert Scheerer
Cast: Olivia d'Abo, John P. Connolly

Amanda Rogers, a gifted young medical student, is gaining work experience with Beverly. She is secretly worried by the seemingly superhuman powers she is developing and, despite saving Riker's life, the crew is also concerned. Whilst discussing Amanda, an officers' meeting is interrupted by Q who announces that Amanda is a Q too. Q is eager to take her with him back to the continuum to prevent her from 'running amok'. Picard leaves the final decision to Amanda and, having used her powers to clear the air pollution on Tagra 4, she leaves with Q to discover the extent of her powers.

Stardate: 46192.3

Strange New Worlds: Tagra 4, the ecologically devastated planet in the Argolis cluster.

Picard Manoeuvre: Picard two, Riker one.

Riker's Conquests: Amanda is attracted to Riker (she even transports him into a scene from Charlotte Brontë at one point) much to the disgust of Q ('How do you stand that hair all over his face?'). There's also an unnamed female in Ten Forward.

Dialogue Triumphs: Q on Beverly: 'Crusher gets more shrill with each passing year.' (Hear, hear.)

'What else have you done? Telekinesis? Teleportation? Spontaneous combustion of someone you don't like?'

Notes: 'Everything was normal and then it's like the laws of physics went out of the window.' Best place for them, can we join? So let's get this straight, a child Q manages to reach adolescence without noticing? Yeah, right! Amanda's hand gestures when doing cool Q-like things is like watching Samantha in *Bewitched!* There are some sly references to *The Wizard of Oz* (Amanda was born in Kansas).

There is a weather modification net on Earth that should prevent things like the 'Tornado' that killed Amanda's parents. There are references to 'Encounter at Farpoint', including the first veiled hint that the 'Q trial' in that episode may not have ended yet (see 'All Good Things . . .').

132: 'Rascals'

US Transmission: 31 October 1992
UK Transmission: 21 July 1993
Writers: Allison Hoch,
from a story by Ward Botsford, Diana Dru Botsford,
Michael Piller
Director: Adam Nimoy
Cast: David Tristan Birkin, Megan Parlen,
Cardine Junko King, Isis J. Jones, Mike Gomez,
Tracy Walter, Michael Snyder, Morgan Nagler, Majel Barrett

Ro, Guinan, Keiko and Picard, returning from shore leave, are transported out of a malfunctioning shuttlecraft, and arrive back on the *Enterprise* as children. Although their bodies have regressed their mental capacities are intact. Arriving at Ligos 7 in response to a medical distress call, the *Enterprise* is boarded by renegade Ferengi. Most of the crew are transported to the planet but the ship's children (including Picard's group) are held hostages. The young adults, with help from Alexander, manage to trap several Ferengi and retake control of the ship. The transporter malfunction has been diagnosed and Picard and the others gratefully return to their normal shape and size.

Stardate: 46235.7

Strange New Worlds: Marlonia ('the most beautiful planet in the quadrant'), Ligos 7 (rich in the mineral venderite, prone to spasmodic volcanic activity), Suvin 4 where Dr Langford has an archaeological dig).

Introducing: The O'Briens' daughter Molly (first mentioned in 'The Game').

Technobabble: A great scene with Riker talking complete gibberish to the Ferengi science officer.

Beverly wibbles on about 'rybo-viroxic-nucleic structure' and 'molecular reversion field'.

Picard Manoeuvre: The young Picard is even more of a fidget than his older version.

Dialogue Triumphs: 'Miles Edward O'Brien, I'm still your wife.' 'Technically, yes!'

'Where did you get the idea that being short and awkward is some kind of wonderful gift?'

'That's the wonderful thing about crayons, they can take you to more places than a starship!'

Notes: 'There are some people who would find it difficult to accept a twelve-year-old captain.' Very amusing, with an eerie performance from David Tristan Birkin (Picard's nephew in 'Family'), complete with the mannerisms and syntax of Jean-Luc. Patchy, but fun.

Guinan's father is seven hundred years old. Ro took a course in botany at the Academy. Picard has spent thirty years aboard starships. When presented with the suggestion of returning to the academy he baulks at the thought of becoming Wesley Crusher's roommate. It is also suggested he could become the youngestadmiral in Starfleet history.

There are 1014 people on the *Enterprise* (see 'Remember Me'). The Ferengi are using stolen Klingon Birds-of-Prey (B'rel class). They do not bring their children on starships. Draebidium froctus and calimus are types of Marlonian fauna.

133: 'A Fistful of Datas'

US Transmission: 7 November 1992
UK Transmission: 22 July 1993
Writers: Robert Hewitt Wolfe, Brannon Braga,
from a story by Robert Hewitt Wolfe
Director: Patrick Stewart
Cast: John Pyper-Ferguson, Joy Garrett, Jorge Cereva jr,
Majel Barrett

Worf, Alexander and Troi are enjoying a relaxing gunfight in an Old West holodeck simulation. Meanwhile Geordi and Data attempt to create a new interface between the android and the ship. Energy fluctuations cause various computer functions to take on aspects of Data's personality; most worrying, the holodeck program characters gain all of Data's abilities, and Worf and the others are trapped in the simulation. However, a progressive memory purge rights the problem.

Stardate: 46271.5

Strange New Worlds: Deinonychus 7, where the *Enterprise* is due to meet the supply ship *Biko*.

Deanna Underused?: No, but the leather trousers she wears as Durango deserve a category of their own.

Dialogue Triumphs: 'Were you born that way or did your Mama marry an armadillo?'

'The replicators on decks four through nine are producing nothing but cat food.'

Notes: 'What is our function here?' 'You're the sheriff, I'm the deputy!' *Star Trek* does *Westworld*. Inventive (Stewart's direction is superb), and very amusing, a great Worf episode. The opening 'Picard-can't-get-a-minute's-peace' scene is very well done.

Alexander and Barclay wrote the Deadwood program. Picard

plays Mozart on the Ressikan flute (see 'The Inner Light', 'Lessons'). Beverly's new production is *Something for Breakfast*. She wants Picard to play the butler (two lines!). Will is a participant (see 'Frame of Mind'). When the computer erases the play, it replaces it with Data's 'Ode to Spot' (see 'Schisms'). Data has at least 147 'feline supplements' for Spot. He has recently been analysing the works of Anton Dvorak. Troi loves Westerns (her father used to read them to her). Worf likes Klingon fire wine.

134: 'The Quality of Life'

US Transmission: 14 November 1992
UK Transmission: 23 July 1993
Writer: Naren Shankar
Director: Jonathan Frakes
Cast: Ellen Bry, J. Downing, Majel Barrett

Dr Farallon's experimental mining techniques are investigated by the *Enterprise* crew. Data comes to believe that the robotic Exocomps might be alive, showing a strong instinct for self-preservation, but tests seem to disprove this. However, he is eventually proved correct, an Exocomp sacrificially saving the *Enterprise* crew.

Stardate: 46307.2

Strange New Worlds: Tyrus 7A, where a new mining technology, the particle fountain, is being tried out. If successful the process could be used on Carema 3.

New Life Forms: The Exocomps, based on common industrial servomechanisms, augmented by boridium power convertors, axionic chip networks and micro-replication systems. The upshot of this is that they learn from their jobs, and always have the right tool to hand!

For Klingons the beard is a symbol of courage.

Technobabble: Lots of guff about the computational speed of Data's positronic network having been limited in the past by the physical separation of the positronic links, whereas now his interlinked sequencer works asynchronously. 'How did you resolve the signal fragmentation?' 'The interlinked sequencer is now bidirectional. It compensates for the asynchronous mode distortion arising from the resonant field.'

Poker Game: Riker, Crusher, Geordi and Worf play seven-card stud with wild one-eyed Jacks. After a discussion of beards (including Geordi's: see also 'The Outcast'), the stakes are established that if Crusher wins then the men will shave off their beards, and that if one of the others wins Crusher will change her hair colour (to brunette). Unfortunately, the game is not completed.

Deanna Underused?: She's in one scene.

Notes: 'Recognising new life, whatever its form, is a principal mission of this vessel.' A standard *Trek* tale that gently probes the definition of life and Data's attitude to humanity.

Worf and Crusher have engaged in combat with a Bat'telh sword.

135: 'Chain of Command, Part I'

US Transmission: 12 December 1992
UK Transmission: 26 July 1993
Writers: Ronald D. Moore,
from a story by Frank Abatemarco
Director: Robert Scheerer
Cast: David Warner, Ronny Cox, Natalia Nogulich,
John Durbin, Lou Wagner, Majel Barrett

Picard, Crusher and Worf are sent on a dangerous mission to Celtris 3, believed to be the location of a Cardassian lab that is developing a metagenic weapon. Meanwhile, Commander Jellico assumes control of the *Enterprise*. Although Crusher and Worf escape, Picard is captured by the Cardassians.

Stardate: 46357.4

Strange New Worlds: Celtris 3, an uninhabited world in Cardassian space believed to be the site of a secret Cardassian research lab. On Tormen 5 the *Enterprise* encounters DaiMon Solok.

New Life Forms: Lynars are said to be a kind of Celtran bat.

Technology: Starfleet believe that the Cardassians have developed a metagenic weapon, a genetically engineered virus that would destroy an entire ecosystem. The virus would then break down, leaving the planet and its technology undamaged, ready to be 'conquered'. The Cardassians are believed to be working on a 'safe' carrier for the virus: a sub-space wave carrying dormant material.

A phaser set at level sixteen can melt granite.

Picard Manoeuvre: Just before (reluctantly) shaking Jellico's hand and going off on his mission.

Dialogue Triumphs: Jellico: 'Oh, and get that fish out of the ready room.'

Notes: Great drama: there's a clash between the brusquely authoritarian Jellico and the rest of the crew in the offing, and a secret mission for Picard, Beverly and Worf.

William T. Riker hails from the class of '57, graduating eighth in his class. He has been decorated by Starfleet five times, and has been offered his own ship more than once (see 'The Arsenal of Freedom', 'The Icarus Factor', 'The Best of Both Worlds 1', and 'The Pegasus'). He has served as Picard's first officer for five years. Whilst on the *Stargazer* Picard oversaw tests on theta-band carrier waves. His serial number is SP – 937 – 215.

The Cardassian forces that recently withdrew from Deep

Space 9 (see *DS9*'s 'Emissary' *et al.*) have redeployed along the Federation border. Edward Jellico helped to negotiate the original armistice with the Cardassians two years previously (see 'The Wounded'). Biological weapons were banned 'years ago', and even the Romulans have abided by this. The Cardassian ship featured is the *Reklar*.

136: 'Chain of Command, Part II'

US Transmission: 19 December 1992
UK Transmission: 27 July 1993
Writer: Frank Abatemarco
Director: Les Landau
Cast: David Warner, Ronny Cox, John Durbin,
Heather Lauren Olsen, Majel Barrett

Picard, stripped of his dignity and his rights, is brutally interrogated by the Cardassian torturer Gul Madred. He refuses to reveal the Federation defence plans for Minos Korva, which would involve the *Enterprise*, to Madred's growing annoyance. Back on the *Enterprise*, the unflinching regime of Jellico is causing great resentment, not least in William Riker, who is stripped of command by Jellico. Madred turns the torture into a battle of wills, but he is thwarted when the *Enterprise* uncovers the Cardassians' invasion plans.

Stardate: 46360.8

Strange New Worlds: The rendezvous point for the team to be picked up by the *Enterprise* is in the Lyshan system. The Cardassian invasion fleet is hiding in the McAllister cluster.

The nearest neutral planet to Cardassia is Tohvun 3. According to Gul Madred Cardassia boasts some of the most ancient and splendid ruins in the galaxy. The 'magnificent' burial vaults of the first Hibitian civilisation were unearthed two hundred years ago, and contained many beautiful artefacts made of

Jevonite. The tombs were plundered to finance Cardassian warfare.

New Life Forms: Wompats are Cardassian pets. Boiled Taspar egg is a Cardassian delicacy.

The Cardassians were once a peaceful, spiritual people, although many people starved. Since the military came to power hundreds of thousands have been killed. However, the new resources brought by warfare have allowed rebuilding and agricultural programmes to take place, feeding and housing the masses. Lakat is a Cardassian city.

Technology: Madred has a very nasty torture device.

Dialogue Triumphs: 'There – are – four – lights!'

Notes: 'I believed I could see five lights.' A superb episode, an adult and unflinching look at torture and the treatment of political prisoners that owes much to *1984*. (At Patrick Stewart's suggestion, Amnesty International advised on the torture scenes.) Stewart and Warner are magnificent. What's especially good is that the conflict between Riker and Jellico *isn't* resolved. Picard's admission to Troi – that he did finally see five lights – also puts us far beyond Kirk country. One to show to friends who think *TNG* is a kid's show.

Picard's mother's maiden name was Yvette Gessard, and the family would sing during Sunday dinner. The two other captains with theta-band experience are no longer in Starfleet. Both Jellico and Geordi began their careers as shuttle pilots on the Jovian run, the daily return flight between Jupiter and Saturn. Swinging around Titan is a short-cut.

The Seldonis 4 convention governs treatment of Prisoners of War, including the prohibition of torture.

137: 'Ship in a Bottle'

US Transmission: 23 January 1993

UK Transmission: 28 July 1993
Writer: René Echevarria
Director: Alexander Singer
Cast: Daniel Davis, Stephanie Beacham,
Clement Von Franckenstein, Majel Barrett

Barclay accidentally calls up the Moriarty program. The Professor is angered by Picard's deception and vows to leave the holodeck, or destroy the ship trying. To Picard's amazement, he walks off the holodeck and declares himself sentient. Moriarty also wishes to bring his fiancée, Countess Regina Bartholomew, into the real world. Picard is dubious, but asks Data to look into the possibility. Experiments with transporters prove unsuccessful, then Data discovers that they are all actually still inside the holodeck which Moriarty has reprogrammed. Setting a complex layered trap, Picard lures Moriarty into what he believes to be an escape from the *Enterprise* when he also is still within the holodeck. Moriarty and the Countess are then stored in a program with enough memory for a lifetime of adventures.

Stardate: 46424.1 (four years after 'Elementary Dear Data').

Strange New Worlds: The *Enterprise* is observing the collision of two giant gas planets in the Detrian system (a 'self-sustaining fusion reaction').

Meles 2 is the nearest inhabited planet (the people are 'friendly').

New Life Forms: Moriarty and Countess Regina, theoretically (sentient holographic beings).

Technobabble: 'Uncouple the Heisenberg compensators.'

Dialogue Triumphs: 'When this is over you will walk out of this room to the real world and your own concerns, and leave me here trapped in a world I know to be nothing but illusion. I cannot bear that.'

'Policemen. I'd recognise them in any century!'

'My God, we are adrift in the heavens.'

'I feel it necessary to point out that criminal behaviour is as unacceptable in the 24th century as it was in the 19th. And very much harder to get away with.'

'I am a man out of time.'

'He's an arch criminal!' 'Only because he was written that way!'

'Our reality may be very much like theirs, and all this may be an elaborate simulation running inside a little device sitting on someone's table.'

And the classic closing line: 'Computer, end program!'

Notes: 'I'm just a fictional character. I have nothing to lose.' The long-awaited sequel to 'Elementary, Dear Data', this is a triumph of clever twists, brilliant dialogue and a labyrinthine plot (holodecks within holodecks), even if Moriarty's character is made into more of a super-villain. And there's an actor in it called Clement Von Franckenstein!

Barclay has never been to Africa. Moriarty had brief, terrifying moments of disembodied consciousness during his four years trapped in the program ('it seemed longer'). He quotes Descartes (*'cogito, ergo sum'*).

Both the transporter and the holodeck convert matter in a similar manner, although Data, Geordi and Barclay's experiments in stabilising holodeck matter off the grid prove unsuccessful.

138: 'Aquiel'

US Transmission: 30 January 1993
UK Transmission: 29 July 1993
Writers: Brannon Braga, Ronald D. Moore,
from a story by Jeri Taylor
Director: Cliff Bole
Cast: Renee Jones, Wayne Grace, Reg E. Cathey,
Majel Barrett

Geordi leads an investigation into a death at a communication relay station near the Klingon border. As he runs through the evidence he becomes increasingly entranced by the personal logs of Lt Aquiel Unhari. Her dislike of her superior officer Rocha is very clear. However, the finger of suspicion seems to point at the Klingons, whose patrols came close to the relay station, but they produce Unhari alive. Geordi has to explain the depth of his knowledge to Unhari, who now seems to have been the murderer rather than the victim. Soon the real culprit is revealed: a shapechanging organism that infected first Rocha and then Unhari's dog. The creature is destroyed.

Stardate: 46461.3

New Life Forms: Lt Aquiel Unhari is a Haliian, and thus partially telepathic. Haliians use a device called the Canar to amplify their telepathy in order to bond.

The coalescent organism infected Rocha in the Triona system.

Deanna Underused?: She's in one scene.

Notes: A soppy love story twists half-way through into *The Thing*. It's a bit obvious, but reasonably enjoyable.

There hasn't been a Klingon raid against the Federation for over seven years. Mention is made of Muskan seed punch. 'Lu Pivos' is a Klingon insult, as is 'Pahtk', used contemptuously of Starfleet and/or the Federation. According to Aquiel, not many people read gothic fiction 'nowadays' (the books she has include *Cold Moon Over Black Water* and *Fatal Revenge*). La Forge's family travelled around a lot when he was growing up (see 'Imaginary Friend'), during which time he picked up a number of languages, including Haliian.

139: 'Face of the Enemy'
US Transmission: 6 February 1993

UK Transmission: 30 July 1993
Writers: Naren Shankar,
from a story by René Echevarria
Director: Gabrielle Beaumont
Cast: Scott MacDonald, Carolyn Seymour, Barry Lynch,
Robertson Dean, Dennis Cockrum, Pamela Winslow,
Majel Barrett

Deanna wakes up – and finds herself on a Romulan ship, her face altered and her 'mission' unclear. Troi is told to assume the identity of Major Rakal of the Tal Shiar, and immediately faces opposition from the suspicious Commander Toreth. The *Enterprise* travels to Research Station 75 to pick up Ensign Stefan DeSeve – a human who defected to Romulus many years ago – who brings a message from Ambassador Spock regarding 'cowboy diplomacy'. The ship is carrying an 'important' cargo (in actual fact Vice-Proconsul M'ret and two aides, held in stasis and wanting to defect). Thanks to Deanna's coolheadedness the defectors are delivered safely to the Federation.

Stardate: 46519.1

Strange New Worlds: Deanna was attending a neuropsychology seminar on Borka 6 before being kidnapped.

New Life Forms: Corvallens are described as mercenaries.

Technobabble: Mention is made of the Federation gravitic sensor net and tachyon subspace listening posts.

Picard Manoeuvre: When questioning Ensign DeSeve, and when standing to address the 'Romulan' Troi.

Notes: At last Troi gets a story pretty much to herself, and Sirtis excels. The interplay with the Romulan Commander is wonderful. Romulus – previously a thin parody of Germany in the 40s (or the 1980s, as in 'Unification') – suddenly becomes the

Soviet Union with a 'dissident' faction.

The Tal Shiar is the imperial intelligence service. Toreth's ship is the *Khazara*. The Corvallen freighter is an Antares-class vessel.

140: 'Tapestry'

US Transmission: 13 February 1993
UK Transmission: 2 August 1993
Writer: Ronald D. Moore
Director: Les Landau
Cast: Ned Vaughan, J.C. Brandy, Clint Carmichael,
Rae Norman, Clive Church, Marcus Nash, Majel Barrett

Attacked by Lenarians outside a conference room, Picard is beamed back to the *Enterprise* but dies on the operating table. Q appears, whisking Picard back into his past, giving him the chance to change things. Picard ruins his relationship with one friend by having sex with her, and seeks to stop a fight with the Nausicaans that led to him being stabbed through the heart and having an artificial replacement. Q then shows him his new future: he's a nobody. Picard relives his past again, this time as it really happened – and wakes up on the *Enterprise*, its captain once more.

Stardate: Not stated.

New Life Forms: The Nausicaans, the ugly, bad-tempered aliens who brawled with the young Picard, stabbing him through the chest with a dagger. They cheat at Dom-Jot. Picard also came into contact with the Nausicaans during his sophomore year, assigned to Morricom 7, near a Nausicaan asteroid outpost.

Technology: Picard's fatal wounds were caused by a compressed terion beam. Dom-Jot is a high-tech version of Billiards.

Dialogue Triumphs: Picard to Q: 'I refuse to believe that the after-life is run by you. The universe is not so badly designed!'

Q, after Picard has wobbled on about changing 'history': 'Please, spare me your egotistical musings on your pivotal role in history. Nothing you do will cause the Federation to collapse or galaxies to explode. To be blunt, you're not that important.'

Q, as a flower deliverer: 'Is there a John-Luck Pickerd here?'

Notes: 'Welcome to the after-life, Jean-Luc. You're dead!' A clever use of elements from *It's a Wonderful Life* and *A Matter of Life and Death* leads to one of the best-ever stories. It's packed to overflowing with witty lines and superb performances, and is worth watching just for the clever scene with Picard in bed with Q. It makes some interesting points about the value of facing one's own mortality and the need for both risk and restraint in life. Seeing Picard ruin his past friendships (one sexually), and stripped of his ability and esteem as a junior officer, only helps to bring his character into sharp relief. The thing is tightly constructed (Picard's laugh on being stabbed), but would have been even better without the coda. Still, at least it doesn't ruin everything by coming up with a definitive explanation for what happened.

We see the exact circumstances surrounding Picard's artificial heart (see 'Samaritan Snare') and details of his life after graduating from the Academy. His friends during this period were Corey Zweller and Marta Batanides, and Picard was known as 'Jonny'. His old flames include Penny from Rigel and Corlena. Picard's father is seen, warning him not to go off to the Academy. In the alternative future Picard is lieutenant, junior grade, and an assistant astrophysics officer. The *Enterprise* is commanded by Captain Thomas Halloway. Real events in Picard's Starfleet career included leading the away team on Milika 3 to save an ambassador and taking charge of the *Stargazer* after its captain was killed.

141: 'Birthright, Part I'

US Transmission: 20 February 1993
UK Transmission: 3 August 1993
Writer: Brannon Braga
Director: Winrich Kolbe
Cast: James Cromwell, Cristine Rose, Jennifer Gatti,
Richard Herd

Whilst the *Enterprise* is docked at station Deep Space 9, Data is knocked 'unconscious' and experiences a dream involving Dr Soong. He takes up painting in an attempt to express himself, and discovers that his dreams are the result of previously dormant neural circuits implanted by Dr Soong. Meanwhile, Worf receives word that his father might have survived the Khitomer massacre, and he makes his way to a Romulan camp where Klingon prisoners are still being held.

Stardate: 46578.4

Strange New Worlds: The 'prisoner of war' camp on the edge of Romulan space in the Carraya sector.

New Life Forms: The Yridian, who informs Worf that his father is in a Romulan prisoner of war camp.

Worf states that Klingons would rather die than be captured in battle (the resultant dishonour would be passed down three generations).

The hammer variously symbolises power (Klingon), hearth and home (the Takwah tribe of Naygor) and sexual prowess (Ferengi).

Notes: The sub-plot – Data's surreal dream sequences and his breath-taking paintings – is rather more interesting than the ostensible subject matter (Worf's search for his father).

The *Enterprise* docks at DS9 in order to assist with the re-building of Bajoran aqueducts damaged during the Cardassian occupation. Dr Crusher says that the station's holosuites have a relaxation program from Alture 7. One of Geordi's favourite meals is pasta al fiorella, and he is excited by the Ktaran antiques booth's 21st-century plasma coil that is in almost perfect condition. Data can adjust his rate of 'follicle replenishment' (i.e. his hair grows), but has not yet had a reason to adjust its length. He also has a functional respiratory system, which helps maintain 'thermal control of internal systems' (he can survive in a vacuum for a considerable time and therefore must be able also to lower his internal pressure), and has a 'pulse' (his circulatory system produces biochemical lubricants and regulates micro-hydraulic power). Data decides to 'switch off' for a period each day in order to dream. Worf is scarred from a ritual hunt he went on when he was very small, during which he tried to take on 'the beast' with his bare hands. Later Worf's adoptive parents arranged for him to take part in the rite of MajQa, a deep meditation in the lava fields of No'Mat, where the heat induces hallucinations.

142: 'Birthright, Part II'

US Transmission: 27 February 1993
UK Transmission: 4 August 1993
Writer: René Echevarria
Director: Dan Curry
Cast: Christine Rose, James Cromwell, Sterling Maccor Jr, Alan Scarfe, Jennifer Gatti, Richard Herd

Worf finds himself on a world where Romulans and Klingons live in harmony, populated by the survivors of Khitomer and their Romulan 'jailors'. The elder Klingons – who would be dishonoured if they ever returned home – and Romulans are now outcasts from their respective societies. Worf, although attracted by the girl Ba'el, is shocked by the young Klingons' ignorance of their true heritage, and angers the elders by teaching them songs and showing them how to use the traditional weapons. Worf is imprisoned and then sentenced to execution as a disruptive influence, but the young people are willing to die alongside him. The elders realise that their society is no longer tenable, and a way is found of sending the children back to their home worlds.

Stardate: 46759.2

Strange New Worlds: The Aquincia and Aquaya systems are mentioned as the *Enterprise* tries to find Worf.

New Life Forms: Ba'el, the half-Romulan, half-Klingon otherwise known as Worf's Conquest.

Deanna Underused?: Deanna AWOL.

Notes: Tedious, repetitive and fascist Klingon version of *Dead Poets Society*. Worf's actions, although very much in character, destroy the peace that existed between the Klingons and Romulans in the 'prison camp'. And the plot is so full of holes it resembles a piece of Gruyère. (For starters, why did the Yridian get Worf involved? And wouldn't Worf's story about the shuttle crash fall apart the moment the Klingons checked it out?)

Worf's father *did* die in the battle of Khitomer. The pintok spear and d'k tahg (a dagger) are both Klingon weapons, and the Kathwa is the ritual hunt. Their equivalent of T'ai Chi is known as Mok'bara, and a jinag (a piece of jewellery) is given to a Klingon girl when she has come of age.

143: 'Starship Mine'

US Transmission: 27 March 1993
UK Transmission: 5 August 1993
Writer: Morgan Gendel
Director: Cliff Bole
Cast: David Spielberg, Marie Marshall, Tim Russ,

Glenn Morshower, Tom Nibley, Tim deZarn,
Patricia Tallman, Arlee Reed, Alan Altshuld, Majel Barrett

The *Enterprise* is docked at the Remmler Array in order to undergo a baryon sweep, which will neutralise the build-up of harmful particles. At a function organised by 'Hutch' at the Akaria Base Data revels in his new aptitude at small talk. Picard returns to the deserted ship for his saddle, only to find himself captured by some very resourceful criminals, who are in the process of stealing trilithium resin, a highly toxic and volatile engine by-product. Picard pretends to be the barber, Mr Mot, and escapes, relying on his resourcefulness to outwit the terrorists. Meanwhile, Riker and the others are held hostage, but trick their captors and disable the baryon sweep, moments before it would have killed Picard.

Stardate: 46682.4

Strange New Worlds: Hutch says that he knew a Captain Edwell who was born on Gaspar 7. Tyrellia is one of only three known planets without a magnetic pole, and one of only seven with no atmosphere whatsoever.

New Life Forms: Arkarian society is egalitarian. The Sheliak (see 'The Ensigns of Command') are said to prefer that their body temperatures equal room temperature rather than the reverse. The mating habits of the Arkarian horn fowl are 'quite interesting' according to Hutch.

Data's Jokes: An explanation for his 'small-talk': 'I am attempting to fill a silent moment with non-relevant conversation.'

Notes: *Die Hard* goes cosmic! This is an enjoyable, unpretentious adventure story, with Picard given the lion's share of the action.

According to Data, there are five Tyrellians aboard the *En-*

terprise. Starbase G7 is, according to Hutch, 'an awful place'.

Neither Deanna nor Geordi are interested in ornithology. Picard appears to use some kind of nerve-grip on one of the terrorists. He has his own saddle which he has 'broken in' over the years.

144: 'Lessons'

US Transmission: 3 April 1993
UK Transmission: 6 August 1993
Writers: Ronald Wilkerson, Jean Louise Matthias
Director: Robert Wiemer
Cast: Wendy Hughes, Majel Barrett

Lt Commander Neela Daren comes aboard the *Enterprise*, and her patient interest in Picard's musical abilities draw the two to each other, despite Picard's reservations about becoming involved with a member of his crew. Although Riker feels under pressure from Daren to make exceptions for her, Picard states that he will not allow himself or anyone else to treat her differently. True to his word, he allows Daren to join the away team involved in a rescue mission on Bersallis 3. When she does not return Picard fears the worst, and cannot come to terms with what has happened. Daren does survive the rescue mission, but she and Picard conclude that because of their depth of feeling for each other they cannot continue working on the same ship.

Stardate: 46693.1 (when the *Enterprise* arrives at Bersallis 3).

Strange New Worlds: There is a Federation outpost on Bersallis 3. Solar radiation interacts with plasma in the atmosphere to produce fire storms, which pass through a seven-year cycle. The base is built to withstand most storms, but not one of such unusual severity (200 km/h 300°C winds).

At the beginning, Picard wants to talk to Professor Mowray, working on an archeological site on Landris 2. Picard discovered a wonderful desert on Thelka 4. Data once led a team of geologists to study a plasma geyser on Melnos 4.

New Life Forms: According to Daren, Kerelian tenors have a huge vocal range, with aural nuances that only those of their own species can pick up.

Technobabble: Picard, trying to explain to Crusher why he finds Daren's work so fascinating when really all he wants to do is get inside her underwear: 'The whole thing is made possible by a mathematical construct based on fractal particle motion . . .The modelling itself is done by gravimetric wave input.'

Picard Manoeuvre: When talking to Troi in the ready room.

Riker's Conquests: None, but mention must be made of his macho pose when standing next to Data in his first scene.

Dialogue Triumphs: Daren to Picard on his musical ability: 'You're not used to playing with anyone, are you?'

Picard: 'When I believed that you were dead I just began to shut down . . . I was here in my quarters and the only thing I could focus on was my music, and how it would never again give me any joy.'

Notes: A very well-directed and well-acted episode that manages to be genuinely moving without resorting to ridiculous sentimentality. Wendy Hughes is wonderful as Daren.

Neela Daren came aboard the *Enterprise* at Starbase 218, along with other new crewmembers including an (unseen) new obstetric nurse named Beck. Daren's studies include the unusual radioactive emissions of the Borgolis nebula. She, Data and Ensign Cheney perform Chopin's *Trio in G Minor* in Ten-Forward. Picard played the piano when he was younger but describes himself as a musical amateur. He has been playing the Ressikan flute (see 'The Inner Light') for a long time, and tells Daren that they're not made any more. She has a folding piano from Mataline 2. They play Bach's third *Brandenburg*

Concerto and 'Frère Jacques'. According to Daren, the fourth intersect on Jefferies Tube 25 is 'the most acoustically perfect spot on this ship'. While there she plays the Moonlight Sonata, and Picard plays 'an old folk melody' from Kataan: he notes sadly that its sun went nova more than 1000 years ago.

Picard states that ship's resources and staff allocations are Riker's responsibility.

145: 'The Chase'

US Transmission: 24 April 1993
UK Transmission: 9 August 1993
Writers: Joe Menosky,
from a story by Ronald D. Moore
Director: Jonathan Frakes
Cast: Salome Jens, John Cothran Jr, Maurice Roëves,
Linda Thorson, Norman Lloyd, Majel Barrett

The *Enterprise* is on a three-week mission surveying proto-stars in the Voltaira nebula when Picard is reunited with Professor Richard Galen, his old archaeology tutor. Galen offers Picard the chance to join him on his latest and most important piece of research, but after much thought Picard declines. However, the death of Galen leads Picard to re-examine the old man's work, revealing ancient codes that exist within the DNA of a number of humanoid races. But the crew of the *Enterprise* is not alone in trying to put together the pieces of the puzzle: the Klingons, the Cardassians and the Romulans are all after the ancient secret. The completed code proves to be nothing more than a message of good will from an ancient civilisation, who altered the genetic development of many of the galaxy's life forms.

Stardate: 46731.5

Strange New Worlds: The *Enterprise* crew should have at-

229

tended a diplomatic conference of Atalia 7, but instead they travel to Deep Space 4, Kea 4 and Indri 8 (attacked by a Klingon atmosphere-destroying weapon). The Indri system was first identified by the Federation nearly sixty years ago: its eighth planet is (or, rather, was) L-class (supporting plant but not animal life). Ruah 4 is class M, its life forms including early hominids. Loren 3 is capable of supporting life. The Cardassian Gul Ocett is tricked into going to the Rahm-Izad system. The chase ends in the Vilmoran system: the second planet was once inhabited, but now supports only lichen.

Kurlan Naiskos is a long way outside Federation territory. Galen has been there recently and retrieved some ceramic specimens from the Third Dynasty (c.12,000 years old). The civilisation was three hundred years ahead of its time. Ya'seem is an archaeological location comparable to Troy: it was discovered by a Klingon woman named M'Tell.

New Life Forms: Four billion years ago the ancient civilisation on Vilmor 'seeded' the primordial oceans of many worlds with genetic material, containing a message for posterity. This explains the humanoid form of most creatures in the galaxy.

The information-dealing Yridians (see 'Birthright') attack Galen's shuttle. The Klingons are searching for a weapon, the Cardassians (who bought DNA information from the Yridians) think the secret is an unlimited power source. The Klingon's mum apparently has a good recipe for biscuits. B'aht Qul is a Klingon challenge of physical strength (Data's strength is known even in the Klingon Empire). Tash Kota refers to Klingons dying together as brothers.

The Satarrans of Sothis 3 (see 'Conundrum') disdain mysteries. 'Dream not of today' is the night blessing of the Yash-El.

Picard Manoeuvre: Much tunic-tugging in the ready room.

Dialogue Triumphs: Nu Daq, after the plot has been explained: 'Is that *it*?'

Notes: 'Whatever information this program contains could be the most profound discovery of our time. Or the most danger-ous.' One of *Trek*'s great shaggy-dog stories. Although it's nice to see the Klingons, the Cardassians and the Romulans in one story, the conclusion was always going to be an anticlimax.

Data's upper spinal support is made from a polyalloy. His skull is composed of kortenide and duranium. Seventeen peo-ple on the *Enterprise* are from non-Federation planets.

146: 'Frame of Mind'

US Transmission: 1 May 1993
UK Transmission: 10 August 1993
Writer: Brannon Braga
Director: James L. Conway
Cast: David Selburg, Andrew Prine, Gary Werntz,
Susanna Thompson, Allan Dean Moore

Riker's starring role in Beverly's production of the play *Frame of Mind* is making him nervous. Uncomfortable with some of the psychological aspects of the play, some of the fictional situ-ations begin to spill over into real life. He is also due to go on a rescue mission on Tilonius 4 soon. Whilst performing the play, Riker suddenly finds himself in a Tilonius asylum where he is told he is not a Starfleet officer, and that he recently murdered a man. Constant switches in perspective between performances of the play and the asylum lead to Riker's uncertainty about what is real and what isn't. Eventually Riker discovers that he is being held captive by the Tilonians and fights his way to freedom.

Stardate: 46678.1 (given towards the end of the episode; the events presumably taking place in the days before).

Strange New Worlds: Tilonus 4 (in a state of anarchy after the recent assassination of the Prime Minister).

New Life Forms: The Tilonians have fanatical political factions, mental asylums, fascist bully-boy guards and spoons. Spiny lobe-fish is a Tilonian dish. 'Nisroh' is a ceremonial knife used by Tilonian traders in barter.

Picard Manoeuvre: Twice.

Riker's Conquests: Well, Deanna's been using 'relaxation techniques' on him. They don't seem to work for Will.

Dialogue Triumphs: 'Sometimes it's healthy to explore the darker side of the psyche. Jung calls it "owning your own shadow".'

Notes: 'Don't let them tell you you're crazy.' A Hitchcock movie (who said *Spellbound*?) reduced to four acts with some genuinely freaky special effects (the 'shattering' images), and a really outstanding, twitchy performance from Jonathan Frakes. The thing we like about this episode is that every standard cliché turns out to be a red herring (especially the daring Data/Worf rescue, a mirror image of the one in 'The Best of Both Worlds'). A story that throws light on Riker's hollow character by showing him to be an actor in every sense. Revealing, and scary.

Will's first year at the Academy was problematic (he still seems to feel paranoid about this period). The play *Frame of Mind* concerns dementia, asylums and torture by doctors.

147: 'Suspicions'

US Transmission: 8 May 1993
UK Transmission: 11 August 1993
Writers: Joe Menosky, Naren Shankar
Director: Cliff Bole
Cast: Tricia O'Neil, Peter Slutsker, James Horan,
John S. Ragin, Joan Stuart Morris, Majel Barrett

Beverly, contemplating a dishonourable discharge, tells Guinan of her interest in the work of Ferengi scientist Dr Reyga. His metaphasic shielding technology impressed her enough to invite him and several other scientists on to the *Enterprise* to discuss his ideas. Jo'Bril, a Takaran, offered to pilot a shielded shuttle into a stellar corona to test his theories, but the alien died in mysterious circumstances. Soon after Reyga was found dead, but his family refused permission for an autopsy. Beverly went ahead with the autopsy, but found nothing. She did, however start a diplomatic incident, and now faces being struck off. Guinan encourages Crusher to investigate further, and Beverly pilots a shuttle herself to show how the shields were sabotaged. Jo'Bril is in fact alive, and has hidden himself on the shuttle, planning to steal the shields to use as a weapon. Beverly fights him off and he dies. The shuttle successfully navigates the star, and Crusher is reinstated.

Stardate: 46830.1

Strange New Worlds: Vaytan, a star with an unstable corona. We hear of Starbase 23.

New Life Forms: Takarans, green-skinned and blue-veined, with no discrete organs, who control their physiology at a cellular level.

The Ferengi Death Ritual requires that a body cannot be violated before it's buried (cf. *DS9*'s 'The Nagus'). It's very rare for the Ferengi to produce scientists, and the Klingons don't respect theirs.

Technology: Anapropalin is a medicinal drug. Cortical stimulators resuscitate a patient. A metaphasic shield allows a ship to pass close to the surface of a star. A plasma infuser is a potentially deadly tool. Exposure to tetrion fields can be fatal.

Deanna Underused?: She gets about a line and a half.

Notes: This one never really gets past the credibility barrier of why a ship's doctor would host a scientific conference of this nature. Isn't Geordi interested?

T'Pan has been the director of the Vulcan Science Academy for the last fifteen years: she's a legend in sub-space morphology. Admiral Brooks is in charge of Starfleet Medical on Earth. The Altine Conference is one where subspace technology is discussed.

Guinan always sees Crusher with her medical problems. She's never been to a formal inquiry and she doesn't play tennis.

One of the *Enterprise* shuttles is the *Justman*.

148: 'Rightful Heir'

US Transmission: 15 May 1993
UK Transmission: 12 August 1993
Writers: Ronald D. Moore,
from a story by James E. Brooks
Director: Winrich Kolbe
Cast: Alan Oppenheimer, Robert O'Reilly, Norman Snow,
Charles Esten, Kevin Conway, Majel Barratt

Suffering from a loss of faith, Worf is given leave by Picard to go to Borath, where the Klingon High Clerics are as ever awaiting the return of their great leader Kahless. Worf discovers that Kahless is alive, and the *Enterprise* is about to take Kahless back to the Klingon Homeworld when Gowron arrives. After Gowron challenges Kahless in combat and wins, the clerics admit that Kahless is a clone with memory implants, but Worf advises Gowron that if the deception is revealed a civil war is inevitable. Worf proposes that Kahless be made emperor, with the power still kept by the Council. Reluctantly, Gowron agrees.

Stardate: 46852.2

Strange New Worlds: Boreth, the icy Klingon world where followers of Kahless await his return. It's about twelve days by shuttle from the Alawanir Nebula.

New Life Forms: There hasn't been a Klingon emperor in three hundred years. The knife of Kirom, which has the blood of Kahless on it, is kept in a sacred vault. Kahless united the Klingons and left, promising to return, 1500 years ago, telling his followers to seek him on a particular star (about which Boreth orbits). A Bat'telh, the sword of honour, was used to kill Molor. (See 'New Ground', 'Birthright', 'First Born', and the original series episode 'The Savage Curtain'.)

Deanna Underused?: Completely absent.

Notes: This is wonderful, full of drama and realpolitik. An unusually non-patronising look at religion.

Klingons go into a trance state and gaze at fires to see visions of Kahless. Worf had one such vision as a child in the caves of No'Mat (see 'Birthright, Part I'). Kahless told him that he'd do something no Klingon had yet done. Warnog is a Klingon drink, Sto-Vo-Kor is the afterlife where Kahless is. The Klingon Homeworld has a volcano at Kri'stak, near the lake of Lusor. There is a city called Quin'lat.

Worf lives on deck 7. Starfleet officers activated Data on Omicron Theta, and he's taken a leap of faith in believing himself to be more than a machine.

149: 'Second Chances'

US Transmission: 22 May 1993
UK Transmission: 13 August 1993
Writers: René Echevarria,
from a story by Michael A. Medlock
Director: LeVar Burton
Cast: Dr Mae Jemison

Eight years ago Riker led the evacuation of Nervala 4. Now the *Enterprise* has arrived there to retrieve data, and Riker beams down. He is astonished to find another Riker there, a transporter duplicate created during the original evacuation. The other Riker, a lieutenant still in love with Deanna, goes straight to Picard with his own plans for data retrieval, aggravating Commander Riker. He enjoys a romantic relationship with Troi and is given a posting to another ship, but when he asks her to come with him she declines. The two Rikers attempt the data retrieval one last time, and save each other's lives. The new Riker – taking his middle name, Thomas – leaves for his posting, asking Will Riker to look after Deanna. Will gives Thomas his trombone as a parting gift.

Stardate: 46915.2

Strange New Worlds: Nervala 4, where distortion fields prevent transporter use, except when the sun affects them every eight years. At least one planet in the Lagana sector, four months away, needs terraforming.

Technology: Cloning produces measurable genetic drift (cf. 'Up the Long Ladder'). Brain organisation patterns are as unique as fingerprints.

Poker Game: Riker wins two games in a row, one against Worf and Data, and then another where they're joined by his new self.

Riker's Conquests: Lieutenant Riker leads Deanna on a treasure hunt of flowers and chocolate.

Future History: Eight years ago, the USS *Potemkin* evacuated the Starfleet research site on Nervala 4.

Notes: This is gorgeous, a wonderful script, with Frakes giving the new Riker a truly separate character. And it avoids the obvious ending.

Lt Riker last saw Deanna at the Janaran Falls on Betazed, the day before leaving on the *Potemkin*. He was promoted, and separated, as a result of his courage in the evacuation, and thus failed to meet Deanna, as arranged, six weeks later on Raisa.

They didn't meet again until the events of 'Encounter at Farpoint', now six years ago, and in those two years, drifted apart. (Compare with several first season episodes.) Commander Riker plays jazz trombone, and has been trying to perfect the solo in 'Nightbird' for ten years. He wanted to make captain before the age of 35 (having already turned down three commands he's going about it in a strange way!). Commander Riker never cared for the name Thomas. Lieutenant Riker takes up a posting to the USS *Ghandi*, on a terraforming mission to the Lagana Sector. He'll be allowed to bring family aboard after six months.

Troi and Crusher meet for Mok'bara (the move called the KoH'-man-ara is similar to the Crane Block in T'ai Chi) as well as aerobics. Troi drinks Valerian root tea.

150: 'Timescape'

US Transmission: 12 June 1993
UK Transmission: 16 August 1993
Writer: Brannon Braga
Director: Adam Nimoy
Cast: Michael Bofshever, John DeMita, Joel Fredericks

Picard, Troi, Geordi and Data are returning to the *Enterprise* from a conference in a runabout when they discover that the way back to the ship is littered with pockets of temporal instability. The *Enterprise* is frozen in time, seemingly in combat with a Romulan Warbird. However, in the engineering section Data ascertains that time has merely slowed down. There is a warp core breach in progress, which will destroy the ship in nine hours. The *Enterprise* is transferring power to the Warbird, which caused the core breach, and the Romulans are in fact in the process of evacuating. The Romulan engine core is swirling with dark spots, which turn out to be organic life. A power burst from the tricorder sends time flowing ahead, and the *En-*

terprise explodes, only for time to reverse again immediately afterwards. Geordi is attacked by an alien disguised as a Romulan. The creature uses black holes as nests for its young, and they mistook the Romulan power source for such a singularity. Picard uses the tricorder on the Romulan power source in an attempt to prevent the core breach, but Data is attacked by another disguised alien. Picard remotely sends the runabout into the path of the energy transfer, and time is put back on a safe course.

Stardate: 46944.2

Strange New Worlds: The *Enterprise* crew used subspace force fields on Davidia 2.

New Life Forms: Extra-temporal shape-shifting beings whose young are incubated in black holes. Katarians are an intelligent species.

Technology: Touching a plasma field is something not done very often. It is possible to scan for temporal anomalies. As in *DS9*, runabouts have warp drive, and measure tiny speeds in metres/second. Emergency transporter armbands have subspace relays for communication and force fields. The Romulans power their ships using an artificial quantum singularity.

Technobabble: Temporal narcosis. Walking into a different timeframe affects the brain.

Data's Jokes: He experiments to see if 'a watched pot never boils'.

Notes: Sorry, the reviewer's mind wasn't on this episode at all, but on wondering whether or not he was going to get any more blackberry muffins. Good, though.

Data has an internal chronometer. Parrises Squares is mentioned again (see '11001001' *et al.*). Riker hates cats, and is attacked by Spot. Beverly loves them. At the conference on the psychological effects of long term deep space assignments were

Dr Vassbinder (Phisignonomy), Prof. Wagner (Philobiology), and the Katarian (and apparently Scouse) Dr Mizan (Inter-Species Mating).

151: 'Descent'

US Transmission: 19 June 1993
UK Transmission: 31 July 1994
Writers: Ronald D. Moore,
from a story by Jeri Taylor
Director: Alexander Singer
Cast: John Neville, Jim Norton, Natalia Nogulich,
Brian J. Cousins, Professor Stephen Hawking,
Richard Gilbert-Hill, Stephen James Carver

The Borg are attacking Federation outposts. When an away team encounter them, the automatons seem to have adopted individualism. Data is troubled by his sudden acquisition of primitive emotions during the confrontation. Later, when speaking to a captured Borg, he is given the choice of killing a friend or experiencing more emotions. The next thing the crew know, Data has left in a shuttlecraft with the Borg, named Crosis. The *Enterprise* follows the shuttle to an unexplored planet and virtually the entire crew transports to the surface, leaving Beverly in command. Picard, Geordi and Deanna are captured by the Borg and meet their new leader, Lore. Data appears beside his brother and says that the sons of Soong have united.

Stardate: 46982.1

Strange New Worlds: Ohniaka 3, New Berlin Colony and the MS1 Colony – all Federation outposts. A nameless planet 65 light years from Federation space accessible through a transwarp conduit.

Poker Game: Data plays on the holodeck with an angry Sir

Issac Newton, an affable Albert Einstein and a (real) Stephen Hawking, who wins.

Picard Manoeuvre: Dr Crusher does it when in command.

Dialogue Triumphs: 'For the last six hours, I have attempted to induce an emotional response by subjecting myself to various stimuli. I listened to several operas known to be uplifting, I watched three holodeck projections designed to be humorous and I made four attempts to induce sexual desire by subjecting myself to erotic imagery.' 'What happened?' 'Nothing!'

Crosis on killing: 'Klingon: shatter cranial exo-skeleton at the tricipital lobe. Death is immediate . . . Human: sever spinal column at third vertebra. Death is immediate.'

Notes: 'I do not have a designation. My name is Crosis . . . It was given to me by The One.' Good focus on Picard's self-conflict over his actions in returning Hugh to the Borg collective in 'I, Borg' (Admiral Necheyev's fascist lack of sympathy is revealing). It's a great Data story too, although there are silly loopholes (why transport 99 per cent of the crew down to the planet, and why have three command officers in one four-man team?). There's a fantastic bit of continuity as Picard watches a scene from Hugh's interrogation in 'I, Borg' – the Stardate given (45855.4) is consistent with the timescale of that story.

There are fifteen Federation ships in the area, including the *Gorkon*, the *Crazy Horse* and the *Agamemnon*. Ferengi trading ships are mentioned. With Picard, Riker, Data, Worf and Geordi all on the planet surface, Beverly is left in command (see 'Thine Own Self').

Seventh Season

24 45-minute and one 90-minute episodes

Created by Gene Roddenberry

Executive Producers: Rick Berman, Michael Piller, Jeri Taylor **Producers:** Peter Lauritson, Ronald D. Moore **Co-Producers:** Brannon Braga, Wendy Neuss **Supervising Producer:** David Livingston **Consulting Producer:** Peter Lauritson (165–176) **Line Producer:** Merri D. Howard **Executive Story Editor:** René Echevarria **Story Editor:** Naren Shankar

Regular Cast: Patrick Stewart (Captain Jean-Luc Picard), Jonathan Frakes (Commander William T. Riker[1]), LeVar Burton (Lt Commander Geordi La Forge), Michael Dorn (Lt Worf), Gates McFadden (Dr Beverly Crusher), Marina Sirtis (Counselor Deanna Troi), Brent Spiner (Lt Commander Data), Patti Yasutake (Nurse Ogawa, 162[2], 166, 170, 176), Dwight Schultz (Lt Reg Barclay, 170), Majel Barrett (Lwaxana Troi, 158), Wil Wheaton (Ensign Wesley Crusher, 162[3], 171), Armin Shimmerman (Quark, 172), Michelle Forbes (Lt Ro, 175), John de Lancie (Q, 176), Colm Meaney (O'Brien, 176), Denise Crosby (Yar, 176)

152: 'Descent 2'

US Transmission: 18 September 1993
UK Transmission: 7 August 1994

---

[1]The 'T.' is unique to this season's credits.
[2]Dr Ogawa.
[3]Lt Crusher.

Writer: René Echevarria
Director: Alexander Singer
Cast: Jonatahn Del Arco, Alex Datcher, James Hordan, Brian Cousins, Benito Martinez, Michael Reilly Burke

Lore has given Data the feelings he has always dreamed of, but the price is to kill his friends. Beverly is forced to take the *Enterprise* out of orbit when a Borg ship appears, though she later returns to get most of the crew off the planet's surface. Worf and Riker have met a rebel Borg group led by a bitter Hugh, who blames the *Enterprise* for the pathetic state of his race, leaving the way for Lore to mould the Borg in his own image. Nevertheless, on learning that Geordi is one of those captured, Hugh agrees to take Worf and Riker into the Borg headquarters. Lore, suspicious that Data may not be totally under his control, orders his brother to kill Picard. When Data proves unable to do so, Lore seems ready to kill Data but for the intervention of Hugh, Worf and Riker. During the ensuing battle, Data defeats Lore and deactivates him. He is left with the seemingly useless emotion chip Dr Soong created for him.

Stardate: 47025.4 (given towards the end).

Picard Manoeuvre: Beverly again involved in shirt-tugging.

Data's Jokes: Lore: 'Maybe we should work on your sense of humour.'

Notes: 'I am not your puppet any more.' Again (for the third season running), a disappointing conclusion to an excellent set-up. Beverly's command of the ship is actually pretty good, though these segments are ruined by the sub-plot involving the smug, uppity ensign Tait, which strains the viewer's tolerance. Data's torture of his best friend, Geordi, is horrible (emotionally as well as physically), and the whole thing seems to work on auto-pilot, though the final scenes are suitably enigmatic.

Data and Geordi once went boating on Navalo lake. Data's

attempts at swimming resulted in his sinking, and having to walk a mile on the lake bed to the shore.

153: 'Liaisons'

US Transmission: 25 September 1993
UK Transmission: 14 August 1994
Writers: Jeanne Carrigan Fauci, Lisa Rich,
from a story by Roger Eschbacher, Jaq Greenspoon
Director: Cliff Bole
Cast: Barbara Williams, Eric Pierpoint, Paul Eiding,
Michael Harris, Rickey D'Shon Collins

The *Enterprise* plays host to a trio of Eyaran Ambassadors. Deanna and Riker are selected to accompany them, but one insists on having Worf as his guide, and then makes the Klingon's life a misery with his constant taunts. Deanna's guest, meanwhile, seems only interested in gluttony. Picard takes a shuttlecraft with the third Ambassador to Eyar, but it crashes on a hostile world. Picard is injured and is found by a marooned Earth woman, Anna. However, things are not as they seem: the Eyarans are interested in various human emotions and have trapped Picard deliberately to observe love. Similarly, Deanna and Worf's charges are testing other emotions. The Eyarans seem satisfied with what they have learned.

Stardate: Not given, sometime between 47025.4 and 47215.5 (and seven years after 40812).

Strange New Worlds: The Eyaran Homeworld has some of the most spectacular crystal formations in the galaxy.

New Life Forms: The Eyarans procreate by 'post-cellular compounding' (they emerge from natal pods fully grown). The Terellians have four arms.

Poker Game: Riker, Deanna and Worf play with Ambassadors Byleth and Loquell. It all ends in a brawl.

Data's Jokes: Worf: 'Ambassador Byleth is demanding, temperamental and rude.' Data: 'You share all of these qualities in abundance.'

Dialogue Triumphs: 'That is an incredibly outmoded and sexist remark. I'm surprised at you. Besides, you look good in a dress!'

Deanna's reaction to Papella juice: 'Yum!'

'If you were not an ambassador, I would disembowel you right here.'

Notes: 'I am going to kill him with my bare hands.' Rather ordinary, despite a great Worf subplot.

The *Enterprise* engineering section encompasses twelve decks of the secondary hull. Deck 42 is the anti-matter storage facility.

Klingons do not, according to Worf, procrastinate. Hitarian chocolate puff is a favourite of Deanna's. It is made with seventeen different kinds of chocolate (this chocoholic stuff is all very well, but doesn't Deanna realise that an excess of dairy products will give her heart disease and acne?).

154: 'Interface'

US Transmission: 2 October 1993
UK Transmission: 21 August 1994
Writer: Joe Menoksy
Director: Robert Wiemer
Cast: Madge Sinclair, Warren Munson, Ben Veeren

A new virtual reality interface keyed to Geordi's brain patterns is to be used on a mission to help the *Rhamon*. But then he receives the terrible news that his mother's ship is lost. Geordi proceeds with the interface experiment but on the *Rhamon* he sees his mother, who tells him that her crew are trapped in the lower atmosphere. Despite warnings not to go back, Geordi returns with Data's help. He discovers that the image of his mother is actually being fed to him by sub-space creatures trapped on the *Rhamon*.

Stardate: 47215.5

Strange New Worlds: Mardgny 7, a gas giant.

New Life Forms: The sub-space beings who live in the lower atmosphere of the planet. The Ferengi are mentioned in passing.

Technobabble: The *Hera* used 'trionic initiators in the warp coil'. Beverly suggests creating an 'inverse warp cascade'.

Picard Manoeuvre: Once.

Notes: 'She's a starship captain. She's got herself into and out of impossible situations before.' A good Geordi episode with lots of excellent characterisation. Geordi's close relationship with his mother is well handled. The denouement is clever, with TV conventions leading the viewer to expect an ending far different to the one they actually get.

Geordi's mother has been captain of the *Hera*, a ship with a mostly Vulcan crew, for seven months. She is said to be a great judge of character. The *Excelsior* and the *Noble* are searching for the missing *Hera*. Geordi also has a sister, Areana. Riker had problems accepting his mother's death as a small child.

Admiral Marcus Holt is stationed at DS3. Data is studying ancient Uzidarian poetry which largely consists of lengthy pauses (sometimes lasting for several days) during which the poet and the audience are encouraged to acknowledge the emptiness of the experience.

Like Worf in 'Reunion', Geordi now has a permanent note on his record for disobeying orders (so, presumably, has Data).

155: 'Gambit'

US Transmission: 9 October 1993
UK Transmission: 28 August 1994
Writers: Naren Shankar,
from a story by Christopher Hatton, Naren Shankar
Director: Peter Lauritson
Cast: Richard Lynch, Robin Curtis, Caitlin Brown,
Cameron Thor, Alan Altshuld, Bruce Gray, Sabrina Le Beauf,
Stephen Lee, Derek Webster

In the seedy surroundings of a Desikan bar, Riker, Deanna, Worf and Beverly discover that Picard has apparently been killed. When Riker is kidnapped whilst leading an away team, Data assumes the captaincy. Riker finds himself on a mercenary ship smuggling archaeological artifacts. A crewman, Galen, is Picard, who manages to tell Riker (between threats to kill him) that his 'death' was the result of a new type of transporter. The pair continue with their subterfuge hoping to find out the mercenaries' plans which seem to involve Romulan artifacts, whilst the *Enterprise* tracks them.

Stardate: 47135.2

Strange New Worlds: Desika 2 where Picard 'dies'. The mercenaries were heading for the Borada system which has one class-M planet, the uninhabited Boradas 3 which was used as an outpost by the De Brun 2,000 years ago. Other potential targets for the mercenaries are Calder 2, Draykin 4 and Yadala Prime.

New Life Forms: The De Brun, an ancient off-shoot of the Romulans.

Picard Manoeuvre: With Picard absent, everybody's at it. Riker, Data (when in command) and even Worf.

Dialogue Triumphs: Riker to alien: 'Great story, I'll remember it the next time I'm in a knife fight.'

'This isn't about revenge, it's about justice. The captain died in a bar fight for nothing. Somebody has to answer for that. Then I can mourn.'

Notes: 'I was right. You do like living dangerously.' Great pre-title sequence (another tribute to the *Star Wars* cantina scene?), and a fine angry Deanna/Riker confrontation in the aftermath of Picard's 'death', but this quickly gets bogged down in too much plot.

Riker's Starfleet number is 231/427. Picard uses the pseudonym Galen (after his archaeological mentor, see 'The Chase'). During Riker's initial interrogation on the mercenary ship, 'Galen' says Riker was once relieved of duty during the Cardassian incident at Minos Cauber, and had a history of insubordination aboard the *Hood*, though he's probably lying. Gold-pressed latinum, the universal currency often mentioned in *DS9*, makes its first *Next Generation* appearance.

156: 'Gambit Part 2'

US Transmission: 16 October 1993
UK Transmission: 4 September 1994
Writers: Ronald D. Moore,
from a story by Naren Shankar
Director: Alexander Singer
Cast: Richard Lynch, Robin Curtis, Caitlin Brown,
Cameron Thor, James Worthy, Sabrina Le Beauf,
Martin Goslins

The search for the artifacts continues, with Riker seemingly having turned traitor. Picard thinks there may actually be an ancient Vulcan relic called the Stone of Gal. The mercenaries obtain a second piece of the relic from the *Enterprise*, an action involving Picard and Riker. Data plays along with their charade and the search ends on Vulcan where the mercenary Tellera reveals herself to be a member of an extremist Vulcan group. The Gal is reassembled but positive thinking by the *Enterprise* crew renders the lethal weapon harmless.

Stardate: 47160.1 (given by Data).

Dialogue Triumphs: Deanna, after Picard has shot Riker: 'He's only stunned.' Data: 'I must admit, I'm experiencing a similar sensation.'

'You've been declared dead, you can't give orders around here.'

Notes: 'This is the power of the mind.' There's a really great scene with Data (as Captain) reprimanding Worf (as first officer) for questioning his orders, which becomes a discussion on styles of command, the role of first officer and friendship. There is also much good acting from the regulars, but the denouement is risible, and the final scenes are more corny than amusing. A big disappointment.

Worf has programmed the replicators for Klingon blood wine (see 'A Fistful of Datas'). Romulans have 'labour camps'. Riker speaks of 'fifteen years of Starfleet technical knowledge', though presumably this includes the time he spent at the Academy (see 'The Pegasus'). Tallera claims to be a Vulcan undercover security officer (Vi'shar) called T'Par.

During Vulcan's savage past, telepathy was used as a weapon. The Stone of Gal – a psyonic resonator – was believed to have been destroyed (by 'the gods') during 'the awakening' (the period when the Vulcans threw off their past and embraced logic).

Picard quotes Sir Walter Scott's *Marmion*.

157: 'Phantasms'

US Transmission: 23 October 1993

UK Transmission: 11 September 1994
Writer: Brannon Braga
Director: Patrick Stewart
Cast: Gina Ravarra, Bernard Kates, Clyde Kusatsu,
David L. Crowley

Data is having nightmares full of strange images. When these start spilling into reality, he seeks Deanna's advice and that of Sigmund Freud via a holodeck program. When he stabs Deanna in the turbo lift, his explanation is that he saw a 'mouth' on her shoulder. Tests reveal that many of the crew have similar invisible parasites on them. Picard and Geordi enter a simulation of one of Data's dreams and piece together several clues to discover that the ship has been infested with a dangerous organism. Data uses a specific sonic pitch to disperse the parasites.

Stardate: 47225.7 (nine months after 'Birthright').

Strange New Worlds: Thanado 7, where the *Enterprise*'s warp core was manufactured.

New Life Forms: Invisible leech-like organisms who feed off the crew's neural cellular peptides and exist in an inter-phasic state.

Picard Manoeuvre: Yes, three times.

Dialogue Triumphs: Data asks Worf to look after Spot for him: 'He will need to be fed once a day. He prefers feline supplement 25. And he will require water, and you must provide him with a sand box. And you must talk to him. Tell him that he is a pretty cat, and a good cat . . .' Worf: 'I will feed him.'

Beverly, sucking Riker's brains out with a straw: 'Do you want some? It's delicious!'

Data: 'What would Dr Freud say about the symbolism of devouring oneself?' Deanna: 'Sometimes a cake is just a cake!'

Notes: 'Strange is not a sufficient adjective to explain the experience.' Odd, disturbing and very funny (often all at the same time). Though the plot ends somewhat buried in rushed explanations, the images of Deanna as a cake and the terrifying lift scene remain with the viewer. The scene of Data asking Worf to look after his cat is a comic highlight.

Picard has been invited to the annual Starfleet Admirals Banquet. He has managed to avoid it for the last six years (and also here, though more by luck than good management). Data has experienced 111 dreams since 'Birthright'. He seems to go to bed in his uniform (boots and all).

Riker has given Alexander a Jazz music program. Worf complains he plays it 'all night'.

158: 'Dark Page'

US Transmission: 30 October 1993
UK Transmission: 18 September 1994
Writer: Hilary J. Bader
Director: Les Landau
Cast: Norman Large, Kirsten Dunst, Amick Byram,
Andreana Weimer

The Kerhen are a gentle race of pure telepaths seeking to join the Federation. Lwaxana Troi is helping to teach them the concept of spoken language. However, contact with a child of the Kerhen awakens a dreadful secret from Lwaxana's past and she lapses into a coma. Deanna, with the help of the Kerhen, enters into her mother's psyche and discovers Lwaxana's secret – that Deanna had an elder sister who tragically died. The healing process begins as Lwaxana is drawn out of the coma.

Stardate: 47254.1

New Life Forms: The Kerhen, an empathic race with no concept of spoken language.

Dialogue Triumphs: Lwaxana: 'Aren't you going to mingle, Mr Woof?' Worf: 'I do not care for telepaths. They make me uneasy.'

'Stay away from my daughter!'

Notes: 'Bad thoughts hurt her. The dark place!' The best Lwaxana story by miles. For the second episode running the psyche is explored, although this is a much darker and intense story than 'Phantasms' (to which Data refers). Deanna is beautifully characterised throughout.

Ian and Lwaxana Troi were married in the year that included Stardate 30620. They lived at Lake Alnar on Betazed when Deanna was a baby. Unknown to Deanna she had an older sister, Kestra, born about six years before her. Kestra died (the exact circumstances aren't stated although it is implied she drowned whilst chasing the family dog) when Deanna was a baby. Lwaxana always blamed herself for the tragedy to the extent of erasing her journals covering Kestra's life.

Deanna was seven when her father died. She was good at languages as a child. She quotes John Milton.

The jewel plant of Tholar 3 secretes a resin which hardens into a gem.

159: 'Attached'

US Transmission: 6 November 1993
UK Transmission: 25 September 1994
Writer: Nicholas Sagan
Director: Jonathan Frakes
Cast: Robin Gammell, Lenore Kasdorf, J.C. Stevens

Whilst evaluating a request from the Kes on the planet Kes-Prit 3 to join the Federation, Picard and Beverly are kidnapped by the xenophobic Prit and telepathically linked to each other. They escape but remain unable to split up, and discover their true feelings for each other. Riker forces the Kes and the Prit to meet, and begins a tentative dialogue between the two as Picard and Beverly return to the ship. Their relationship, it seems, may not be over yet.

Stardate: 47304.2 (seven years after 'Encounter at Farpoint').

Strange New Worlds: Kes-Prit 3, a divided world.

New Life Forms: The Kes, driven by suspicion, deviousness and paranoia. The Prit, a fiercely xenophobic race. It has been nearly a century since the last formal contact between the two.

Deanna Underused?: Missing completely, as is Geordi.

Dialogue Triumphs: 'One of us is hungry.' 'That'll be me.' 'Do you mind thinking of something else – you're making *me* hungry!'

'Why didn't you ever tell me you were in love with me?' 'You were married to my best friend.'

Future History: The World Government was created in 2150.

Notes: 'It seems as if we're stuck with each other.' *The Thirty-Nine Steps* with psychic bonding instead of handcuffs! Very much a first season-type story, with a pointless three minute sequence of Picard and Beverly trying to escape pursuing guards when, at the same time, Riker is negotiating their release. Good in parts, however, with the Picard/Beverly relationship hinted at in 'Encounter at Farpoint' and others (especially 'The Naked Now') coming full circle (see also 'All Good Things . . .').

Beverly gossips about Nurse Ogawa and Ensign Marksen. She is afraid of heights. Her grandmother used to make good vegetable soup. She says her mouth was always landing her in trouble. She once dated a boy called Tom Norris.

Picard likes coffee and croissants for breakfast.

160: 'Force of Nature'

US Transmission: 13 November 1993
UK Transmission: 2 October 1994
Writer: Naren Shankar
Director: Robert Lederman
Cast: Michael Corbet, Margaret Reed, Lee Arenberg,
Majel Barrett

The *Enterprise* is searching the Hekaris Corridor for a missing ship, the *Fleming*. The corridor is a passageway through an area of tetrion fields, which inhibit warp engines. The ship finds a Ferengi vessel, disabled by a mine that overloads warp drives. Its crew tells Picard the course of the *Fleming*, and the *Enterprise* follows it to a field of debris. In the field is a probe disguised as a buoy, which cripples the *Enterprise*. A small ship arrives, and Dr Rabal and Dr Serova beam aboard. They have planted the probes, their research indicating that their world is threatened by warp drives which continually wear thin the fabric of space-time in the Corridor. Geordi is sceptical, but, in return for reactivating the *Enterprise*, Picard promises further study. Arriving at the *Fleming*, Serova is distressed by the lack of belief in her work, and, stealing a shuttle, sacrifices herself in a deliberate warp core breach. A rift, sure enough, opens in space, and sucks in the two ships. When the *Fleming* uses its warp drive to escape, the *Enterprise* only survives by surfing out on a distortion wave. In forty years, the Corridor may be a single subspace rift, so the Federation puts a speed limit on warp drive.

Stardate: 47310.2

Strange New Worlds: The Hekaris Corridor, a twelve light year-long passage through a warp-inhibiting tetrion field established by the Federation. Hekaris 2 is in the corridor.

New Life Forms: The Hekarians, ridge-foreheaded humanoids who possess warp drive capability.

Technology: Bio-mimetic gel is valuable. A verteron pulse can disable a starship. Starships are made of duranium and polycomposites. A ship's log recorder can survive one's destruction. Warp drive has been around for 300 years. Long range sensors extend at least 0.3 light years, a distance which would take weeks at impulse speed.

Technobabble: The whole story . . .

Picard Manoeuvre: Pulls it twice when confronting Ferengi.

Deanna Underused?: Two lines.

Data's Jokes: 'Spot does not respond to verbal commands.'
  'Geordi . . . I cannot stun my cat.'

Notes: At the end of this story, all Federation vessels are limited to warp five due to environmental effects, a conclusion which almost suggests, along with the first season-ish awkwardness displayed towards the characters, that the writer doesn't understand the series. Certainly, *ST:TNG* does and should recognise social trends, but *Trek* is about going to far away places and exploring. Our aspirations should be boundless, then bounded in by reality, not stunted from the start. Certainly, this view puts us on the side of some rather awful Republicans, but the only point in having a speed limit in a fantasy about speed and freedom is if this fantasy is also somehow true. The followers of *Trek* are the people who are already conserving resources, hoping to keep the human adventure going. They don't need a continuing environmental lesson, or an ongoing metaphor about how America is now starting to doubt there's anywhere left to go. They're bigger than one country, and they don't need a speed limit on their dreams.

Ferengi transport ships of the De Kora class carry a crew of 450. The Ferengi are ruled by a council (cf. *DS9*'s 'The Nagus'), and one also governs Federation science policy. Commander Donald Kaplan is the chief engineer of the USS *Intrepid*. Geordi enjoys a friendly rivalry with him. Geordi's sister trained her cat. Spot is female (it's obviously a hermaphrodite, as it's been a 'he' on every previous appearance). Surfing is still an activity.

161: 'Inheritance'

US Transmission: 20 November 1993
UK Transmission: 9 October 1994
Writers: Dan Koeppel, René Echevarria,
from a story by Dan Koeppel
Director: Robert Scheerer
Cast: Fionnula Flanagan, William Lithgow

One of the scientists aiding the *Enterprise* crew in re-liquefying the core of Atrea 4 is Dr Juliana Taner, Data's co-creator and Noonian Soong's wife. Data had his memory of her wiped, along with that of his childhood. She left Soong years ago, but is distressed to hear of his death. Getting to know each other, Taner tells Data that, fearing another bad experience such as that with Lore, she persuaded Soong to leave Data behind when the Crystalline Entity attacked the colony. Taner and Data perform a violin piece together. Then the geological work is interrupted by a cave-in. The two of them beam down to recover some equipment, and in order to save their lives they leap from a precipice. Taner's arm breaks off: she's an android. Data consults Soong on the holodeck, using an information chip from the unconscious Taner's brain. Taner was based on a real, now dead, woman, and doesn't know she's an android. Data agrees not to tell her.

Stardate: 47410.2

Strange New Worlds: Atria 4, a planet with a dying core. Terlina 3 and Murvala 4 are mentioned.

New Life Forms: The Atrians, big-eared humanoids. A

Carvalen trader is mentioned.

Technology: Pattern enhancer poles are needed for beaming out from underground. A Fourier system is used to give Data's blinking the appearance of randomness.

Notes: Rather lovely, and nowhere near as stomach-churning as it might have been.

Dr Juliana Taner, née O'Donnell, married Dr Noonian Soong on Murvala 4, before the government there was overthrown. They created Data on Omicron Theta, after three destroyed prototypes, and Lore, who was dismantled because of the flaws in his emotional make-up. Data was deliberately abandoned on Omicron Theta before the attack of the Crystalline Entity (see 'Data Lore'), his processors wiped so that he had no memory of his 'childhood', some of which he spent walking around naked. He was going to be a girl, but was given a sexuality program, and is anatomically correct. Soong and Taner went to the Terlina system, where Data met Soong in 'Brothers', and eventually separated. Data weighs around 100kg, and is attempting to master all known styles of painting, including painting Lol. He has mastered a violin piece by Handel.

162: 'Parallels'

US Transmission: 27 November 1993
UK Transmission: 16 October 1994
Writer: Brannon Braga
Director: Robert Weimer
Cast: Mark Bramhall, Majel Barrett

Returning from a Bat'telh tournament, Worf arrives on the *Enterprise* to find a surprise birthday party has been arranged for him. However, as the day progresses, subtle differences begin to manifest themselves and Worf finds the *Enterprise* changing. After his error has caused Geordi to be badly injured, he returns to his quarters to find Deanna waiting for him. She claims to be his wife. Worf is in fact bouncing through a multitude of parallel universes, each slightly different from the last. Finding himself on an *Enterprise* in which Riker is Captain, the ship is faced with a fissure in the space-time continuum and a multitude of parallel *Enterprise*s. A way is found for Worf to return to his own universe and restore the fissure.

Stardate: 47391.2 (Worf's birthday).

Strange New Worlds: Worf has been attending a Bat'telh competition on Forgas 3. He won, whilst 'several competitors were maimed'.

New Life Forms: Alexander has a pet Dalvin hissing beetle. Klingons do not have a word for 'jolly'.

Technobabble: Oceans of it. 'It appears to be a quantum fissure in the time-space continuum.'

'The uncertainty principle dictates that time is a variable in this equation.'

Picard Manoeuvre: Worf does it.

Dialogue Triumphs: 'I think Data's painting is making me dizzy.'

Riker: 'You don't remember this, do you?' Worf: 'I *do* remember. I just remember differently.'

'At this rate the sector will be completely filled with *Enterprise*s in three days!'

'Captain, we're receiving 285,000 hails.' 'I wish I knew what to tell them.'

'I knew Klingons preferred to be alone on their birthday. You probably want to meditate, or hit yourself with a painstik.'

Notes: 'Things are changing.' Complex and hugely enjoyable. The highlight of this fine episode is the little glimpses we get into what might have been. We'd like to see more of the timeline in which Riker is captain, and Lieutenant Wesley Crusher saves the ship!

Data's present to Worf is his painting of the Battle of Horos. Worf pilots the shuttlecraft *Curie*. Kurn does not, according to Worf, have his prowess with the Bat'telh. Just as in 'Ethics' he asked Deanna to be Alexander's guardian if he died during surgery, here Worf asks Troi to become Alexander's step-mother (Soh Chim) in case anything happens to him. This would make her his step-sister in human terms. She asks if he realises that this would make Lwaxana his step-mother, which he hadn't.

The Argus Array (see 'The Nth Degree') in various universes has been reprogrammed by the Cardassians to gain information on important strategic Federation installations like Deep Space 5, Starbase 47, the Irridawa colony and the Utopia Planetia shipyards (responsible for new starship development). (See 'Eye of the Beholder'.)

In one of the parallel universes Geordi dies in a plasma explosion. Worf is married to Deanna on one *Enterprise* (in another, they have two children). They have been married for two years, having fallen in love after 'Ethics'. Six months later, Worf asked Riker for permission to wed Deanna (he considered it the honourable thing to do).

Nurse Ogawa is a doctor on one *Enterprise*. In another Worf is first officer under Captain Riker, Picard having died in 'The Best of Both Worlds'. Wesley Crusher is security officer. The Bajorans overpowered the Cardassians and are openly hostile to the Federation.

Finally, in one universe the Borg over-ran the Federation. The *Enterprise* is one of the few ships left, and they don't want to go back!

163: 'The Pegasus'

US Transmission: 4 December 1993
UK Transmission: 23 October 1994
Writer: Ronald D. Moore

Director: LeVar Burton
Cast: Nancy Vawter, Terry O'Quinn, Michael Mack

Twelve years ago, the *Pegasus*, commanded by Captain Eric Pressman and with a young ensign named Will Riker, was lost with only a handful of crew surviving. Now Admiral Pressman arrives on the *Enterprise* with orders that the ship head for the Neutral Zone to find the *Pegasus*. Riker refuses to discuss the events of the ship's loss with Picard, but later reveals that a mutiny took place amongst the officers. Despite the attentions of a Romulan ship, the *Enterprise* locates the *Pegasus* buried in an asteroid. Pressman and Riker board the *Pegasus* and bring back a piece of scientific equipment which Riker reveals to be an experimental cloaking device. Escaping from the asteroid, Picard informs the Romulans of the illegal machine's existence and arrests Pressman and Riker, though the first officer is later released.

Stardate: 47457.1

Strange New Worlds: The *Enterprise* is conducting energy output studies of the Macorea quasar. They are sent to the Delovin system and discover the *Pegasus* at asteroid Gamma 601.

Picard Manoeuvre: Once.

Deanna Underused?: Missing completely.

Dialogue Triumphs: 'Twelve years ago I needed an officer that I could count on in a crisis. Someone who would support and obey my decisions without question . . . And that someone was Will Riker.'

'I was seven months out of the Academy, my head still ringing with words like 'duty' and 'honour'. When they turned on him, I thought they were a bunch of self-serving disloyal officers, so I grabbed a phaser and defended my captain.'

Notes: 'I wasn't a hero, and neither were you. What you did was wrong and I was wrong to follow you, but I was too young and too stupid to see it!' After a great Worf episode comes a *great* Riker episode, which sees *Star Trek* doing *A Few Good Men* and coming up with a cynical look at what Starfleet has become. Jonathan Frakes' Picard impression is amusing rather than accurate.

Captain Picard Day is an art competition for the *Enterprise*'s children. Warp speed limitations are mentioned (see 'Force of Nature'). Starfleet have an operative in Romulan High Command. Worf breaks one of Riker's ribs in a Bat'telh contest.

Riker says he's had his beard for 'about four years' (it's closer to six). He was getting tired of hearing how young he looked. Lieutenant Boylan (on the *Pegasus*) used to call him 'Ensign Babyface'. The Treaty of Algeron (see 'The Defector') prohibits Federation cloaking technology. Picard says the treaty is the reason the Federation has had sixty years of peace with the Romulans.

Picard tells Pressman that he chose Riker for his first officer without having met him, on the strength of Riker's actions with Captain De Soto on Altair 3 (see 'Encounter at Farpoint').

This episode measures Riker's career: he left the Academy nearly thirteen years ago (class of '57: see 'Chain of Command'), spent seven months on the *Pegasus*, where his 'heroism' earned him a promotion to lieutenant on the *Potemkin* (see 'Peak Performance', 'Second Chances'). Thereafter he was first officer on the *Hood* where he turned down a first captaincy (see 'The Arsenal of Freedom'). If this timescale is correct, and Riker has been aboard the *Enterprise* for seven years, then he ascended from the Academy to the verge of captain in little over five years. Phenomenal even by Picard's standards.

164: 'Homeworld'

US Transmission: 11 December 1993

UK Transmission: 30 October 1994
Writer: Naren Shankar,
from a story by Spike Steingasser
Director: Alexander Singer
Cast: Penny Johnson, Brian Markinson, Edward Penn,
Paul Sorvino, Susan Christy, Majel Barrett

Worf's foster-brother, Nikolai, is a Federation cultural observer on the primitive planet Boral 2. The planet's atmosphere is about to dissipate but Picard refuses to intervene and save any of the Borallans. Nikolai beams an entire village to a holodeck simulation of their home. Picard is angry, but has no alternative but to follow Nikolai's plan to find the Borallans a new home. Worf accompanies Nikolai on to the holodeck to help the villagers in their 'trek' to their new home. Problems occur, one of the villagers wandering off the holodeck by mistake, but eventually the *Enterprise* finds an uninhabited world and transports the villagers down. Nikolai decides to stay with them.

Stardate: 47423.9 (it is four years since Worf and Nikolai have seen each other).

Strange New Worlds: Boral 2, where plasmodic reactions are destroying the atmosphere. Drago 4, a suggested new home for the Borallans with a large temperate zone, discounted because of its proximity to Cardassian space. Vacus 6 in the Kabral sector is eventually chosen.

New Life Forms: The Borallans, a simple people with a 'rich and beautiful culture'.

Picard Manoeuvre: Picard one, Riker one!

Dialogue Triumphs: 'Don't worry, it is an omen . . . The sign of La Forge!'
    Beverly: 'He would have died anyway.' Picard: 'But he wouldn't have died alone and afraid.'

Notes: 'I wasn't going to let those people die just because your captain started quoting Federation dogma at me.' A little classic, showing how narrow the Prime Directive can be (Picard spouts a lot of rubbish about not interfering when a world is about to go up in smoke). Even the tragic subplot about the Chronicler Voren is given subtle weight.

Nikolai Rozhenko, was first mentioned in 'Heart of Glory'. He left the Academy after a year, unable to follow the rules. Worf thinks he had many fine qualities.

Atmospheric dissipation is said to be rare.

165: 'Sub Rosa'

US Transmission: 18 December 1993
UK Transmission: 6 November 1994
Writers: Brannon Braga,
from a story by Jeri Taylor
Director: Jonathan Frakes
Cast: Michael Keenan, Shay Duffin, Duncan Regehr,
Ellen Albertini Dow

Following the death of her grandmother, Beverly arranges her funeral on the Scottish-influenced colony of Caldos. A handsome stranger at the burial seems to haunt Beverly as she makes the discovery that her grandmother had a young lover, Ronan. Soon afterwards, Beverly announces that she intends to stay on Caldos. Picard has Geordi and Data track power fluctuations on the planet and confronts Ronan, a 'ghost' who has lived with the women of the Howard family for many centuries. Ronan is an anaphasic energy form, who required their biochemistry to survive. Beverly kills Ronan and returns to the *Enterprise*.

Stardate: None given (presumably between 47458 and 47566).

Strange New Worlds: Caldos, one of the Federation's first terraforming projects almost a century ago. The cornerstone of every building was brought from Edinburgh, Glasgow or Aberdeen as the founders wanted to recreate Scotland in space.

New Life Forms: The anaphasic energy life form masquerading as an 800-year-old ghost.

Dialogue Triumphs: 'Ye dinna understand. He's tryin' t'kill us aal!'

'You have been using . . . my entire family for centuries.' 'And I loved you all!'

Future History: Glamis castle still exists in the 24th century.

Notes: 'There's a caber toss scheduled for tomorrow!' Having done 'Planet of the Irish People (Begorrah)' in 'Up the Long Ladder', here's 'Planet of the Scottish People (Och-Aye)'. Quite silly, with many inexplicable elements and some truly dreadful accents; but also sweet (the scene of the *Enterprise* bridge shrouded in fog). The Beverly/Deanna 'girl's talk' scenes are excellent.

The major inconsistency: Ronan loves 'the Howard women', but none, after the first, should have been named Howard (as Felisia and Beverly were), unless they're a long line of single mothers. None of these females can have married male Howards since it is that particular biochemistry that Ronan requires.

Beverly's grandmother, Felisia, was over one hundred years old. Beverly's mother died when she was young (Beverly remembers what she looked like, but little else) and she was raised by her grandmother on Arvada 3 (see 'The Arsenal of Freedom') and then Caldos where Felisia was a 'healer'. Felisia's mother seems to have died only a few years before.

Ronan says he was born in 1647 in Glasgow. After he 'died' he found a home with Jesso Howard, 'a pretty lass with . . . red hair and eyes like diamonds'. He lived with her until her death, and then with her descendants. Beverly speculates that her ancestor's biochemistry was compatible with Ronan's energy matrix, as was the ancient candle-holder heirloom in which he 'lived'.

166: 'Lower Decks'

US Transmission: 5 February 1994
UK Transmission: 13 November 1994
Writer: René Echevarria,
from a story by Ronald Wilkinson, Jean Louise Matthias
Director: Gabrielle Beaumont
Cast: Dan Gauthier, Sannon Fill, Alexander Enberg,
Bruce Beatty, Don Reilly

It is crew evaluation time, and a group of junior officers in Ten-Forward speculate on their chances of promotion. Soon afterwards, a mysterious pod is brought to the *Enterprise*. Some of the young crew members are told not to divulge what they have seen: a Cardassian. After a complicated series of tests, Ensign Sito is informed by Picard that she has been chosen for a dangerous mission to accompany the Cardassian, a Federation spy, back into Cardassian space pretending to be his prisoner. The mission is a success, but Sito is killed 'escaping'. Her friends join Worf in honouring her memory.

Stardate: 47566.7 (three years after 'The First Duty').

Strange New Worlds: The Ogea system, close to Cardassian space.

New Life Forms: The Vetichs of the Janlin order maintain a round-the-clock chant for the benefit of the Bajoran people.

Technobabble: Dr Nils Diaz has been experimenting with warp field integrity techniques at the Tallian Propulsion laboratory.

Poker Game: Two! In the first, Ben, Taurvik, Sito, Lavelle and Ogawa discuss the senior officers, the pod and promotion. Ben wins and then goes to the Big Boys' game. In this Worf, Riker, Beverly, Deanna and Geordi are discussing Lieutenant Powell's infidelity, and Lavelle and Sito's promotability. Riker wins.

Dialogue Triumphs: 'You think Worf's chewing her out?' 'Na, he always looks like that!'

Notes: 'I just cleaned out some junior officers and thought I'd do the same here!' Highly unusual and effective, a story told largely from the point of view of five 'substitutes' for Riker, Worf, Geordi, Beverly and Guinan. Well-plotted (the audience, as well as the junior officers, have little idea what is going on for half the episode) and a sad, but positive, end. Picard's initial interview with Sito is shockingly unjust, though this is later revealed to be a test; it's a relief to the audience to find Jean-Luc isn't turning into Heinrich Himmler.

Crew evaluations are held every three months. Ambassador Spock is mentioned. Riker drinks Trakian ale. He took up poker so he could sit in on the officer's game on the *Potemkin*. Gi'tahl is Klingon for 'to the death'.

Sam Lavelle is like a young Riker (as everyone but the first officer notices). He has a Canadian grandfather and is promoted to lieutenant. His room mate Taurvik is a Vulcan engineer. Sito Jaksa (see 'The First Duty') is a Bajoran security officer, and Worf's star pupil. She has been on the *Enterprise* for seven months (Picard specifically asked for her so that she would have a chance to redeem herself after the Locarno incident). She speaks Klingon. Nurse Alicia Ogawa is engaged to Lieutenant Andrew Powell (see 'Genesis'). Beverly is going to recommend her promotion. Ben (last name unknown) is a civilian worker in Ten-Forward.

167: 'Thine Own Self'

US Transmission: 12 February 1994
UK Transmission: 20 November 1994

Writers: Ronald D. Moore,
from a story by Christopher Hatton
Director: Winrich Kolbe
Cast: Ronnie Claire Edwards, Michael Rothhaar,
Kimberly Cullum, Michael G. Hagerty, Andy Kossin,
Richard Ortega-Miró, Majel Barrett

A Federation deep space probe crashes on the planet Barkon 4, and Data is sent to recover the radioactive material. The mission should be a simple one, although contact with the pre-industrial society is to be avoided. However, the nearby town is soon visited by a pale stranger who has lost his identity. Data's memories begin to return, but he does not realise that the metal he is carrying – which has been fashioned into jewellery for the populace – is radioactive and is affecting the townsfolk. On the *Enterprise* Deanna tries to take her full commander's exams, but fails in one key simulation. Only when Deanna asks the holographic Geordi to sacrifice himself in order to save the ship does she pass. Data, meanwhile, clashes against the received scientific wisdom of the Barkonians, and is branded a plague-carrier. He is 'killed' moments after putting an antidote into the town's water supply, but is later found and reactivated by Crusher and Riker.

Stardate: 47611.2

Strange New Worlds: Barkon 4, the probe crashing some 100kms from the nearest settlement.

The Torenko colony needs medical supplies from the *Lexington*.

New Life Forms: The Barkonians are intelligent humanoids comparable to the people of medieval Earth. Their unit of measurement is the saltan (1km = c.2 saltans), and their unit of currency is the dorik. The mountains where the probe crashed are known as the Velorian mountains, and they believe there to be ferocious creatures there (including the Icemen, of whom Data is believed to be an example). The Barkonians have rock, fire, sky and water as their basic elements.

Technobabble: 'However, based on interstitial transparency and membrane integrity, I do not believe it is an infection or any other form of communicable disease.'

Deanna Underused?: She has just returned from a three-day class reunion on Starbase 231.

Notes: An excellent story that uses its archetypes – Kaspar Hauser and *Frankenstein* – to great effect. It's a shame that more time could not have been given to Data's conflicts with the received wisdom of the Barkonians at the expense of the dull Deanna-takes-her-exams sub-plot. And at the end of the story one has to ask 'Whither Prime Directive?' (no matter how accidental Data's culture-changing has been).

At the start of the episode Crusher is bridge officer, being ranked as a commander in addition to her status as ship's doctor (see 'Descent'). She started thinking about taking the officer's exams eight years ago (but it is not stated when she actually took them). Troi has been considering applying to become a full commander ever since she was in command during 'Disaster' and made such a mess of it. Her authorisation code is omega omega 31.

168: 'Masks'

US Transmission: 19 February 1994
UK Transmission: 27 November 1994
Writer: Joe Menosky
Director: Robert Wiemer
Cast: Ricky D'Shon Collins

Soon after the *Enterprise* comes across a rogue comet, strange ceremonial objects begin to appear on the ship. Data sculpts an alien mask from clay, and esoteric symbols form on computer consoles. The ship's phasers melt the ice around the comet's core, revealing an alien archive. The 'library' uses the *Enterprise*'s sensor beam as a carrier wave to transmit information into the computer and the replicators. Data is 'possessed' by various individuals who warn that Masaka, a semi-mythical, evil queen, is waking. Only Korgano can stop her, but he no longer pursues Masaka. The very fabric of the *Enterprise* transforms into a representation of the ancient culture, but Picard plays out the ancient rituals as Korgano, and Masaka is defeated.

Stardate: 47615.2

Strange New Worlds: The 87 million year-old comet in sector 1156 is said to have originated in the Darsee system. It contains an alien 'library' composed of fortanium and various unknown materials.

New Life Forms: Although there is now no life within the Darsee system the informational archive shows an advanced, ritualistic culture.

Dialogue Triumphs: 'Geordi, what does it feel like when a person is losing his mind?'

'Maybe we'd better talk out here. The observation lounge has turned into a swamp.'

'Well, Data, you never may become fully human, but you've had an experience that transcends the human condition – you've been an entire civilisation.'

Notes: 'Masaka is waking!' A semiologist's nightmare, this darkly surreal story is stonkingly well directed. Spiner's performance, the incredible designs and effects, and some marvellous 'ethnic' music, all contribute to a most engaging fable. The only disappointment is the ending.

Crusher says that Worf will show them some Mok'bara throwing techniques. Data's schizoid characters include a coward, an old man who proves to be Masaka's father, and the rather sinister Ehot, who hails from Masaka City.

169: 'Eye of the Beholder'

US Transmission: 26 February 1994
UK Transmission: 4 December 1994
Writer: René Echevarria,
from a story by Brannon Braga
Director: Cliff Bole
Cast: Mark Rolston, Nancy Harewood, Tim Lounibes,
Johanna McCloy, Nora Leonhardt, Dugan Savoye,
Majel Barrett

A crew member commits suicide, throwing himself into the plasma venting system. Deanna and Worf begin an investigation. The crewman seemed very happy, and nothing in his background suggests any apparent cause, apart from the fact that he worked on the construction of the *Enterprise* eight years ago. Deanna next suffers a 'vision' of what seems to be a murder that took place during the building of the *Enterprise*. It is eventually discovered that psychic images of the crime have remained, and that empaths are particularly vulnerable to them, Worf saving Deanna from a grizzly fate.

Stardate: 47622.1 (given in Lieutenant Kwan's log). Picard's first entry is at 47623.2 (eight years after 40987).

Strange New Worlds: The *Enterprise* is *en route* to Barson 2, which is suffering a medical emergency.

Poker Game: Worf notes that Deanna never bluffs (not actually true: see 'Ethics').

Riker's Conquests: Lieutenant Correll, a stunning blonde in Ten-Forward. Number One doesn't know if he's 'involved' with her yet, but we bet he's going to have fun finding out.

Notes: 'Something terrible happened in that room. I felt it.' A good murder mystery with several unusual twists and an engaging suicide sub-plot. The first Worf/Deanna screen-kiss seems to develop into a night of hot rumpy-pumpy (though we're spared the intimate details).

Data's first sentient months were difficult, as his neural net struggled to adapt. He considered shutting himself down, which Geordi equates to contemplating suicide.

Starfleet warp limits are again mentioned (see 'Force of Nature'). Dan Kwan's mother was Napian (a partially empathic race). He was having a relationship with medical ensign Calloway. He worked on the *Enterprise*'s construction at Utopia Planetia eight years ago (see 'Parallels').

Walter Pierce (whose maternal grandmother was a Betazoid) and Marla Finn, along with an unnamed male companion, were killed by a plasma discharge during the *Enterprise* construction (it was actually murder and suicide).

Deanna had empathy as a child (which flatly contradicts 'Tin Man'). Her grandfather used to tell her stories empathically by the fire. Picard has never had a suicide under his command before.

170: 'Genesis'

US Transmission: 19 March 1994
UK Transmission: 11 December 1994
Writer: Brannon Braga
Director: Gates McFadden
Cast: Carlos Ferro, Majel Barrett

Data and Picard return from a three-day photon torpedo hunt to find that things have rather degenerated in their absence. The *Enterprise* crew have 'de-evolved', and Data must try to find a solution. Not only is Picard affected by the regressive virus, he must escape the attentions of the armoured killer that was once Worf.

Stardate: 47653.2

Old Life Forms: Riker has become an australopithicene, Deanna an aquatic creature, Spot an iguana, Barclay a spider, and Worf develops a poisonous spit before turning into a prickly, armoured *Alien* reject. Picard seems to be turning into a lemur.

Technobabble: Data says that Deanna's DNA is in a state of ribosiatic flux.

Riker's Conquests: Riker has been getting amorous with Rebecca Smith, the new tactical officer, in the arboretum. He ended up impaled on a Sypherian cactus.

Notes: 'Captain, I believe the crew is de-evolving.' A charming scene in the medicentre leads into a gripping story containing some genuinely shocking moments. Like any horror film the premise is ultimately rather silly, but if you're in the right mood this is a most enjoyable romp. Worf's pyjamas are hysterical.

Barclay's hypochondria leads him to think he is suffering from Terellium death syndrome or Symbeline blood burn. In fact he has Yridian 'flu. The synthetic T cell used to treat Barclay produces an intron virus: the condition will forever more be known as Barclay's Protomorphosis Syndrome.

Alysa and Spot are both pregnant. Data doesn't know who Spot mated with: she has escaped from his quarters on various occasions, and Data intends to find out which of the twelve male cats on board did the dirty deed via a DNA test when the kittens are born. Spot gets on with Barclay but is hostile towards other crew members (see 'Timescape').

The *Enterprise* weapons and tactical systems are being upgraded (the photon torpedo targeting has been improved and the explosive yield has increased by eleven per cent). Picard describes himself as a 'reasonably qualified' shuttle pilot (see 'In Theory').

Troi eats Unzillan caviare.

171: 'Journey's End'

US Transmission: 26 March 1994
UK Transmission: 17 December 1994
Writer: Ronald D. Moore
Director: Corey Allen
Cast: Tom Jackson, Natalija Nogulish, Neo Romero,
George Aguilar, Richard Poe, Eric Menyuk, Doug Wert

The *Enterprise* is asked to move a colony of native Americans that is now on the wrong side of the Cardassian border, but the settlers are well-established and refuse to leave. Wesley Crusher returns from Starfleet Academy, where he is doing badly, and arrogantly offends his mother and many of his friends. Wesley seeks answers to his deep questions in the rituals of the American aboriginals, and finds that he can pull himself out of time. The Traveler will accompany him on a fantastic journey: this, and not Starfleet, is his true destiny. Picard, mindful of an ancestor's role in the subjugation of the 'Indians', is shocked when the dispute almost leads to a renewal of Federation/Cardassian hostilities. However, a compromise solution is reached, with the native Americans allowed to stay where they are as long as they accept Cardassian rule.

Stardate: 47751.2

Strange New Worlds: Dorvan 5, on the Cardassian side of the DMZ. A number of North American aboriginals have established a village in a small valley on the southern continent. They have been there for about twenty years. Their ancestors left Earth two hundred years ago in order to conserve their cultural identity.

Future History: New Mexico still exists in some form in the 24th century.

Notes: 'You have wiped clean a very old stain of blood.' *Next*

Gen bids goodbye to Wesley – now thankfully not going to end up as a Starfleet fascist – and grapples bravely with the guilty American psyche. Where the original series looked aghast at Vietnam, 'Journey's End' remembers with sorrow the attempted genocide carried out against the native Americans.

Picard has a meeting at Starbase 310 with Fleet Admiral Nechayev (see 'Chain of Command', 'Descent') regarding Wesley. There is a 'certain amount of tension' between Picard and Nechayev. Picard's father strongly believed in passing on family history, and his family's roots in Western Europe go back to the time of Charlemagne. One of Picard's ancestors, Alvarez Marebona Picard, was involved in the bloody Spanish reprisals after the Indian uprising in New Mexico in 1680. (This was more than 700 years – or 23 generations – ago.)

The Traveler from Tau Ceti can control warp fields with his mind (see 'Where No One Has Gone Before'). He told Picard that Wesley was very important 'like Mozart', destined for something quite different 'from the rest of us'. Wesley will travel to a new plane of existence which few humans have experienced.

A Cochran is a measurement of warp-field stress (see 'New Ground' and the original series episode 'Metamorphosis').

172: 'Firstborn'

US Transmission: 2 April 1994
UK Transmission: 24 December 1994
Writers: René Echevarria,
from a story by Mark Kalbfeld
Director: Jonathan West
Cast: James Sloyan, Brian Bonsall, Gwynyth Walsh,
Barbara March, Joel Sweton, Colin Mitchell, Michael Danek,
John Kenton Shull, Ricky D'Shon Collins, Majel Barrett

Worf, already discouraged by Alexander's lack of interest in becoming a warrior, is further aggrieved when an adviser to the house of Mogh challenges Worf's competence to be his father. A weapon that implicates the Duras family bears an anachronistic family crest, leading the adviser to admit that he is Alexander. He has travelled back in time to change his past: Worf will be killed on the floor of the great council chamber because Alexander was too weak to protect him. Instead of becoming a warrior Alexander became a diplomat and decided that the house of Mogh would be the first to end the feuding. However, young Alexander is left to make up his own mind on who he wants to be.

Stardate: 47779.4

Strange New Worlds: Picard is going to visit the ancient ruins of the Hatarian system. A magnesite deposit (see the original series episode 'Friday's Child') in the Kolus system belongs to the Pakleds (see 'Samaritan Snare'). The magnesite has been sold on to a Yridian trader in the Ufandi system.

The Alexander from the future says that he met a man in the Kember system who gave him the ability to travel in time.

New Life Forms: The *Enterprise* is holding its position until its rendezvous with the Kiersars.

Dialogue Triumphs: Quark on the Duras sisters: 'Big talk, small tips.'

Notes: 'Mother always said that I didn't have to do any of this Klingon stuff if I didn't want to.' Depending on your viewpoint, this is either preposterous nonsense or a hearty final *Next Generation* look at the Klingons. The time-travelling plot is a bit suspect, as is the brief use made of the Duras sisters, but the story cleverly subverts expectations regarding Worf's reactions and attitudes to his son.

Worf believes that it is time for Alexander to prepare for the first Rite of Ascension (the second one involves the painstiks: see 'The Icarus Factor'). The tests for this cover fighting skills and knowledge of the teaching of Kahless. Kor T'vo candles represent the fires that burn within the heart of a warrior: lighting one declares willingness to become a warrior. This ceremony must take place before the age of thirteen or a Klingon cannot truly become a warrior. The Festival of Kote B'vall is celebrated on the Klingon outpost on Maranga 4. It involves a reconstruction of the twelve-day fight between Kahless and the tyrant Molor, which was apparently Kahless teaching Molor a lesson for telling a lie. (There appears to be some confusion in this story between the tyrant Molor ('Rightful Heir') and Kahless' lying brother Morath ('New Ground').) Y'nara Kor is the Klingon procedure regarding an unfit parent. There is a Klingon training academy at Ogat.

Alexander was three years old when his mother died (which doesn't tie in with the timescale of 'The Emissary', 'Reunion', and 'New Ground'). Worf's brother has no male heir. His house has a very clean lake. Alexander has never been to the Klingon Homeworld. The Duras sisters were seen on Deep Space 9 trying to sell belitrium explosives 'months ago' (see *Deep Space Nine*'s 'Past Prologue').

According to Quark, Riker is the only man to win triple Dabo on one of his tables. Quark didn't have enough latinum (twelve bars) to cover his winnings, and so he issued Riker with some vouchers – which are only redeemable at Quark's!

Stellar Dynamics are studying the Vodree Nebula.

173: 'Bloodlines'

US Transmission: 9 April 1994
UK Transmission: 1 January 1995
Writer: Nicholas Sagan
Director: Les Landau
Cast: Ken Olandt, Lee Arenberg, Peter Slutsker, Amy Pietz, Michelan Sisti, Majel Barrett

DaiMon Bok appears on the *Enterprise*, claiming that Picard has a son. The Ferengi's murderous intentions are clear, and the young man – Jason Vigo – is swiftly rescued. DNA tests prove the seemingly unthinkable: Vigo is Picard's child. However, Vigo's genetic disorder eventually convinces Crusher that his DNA has been altered by Bok, and the Ferengi's schemes are exposed.

Stardate: 47829.1 (six years after 'The Battle').

Strange New Worlds: Vigo was born on New Gaul (cf. the New France Colony mentioned in *DS9*'s 'The Forsaken'). Kaymore 5 is an inhospitable planet with agriculture only possible on the southern continent.

Picard Manoeuvre: When talking to his 'son' and during other moments of embarrassment.

Dialogue Triumphs: Picard to Jason: 'Like it or not, I'm your father. I don't know what that means . . . One thing is clear: you'll never look at your hairline again in the same way.'

Notes: Although covering the same old ground as 'The Battle', Picard's reaction to his 'son' is wonderful to behold.

Picard met Miranda Vigo, a botanist, through a friend when on shore leave about 25 years ago. The following fortnight was 'romantic' and 'intense'. They kept in touch for a while but never met again. Jason Vigo and Miranda left Earth twelve years ago and settled on Kaymore 5, Miranda working with children orphaned in the Cardassian war. She died at the hands of thieves some years later. Jason is now 23 years old, and has a lengthy criminal record: three charges of petty theft, two for disorderly conduct, 'several dozen' for trespassing (indulging his passion for caving). Picard calls himself a 'not inexperienced' climber. Vigo is said to suffer from Forrester Trent syndrome, a degenerative and very rare neurological disorder that if left untreated will cause paralysis or death. Although hereditary, Jason's condition is the result of having his DNA re-sequenced by Bok.

Bok bought his freedom from Rog prison two years ago, and was last seen in the Doryas cluster (which contains over twenty solar systems). Once again, Bok's plan is exposed and his underlings conclude 'There is no profit in this for us.'

Picard has some archeological fragments (a Sylvan glyphstone, a Gorlan prayer stick) which he received in exchange for Saurian brandy.

174: 'Emergence'

US Transmission: 16 April 1994
UK Transmission: 8 January 1995
Writers: Joe Menosky,
from a story by Brannon Braga
Director: Cliff Bole
Cast: David Huddleston, Vinny Argiro, Thomas Kopache,
Arlee Reed

Having encountered a magnascopic storm, the *Enterprise* systems begin to play very strange tricks on the crew. The holodeck jumbles up many of its programs into a single one. Data, Worf and Riker enter the holodeck and are informed by various characters that the destination of the train on which they find themselves is 'Keystone City'. It transpires that the *Enterprise* is using virtiform particles, a side-effect of the storm, to create a new life form. Having succeeded, the emergent being leaves the ship.

Stardate: 47869.2

Strange New Worlds: Tambor Beta 6, a white dwarf star. The McPherson nebula, a supernova remnant. Dylcon Alpha, a class 9 pulsar.

New Life Forms: With the aid of virtiform particles, a neural matrix of 'nodes' created by a magnascopic storm is in the process of forming an elementary neural net. The new life form is variously described as a 'thing' and an 'object'.

Technobabble: Virtiform particles are emitted by white dwarf stars and are extremely rare. By exploding a photon torpedo into a pulsar, Geordi 'manufactures' them.

Dialogue Triumphs: 'I was right. He was trying to make off with my brick!'

Notes: 'The ship was protecting itself again.' Scientifically ludicrous! The holodeck scenes are amusing (though frequently unintelligible).

Data's initial holodeck sequence is Prospero's soliloquy from *The Tempest* (Act VI). Once the ship takes over, at least seven distinct holodeck programs are merged, including Beverly's Orient Express simulation, what seem to be one of Alexander's Westerns and a Dixon Hill story, and one involving an android.

175: 'Preemptive Strike'

US Transmission: 23 April 1994
UK Transmission: 15 January 1995
Writer: René Echevarria,
from a story by Naren Shankar
Director: Patrick Stewart
Cast: John Franklyn-Robbins, Natalia Nogulich,
William Thomas jr, Shannon Cochrane, Richard Poe

Further Maquis attacks on Cardassian ships in the demilitarised zone lead Admiral Necheyev to ask Picard for one of his crew to go undercover. Ro Laren, recently returned from tactical training school, is chosen, and she travels into the Cardassian sector to Onaga, a Maquis stronghold. Although her loyalty to Picard is strong, Ro is drawn into the Maquis' aims and, rather than lead them into a trap, betrays the Federation, joining the outlaws.

Stardate: 47941.4

Strange New Worlds: Onara, a Maquis stronghold.

New Life Forms: Cardassians are believed to possess biogenic weapons (cf. 'Chain of Command'). The Pakled, Ferengi and Yridians are all mentioned as dealing in the demilitarised zone.

Faraiga and Hasparat are Bajoran food-types (the latter is a spicy kind of stew). Bolarian canapés are said to be extremely fattening. The clarion is a Bajoran musical instrument (Ro's father played one).

Riker's Conquests: Slight evidence of a relationship with Ro (she calls him Will when defecting, instead of Commander).

Dialogue Triumphs: 'Even sympathy has to end at some point.'

'There are worse things a person can do than kill a Cardassian.'

Notes: 'I never thought we'd be firing on our own people to protect a Cardassian ship.' Really well set-up, continuing the themes from 'Journey's End' and the two-part Maquis *Deep Space Nine* storyline. Ro's return is welcome, although her Electra relationship with both Picard and Macias is signposted with a big white arrow. And Ro's defection to the Maquis seems inevitable: given her background, it's surprising she hasn't been leading them for years.

Ro has been studying tactical training for a year, and has been promoted to lieutenant. Picard notes that the course is very hard and that half the class 'washes out' every year. Deanna's promotion in 'Thine Own Self' is mentioned.

Armed Cardassian civilians in the demilitarised zone destroyed a Jouretan freighter a week ago (see 'The Best of Both Worlds'). Ro refers to her father's death and her imprisonment on Jaros II (see 'Ensign Ro').

176: 'All Good Things . . .'
90 Minutes
US Transmission: 30 April 1994

UK Transmission: 22 January 1995,
29 January 1995 (in two parts)
Writers: Ronald D. Moore, Brannon Braga
Director: Winrich Kolbe
Cast: Andreas Katsulas, Clyde Kusatsu, Pamela Kosh,
Tim Kellener, Alison Brooks, Stephen Matthew Garvin,
Majel Barrett

Past, present and future collide for Picard as he finds himself
bouncing around through three different time zones: an alternative Farpoint mission, the present, and a future in which many
changes have affected *Enterprise* crew. A spatial anomaly,
present in two of the time zones, baffles Picard, whilst in the
future, an aged Picard gathers his crew together one last time to
try and find the source. Meanwhile, in the past, Picard finds
himself back in Q's court once again on trial for humanity. Although as annoyingly playful as ever, Q tells Picard that the
captain will be responsible for the destruction of humanity and
continues to give him clues as Picard stumbles back and forth
in time. Eventually, Picard guesses that the *Enterprise* of the
future is causing the spatial anomaly and all three *Enterprises*
join forces to mend the rift in time. Q tells Picard that he has
succeeded and Picard finds himself back in the present. He joins
his officers in a game of poker and tells them that the sky is the
limit.

Stardate: 47988. And 41153 (seven years before in an alternative timeline). And over 25 years into the future.

Strange New Worlds: The Devron system near the Neutral
Zone.

Technobabble: 'A multi-phasic temporal convergence in the
spatial continuum.' 'In English, Data?' ' . . . An eruption of anti-
time!'

Poker Game: Beverly, Riker, Data, Geordi and Worf play. Riker
wins (as usual) and says he cheats. Deanna joins them, as does

Picard, who used to be a good card player. 'I should have done this a long time ago.' 'You were always welcome.'

Picard Manoeuvre: Yes. In all three time zones.

Riker's Conquests: He totally fails to hustle Deanna into a dinner date, losing out to Worf.

Dialogue Triumphs: 'That was an incredible program!'

Q's summing up the series: 'Seven years ago I said we'd be watching you and we have been, hoping that your ape-like race would demonstrate some growth . . . What have we seen instead? You, worrying about Commander Riker's career! Listening to Counselor Troi's pathetic psychobabble! Indulging Data in his witless exploration of humanity!'

Notes: 'It's time to put an end to your trek through the stars!' A complicated script, acted beautifully. The final scene, which could (in lesser hands) have been truly dreadful, is sweet and charming. The use of Q as a viewer-substitute brings the series full circle – together with the stunning recreation of the 'Encounter at Farpoint' era (including Troi's haircut and mini-skirt). Epic themes mix with friendship and the effect of time on relationships.

Worf takes Deanna on a holodeck beachwalk near the Black Sea ('very stimulating'). Deanna thinks he will love Lake Kataria on Betazed.

In the alternative past, it is confirmed that O'Brien was an initial member of the crew. He spent his childhood making models of Starfleet engines. Deanna says she and Will had a 'prior relationship several years ago' (cf. 'Encounter at Farpoint', 'Second Chances', 'Violations', and most of the first season).

Peredoxin is a drug used to treat Irumodic syndrome (though it is not a cure). Alyssa Ogawa is pregnant during the episode (see 'Genesis') but loses the baby due to the time distortion.

In the future timeline, Geordi has (synthetic?) eyes. He is married to Leah Brahms (who has just been made director of the Daystrom Institute). They have three children (Brett, Alandra and Sydney), and are living on Rigel 3 where Geordi is a novelist. Picard has retired, having been a Federation ambassador. He has advanced Irumodic syndrome, a neurological disorder, and is living in the family vineyard in France. He married Beverly, they later divorced.

Data holds the Lucasian Chair at Cambridge University, living in Issac Newton's old house. He has streaked his hair grey (to appear 'distinguished'!) and still keeps (several) pet cats. Riker is an admiral stationed at Starbase 247. The *Enterprise* is his flagship. Deanna is dead (in unrevealed circumstances). Riker and Worf have barely spoken since the funeral. Worf was a member of the Klingon council and is now the governor of the colony of Hatoria. Beverly Picard (she kept her married name) is captain of the science vessel *Pasteur*.

There is no Neutral Zone, the Klingons having taken over the Romulan empire and closed the borders to all Federation ships. There has recently been an outbreak of Terrelian plague on Romulus. Federation ships now have cloaking devices (see 'The Pegasus'). Warp 13 seems to be an acceptable speed (see 'Force of Nature').

Deep Space Nine
First Season

18 45-minute and one 90-minute episodes

Created by Rick Berman, Michael Piller,
based on *Star Trek*, created by Gene Roddenberry

Executive Producers: Rick Berman, Michael Piller
Producer: Peter Lauritson **Co-Producer:** Peter Allan Fields
(2–19) **Associate Producer:** Steve Oster
Supervising Producers: Ira Steven Behr (2–19),
David Livingston **Line Producer:** Robert della Santina
(10, 13, 19)

Regular Cast: Avery Brooks (Commander Sisko), Rene Auberjonois (Odo), Siddig el Fadil (Dr Bashir), Terry Farrell (Lt Dax), Cirroc Lofton (Jake Sisko), Colm Meaney (Chief O'Brien), Armin Shimerman (Quark), Nana Visitor (Major Kira) Aron Eisenberg (Nog, 1, 3, 10, 13-14), Max Grodénchik (Rom, 1[1], 3, 6, 10-11), Andrew Robinson (Garak, 2), Marc Alaimo (Gul Dukat, 1, 18), Rosalind Chao (Keiko O'Brien, 3, 15, 19), Hana Hatae (Molly O'Brien, 3, 15), Patrick Stewart (Captain Jean-Luc Picard, 1), Majel Barrett (Lwaxana Troi, 16)

[1] Listed in the on-screen credits as 'Ferengi Pit Boss' for this episode.

1: 'Emissary'

90 Minutes
US Transmission: 2 January 1993
UK Transmission: 15 August 1993, 22 August 1993[1]
Writers: Michael Piller, from a story by Rick Berman,
Michael Piller
Director: David Carson
Cast: Camille Saviola, Felecia M. Bell, Joel Swetow,
Stephen Davies, Steve Rankin, Lily Mariye, Cassandra
Byram, John Noah Hertzler, April Grace, Keven McDermott,
Parker Whitman, William Powell-Blair, Frank Owen Smith,
Lynnda Ferguson, Megan Butler, Stehen Rowe, Thomas
Hobson, Donald Hotton, Gene Armor, Diana Cignoni, Judi
Durand, Majel Barrett

Benjamin Sisko is assigned to a former Cardassian space station in orbit around Bajor, an outpost that suddenly gains in importance when a stable wormhole that leads the unimaginably distant Gamma Quadrant is discovered nearby. After a meeting with the Kai, the Bajoran spiritual leader, Sisko travels into the wormhole, and encounters within a mysterious alien consciousness. The Cardassians become interested in the wormhole, but O'Brien is able to move the entire station to the vicinity of the phenomenon. When a Cardassian ship disappears into the wormhole DS9 comes under threat from the former rulers of Bajor – until Sisko returns in the runabout, dragging the Cardassian vessel safely behind it. DS9 will remain in the area, observing the vessels that pass through the wormhole to the Gamma Quadrant, with a once reluctant Sisko now happy to be its commander.

---

[1]'Emissary' was originally made as a 90-minute TV movie, and was split into two 45-minute episodes only for subsequent US (and all UK) showings. (It appears in the former format on video.)

Stardate: 46379.1 (the station log commences on 46388.2).

Strange New Worlds: The closest system to the other end of the wormhole is Idran (less than five light years away). It is a trinary system consisting of twin O-type companions and no class-M planets. Analysis was conducted in the 22nd century by the Quadros-1 probe which explored the gamma quadrant. Idran is 70,000 light years from Bajor.

Within the constructed wormhole there is (or appears to be) a planet with an atmosphere.

New Life Forms: The non-corporeal entities who built the wormhole. They have no concept of linear time.

Introducing: The Ferengi boy Nog, the only person close to Jake's age on the station.

Gul Dukat, station prefect before the Cardassian withdrawal from Bajor.

Picard Manoeuvre: When he talks to Sisko and becomes aware that Sisko encountered Locutus.

Bashir's (Failed?) Conquests: Dax, of course. He doesn't mind the fact that she's got this slug-thing inside her.

Quark's Bar: The main game is Dabo, a roulette-type affair operated by scantily clad and often alien females. (When one wins – which is rare in Quark's – one shouts 'Dabo!')

Dialogue Triumphs: Odo on Quark becoming community leader: 'You have all the character references of a politician.'

Quark: 'I love the Bajorans. Such a deeply spiritual culture, but they make a dreadful ale.'

Kira to Bashir: 'You can make yourself useful by bringing your Federation medicine to the "natives". Oh, you'll find them a friendly, simple folk.'

Sisko to the aliens: 'It is the unknown that defines our existence.'

Sisko, after the aliens have shown him that he is still traumatised by Jennifer's death: 'I never left the ship. I exist here.'

Quark on Kira: 'Oh, I love a woman in uniform.'

Notes: 'Ironic – one who does not wish to be among us is to be the emissary.' The most assured *Trek* debut yet and a flawless exercise in story-telling on a grand scale. Everything from the staggering opening sequence onwards is a delight. And it's lovely to have a decent theme tune at last.

The *Saratoga* was destroyed by the Borg on Stardate 43997 during the battle at Wolf 359 (see 'The Best of Both Worlds 2'). Its commanding officer was a Vulcan, its tactical officer was a Bolian. Lt Commander Benjamin Sisko and his son Jake were among the survivors; his wife, Jennifer, died. Sisko has spent the last three years working at the Utopia Planitia yards. Benjamin met Jennifer on Gilgo beach, soon after graduating from Starfleet Academy, and he proposed to her about fifteen years ago. His father was a gourmet chef with a famous recipe for aubergine stew. He was born on Earth.

The Cardassians occupied Bajor for 56 years, plundering the planet of its resources, but withdrew around two weeks ago. Bajor itself is no longer self-sufficient, and the political situation has become chaotic in the absence of a single unifying foe. Only Kai Opaka – the Bajoran spiritual leader – pulls the Bajorans together. In Bajoran belief the spiritual life force is known as the pagh. Nine orbs – the Tears of the Prophets – have appeared in the sky over Bajor during the past 10,000 years. The orbs have shaped their theology, giving rise to a belief in the Celestial Temple (the 'world' inside the wormhole) and the prophets (the creatures inside the wormhole, who constructed it). Monks have been studying the orbs ever since the first appeared, but now all but one have been taken by the Cardassians (see, however, 'The Storyteller', 'The Circle'). The DS9 end of the wormhole is located within the Denorios Belt (a charged plasma field). In the 22nd century a ship carrying Kai Taluno was disabled for several days within the Denorios Belt, and five orbs were found there. There are also 23 reports of unusual neutrino disturbances within the belt.

The provisional Bajoran government have requested Starfleet's presence in the area. The Cardassians half-wrecked DS9 on their departure, killing four Bajorans who tried to protect their shops. The first contingent of Starfleet personnel, including Miles O'Brien, arrived two days previously to begin repairs. The *Enterprise* departs on Stardate 46390.1 for the Lapola system after off-loading three runabouts (the *Rio Grande*, the *Yangtzee*, and one named in the next story), and returns on Stardate 46393.1, placing these events between 'Chain of Command' and 'Ship in a Bottle'.

Miles O'Brien's favourite *Enterprise* transporter room was number three. Keiko O'Brien's mother lives in Kumomoto in Japan (see 'Dax'). Miles mentions the Setlik massacre during the Border Wars (see 'The Wounded'). Kira, the Bajoran government attaché, has been fighting for Bajoran independence 'since I was old enough to pick up a phaser', and has spent time in a refugee camp. Jadzia Daxis the station's Trill science officer. Her symbiont is about three hundred years old, the host about 28 (this age is confirmed in 'Dax'). The previous host was Curzon, who Sisko knew as an old man. Dr Julian Bashir is the 27-year-old medical officer, and had the pick of any job in Starfleet. Odo is the mysterious shape-shifting security officer. He was found in the Denorios Belt and was raised amongst humans, whom he can just about mimic. He has no idea as to his origins, and serves as DS9's 'constable' (later stories make it clear that this is a nickname rather than a true rank). He does not allow weapons on the Promenade. The Ferengi Quark owns a bar on the Promenade. It seems that he's been on the station for about four years (cf. 'Profit and Loss').

2: 'Past Prologue'

US Transmission: 9 January 1993
UK Transmission: 29 August 1993

Writer: Kathryn Powers
Director: Winrich Kolbe
Cast: Jeffrey Nordling, Gwynyth Walsh, Barbara March,
Susan Bay, Vaughn Armstrong, Richard Ryder

The terrorist Tahna Los is pursued into Bajoran space by the
Cardassians, and is beamed aboard DS9. There the Bajoran,
known to Kira, requests asylum, but the Cardassians demand
his return. The provisional government have their own interest
in the man, believing him to be a member of the banned Kohn-
ma group. The unexpected appearance of the Duras sisters on
DS9 indicates that perhaps his days of terrorism are not at an
end, as he has claimed. Kira discovers and then foils Tahna's
plan to destroy the wormhole with material bought from the
Duras sisters, which he hoped would lead to both the
Cardassians and the Federation losing interest in Bajor.

Stardate: Not stated[1].

Strange New Worlds: There are six colonies on Bajor 8.

New Life Forms: Apparently the Joranian ostrich hides by stick-
ing its head underwater, sometimes until it drowns.

Introducing: Garak, 'plain, simple' Cardassian tailor. Julian
thinks (probably correctly) that he must still have contacts within
Cardassian high command.

Technology: A cylinder of bilitrium is to be delivered by the
Duras sisters to Tahna on the dark side of Bajor 8's lower moon.
Bilitrium is a rare crystalline element that can be an incredible
source of energy if linked to an anti-matter convertor. (Tahna
stole one from the Cardassians.)

---

[1]Many *Deep Space Nine* episodes do not feature a Stardate. The Stardates
featured on the video covers cannot be considered canonical.

Notes: 'My name is Tahna Los. Request political asylum.' Another good terrorism story (cf. *TNG*'s 'The High Ground'), with the regular characters quickly finding their feet.

The Kohn-ma are a Bajoran terrorist group who assassinated a Bajoran First Minister a month ago. Sisko's current superior in Starfleet is Admiral Rollman. He mentions the Duras sisters' involvement in the events of 'Redemption', and says that they are in desperate need of funds. The third runabout is named as the *Ganges* (the full title of the second being *Yangtzee Kiang*).

Bashir drinks Tarkalean tea. Kira still has nightmares about the raids on the Haru Outpost. The currency gold-pressed latinum is mentioned by the sisters and Garak.

3: 'A Man Alone'

US Transmission: 16 January 1993
UK Transmission: 5 September 1993
Writers: Michael Piller,
from a story by Gerald Sanford, Michael Piller
Director: Paul Lynch
Cast: Edward Lawrence Albert, Peter Vogt,
Stephen James Carver, Tom Klunis, Scott Trost, Patrick
Cupo, Kathryn Graf, Diana Cignori, Judi Durand

Odo orders Ibudan, a Bajoran former black marketeer, to leave the station, but the man is later found dead in one of Quark's holosuites. It seems that Odo is the only person who could have committed the murder, and suspicion turns to outright hostility when an ugly mob demands swift justice against the shapeshifter, who they also accuse of collaborating with the Cardassians. Bashir, however, discovers that the corpse is a clone of Ibudan, and that Odo has been framed.

Stardate: 46421.5 (towards the end of the story: Ibudan's personal logs give the date – incorrectly – as 46385).

New Life Forms: Nog has a box of Garanarian bolites, which cause itching and skin colour change in humans.

Curzon and a young Sisko attended the Rujian steeplechase with a pair of 'gorgeous' seven-foot-tall Rujian twin sisters.

Trills have cold hands.

Introducing: Quark's brother Rom, father of Nog. (Rom is glimpsed in the first story, but is only named here.)

Bashir's (Failed) Conquests: Dax again. He tries to impress her by playing an Altonian Brain Teaser (which responds to neuro-theta waves) which she's been trying to master for about 140 years. He's hopeless at it.

Quark's Bar: Quark has found Bashir a dry champagne from Koris 1.

Dialogue Triumphs: Odo on marriage: 'You want to watch the Karo-Net tournament, she wants to listen to music, so you compromise: you listen to music. You like Earth Jazz, she prefers Klingon opera, so you compromise: you listen to Klingon opera. So here you were ready to have a nice night watching the Karo-Net match and you wind up spending an agonizing evening listening to Klingon opera.'

Notes: A good, unpretentious tale, although the sequence with the bolites is best ignored.

Ibudan used to run black market goods through the station. Odo was involved in his imprisonment for the murder of a Cardassian. He was held at Kran-Tobal prison, and returned to the station from Alderaan spaceport.

Odo refers to himself as a shape-shifter for the first time. He has to return to his natural state every 18 hours to regenerate. He stays in a pail at the back of his office. Odo has never, as Quark so delicately puts it, 'coupled'. Dax likes steamed azna. Benjamin thinks that Jadzia is probably the sixth host (see 'Equilibrium'). Curzon Dax regularly beat Benjamin at barefist Juro counter-punch. Sisko's father used to try out his new recipes on the children.

Keiko is a botanist. Molly is about three years old.'
Not surprisingly there is little water in the Yadozi desert.

4: 'Babel'

US Transmission: 23 January 1993
UK Transmission: 12 September 1993
Writers: Michael McGreevey, Naren Shankar,
from a story by Sally Caves, Ira Steven Behr
Director: Paul Lynch
Cast: Jack Kehler, Matthew Faison, Ann Gillespie,
Geraldine Farrell, Bo Zenga, Kathleen Wirt, Lee Brooks,
Richard Ryder, Frank Novak, Todd Feder

O'Brien, under great pressure to fix all of DS9's broken systems, begins to spout gibberish – and it's not just stress. Bashir concludes that for some reason O'Brien is suffering from aphasia – and then Kira comes down with the disease. A terrorist device, planted when the station was operated by the Cardassians, has infected the command level replicators with an ultimately deadly virus – and Quark has been secretly using these replicators in place of his own damaged ones. Bashir begins to work on a cure, and Kira discovers that the Bajoran creator of the virus, Dekon Elig, died in prison some years ago. The situation escalates when the virus mutates into an airborne equivalent, and Bashir comes down with the disease. Kira is forced to use desperate measures to ensure the cooperation of Dr Surmak Ren, the only man capable of curing the problem. Odo and Quark have to deal with the impatient freighter captain Jaheel, whose desire to leave the station threatens the station's safety.

Stardate: 46423.7

Strange New Worlds: Captain Jaheel has a shipment of Tamen Sahsheer for Largo 5. As an example of DS9's technical faults,

Kira says that she asked for the star chart for the Argosian Sector and one for the Glessene Sector came up instead.

New Life Forms: The aphasia-inducing virus randomly reroutes synaptic pathways. Ferengi and shape-shifters would seem to be immune or very resistant to it.

Technology: The device containing the genetically engineered virus has a standard diboridium core for a power source, which hints at Cardassian manufacture. However, the aphasia device was created by the Bajoran underground.

Quark's Bar: Replicator faults means Quark's serves some bad Kohlanese stew. Quark offers Dax and Kira a double-whipped l'danian spice pudding, and gains unauthorised access to a (working) replicator to produce a Ferengi stardrifter (a drink).

Dialogue Triumphs: Some inspired 'babelbabble', beginning with 'She's flowery units about the lad herself', and reaching such heights as 'Major lacks true pepper . . . Let birds go further loose maybe. Shout easy play . . . Round the turbulent quick!'

Odo, on Quark's claim that Rom fixed the replicator: 'Rom's an idiot. He couldn't fix a straw if it was bent.'

Quark, about to transport Odo: 'I must have watched the procedure hundreds of times.'

Notes: A marvellous story that builds to a gripping climax. There are some lovely scenes with Odo and Quark, especially at the end where they seem to be the only ones not affected by the virus. Look out for a sequence where we see an aphasiac's eye view of a computer screen.

DS9 is eighteen years old, and is said to have originally been a Cardassian mining station. Dekon Elig, a member of the Higa Metar sect of the Bajoran underground, created the virus. He died in the Velos 7 internment camp. The computer records on Dr Surmak Ren state that he graduated from the University of Bajor, is a member of the Akira Advanced Genetics Research

Unit, and is suspected of supporting the Kohn-Ma (see 'Past Prologue'). He is now chief administrator of the Ilvian Medical Complex in the north-eastern district. Ren also mentions the Gran Tobal prison.

Dax hasn't been a female for over eighty years (see 'Equilibrium'). Quark served on a Ferengi freighter for eight years.

5: 'Captive Pursuit'

US Transmission: 30 January 1993
UK Transmission: 19 September 1993
Writers: Jill Sherman Donner, Michael Piller,
from a story by Jill Sherman Donner
Director: Corey Allen
Cast: Gerrit Graham, Scott MacDonald, Kelly Curtis

The first creature from the Gamma Quadrant comes through the wormhole – and he's on the run. O'Brien tries to befriend the alien, who only answers to the name Tosk, and sets about repairing his ship, which seems to have been hit by some sort of weapon. Tosk refuses to discuss who attacked his craft, but is caught tampering with the security system by Odo. Another ship comes through the wormhole, its occupants managing to teleport on to the Promenade in search of Tosk. They capture the creature in disgrace, saying that the hunt is over. Sisko tries to argue against the aliens' desire to hunt, but is informed that Tosk are created purely for that purpose. O'Brien, less accepting of the Prime Directive than Sisko, wants at least to allow his friend the possibility of an honourable death, and engineers his escape. The hunters leave the station in pursuit – and O'Brien is reprimanded by Sisko.

Stardate: Not stated.

New Life Forms: Tosk, the reptilian humanoid (who can become invisible and thus may have some sort of personal cloaking device). He requires only seventeen minutes of sleep 'per rotation' and can store liquid within his body. Tosk – a general name for the hunted creatures rather than a personal name – take an oath of silence not to talk about the hunt. The greatest humiliation for a Tosk is to be captured alive and then put on show as an example to others. They are only sentient because the hunters made them so.

The hunters' craft emits a type of radiation that disables DS9's shields, and have some sort of transporter technology. The hunters wear helmets that render Tosk visible, and their arm shields can absorb phaser fire. Underneath, they share certain physical characteristics with the Tosk.

Technology: Tosk's ship utilises coladrium flow for power, which O'Brien has never heard of before. The ship captures space matter which it converts into fuel.

The Cardassians made the station conduits from two metre thick duranium composite. O'Brien has never seen a scanning device that can penetrate this, but the hunters' can.

Quark's Bar: Quark's contracts for the Dabo girls contain a clause legitimising sexual contact between the proprietor and the girl.

Notes: A powerful fox-hunting allegory with some good action scenes to boot.

In this story it is stated that Bajor is 90,000 light years from the Gamma Quadrant (cf. 'Emissary'). On average five or six ships a week pass through the wormhole: Tosk is the first visitor from the other side. Although some cultures have an equivalent of fox-hunting, the use of a sentient being is unknown to Sisko.

Weapons are stored in the habitat ring of DS9 (level 5 section 3), and require security clearance seven and above for access. Odo never uses phasers (and, as first seen in 'Emissary', he doesn't allow them on the Promenade).

6: 'Q-Less'

US Transmission: 6 February 1993
UK Transmission: 26 September 1993
Writers: Robert Hewitt Wolfe,
from a story by Hannah Louise Shearer
Director: Paul Lynch
Cast: Jennifer Hetrick, John de Lancie, Van Epperson,
Tom McCleister, Laura Cameron

Dax returns to DS9 in a runabout almost drained of power. On board is the archaeologist Vash, who has spent the last two years exploring the Gamma Quadrant, despite having never heard of the wormhole. Vash gets Quark to organise an auction for some of the treasures she has brought back with her, and O'Brien is shocked to see Q on the station. He warns Sisko, who is trying to deal with DS9's own power drains. Sisko accuses Q of pushing the station to the brink of destruction, but Q, although angry with Vash for wanting to leave him, says it's nothing to do with him. Dax finds a way of determining the source of the energy depletions – an embryonic creature in one of Vash's treasures. Released into space, DS9 is safe once more.

Stardate: 46531.2

Strange New Worlds: Q tries to tempt Vash into further travels by mentioning the Teletis cluster, the Lantar nebula, which includes Hoek 4 and its Sampalo relics, and the 'charming' Vadris 3. Q almost got Vash killed on Erriakang 7, and is known as the God of Lies on Brax.

New Life Forms: The embryonic 'egg' contains a ray-like space creature from the Gamma Quadrant.

Vash has booked passage on a Mulzirak transport. She says that some of the cultures in the Gamma Quadrant date back millions of years. The first lot in Vash's auction comes from the Verath system, where a civilisation reached its peak 30,000 years ago, spanning around 25 systems interconnected by a highly developed trade and communications network. The statue in question represents Drolock of the 19th dynasty.

Q mentions the Stardancers at Mandahla, and threatens Vash with an insect bite from Aramus Cri (the side-effects seem to include hair-loss).

Vash is very good at oo-mox (see 'Ménage à Troi').

Technobabble: As Q says, 'Picard and his lackeys would have solved all this technobabble hours ago.'

Bashir's (Failed?) Conquests: He seems to have a willing audience for his medical chat-up routine (see Notes), but is interrupted.

Quark's Bar: Makes a good couscous and serves some rather intoxicating Gamzain wine.

Dialogue Triumphs: O'Brien's assessment of Picard and Vash's relationship and the former's taste in women: 'The Captain likes a good challenge, sir.'

O'Brien sees Q: 'Bloody hell.'

Q to Sisko: 'You *hit* me. Picard never hit me.'

Q discusses Earth: 'An abysmal place . . . Don't get me wrong – a thousand years ago it had character: crusades, Spanish inquisition, Watergate. Now it's just mind-numbingly dull.'

Notes: The first of a number of clashes between the darkness of *Deep Space Nine* and the comparative brightness of *TNG*. Q works less well in this format and, although well-written, the episode isn't very engaging.

The assay office is said to be the safest place on DS9. Starfleet had a briefing on Q two years ago which Sisko attended. Tritrium is toxic when highly concentrated but Dax suggests using ionised tritrium gas to trace the source of the power loss.

Bashir is a salutatorian: he would have been a valedictorian if he hadn't mistaken a pre-ganglionic fibre for a post-ganglionic nerve during the Starfleet medical finals oral. (He claims it's a trick question.) Scientists at the Daystrom Institute on Earth, including Professor Woo, are especially anxious to hear of Vash's experiences in the Gamma Quadrant. On two occasions Vash's membership of the institute's archaeological council has been suspended for illegal sale of artefacts. She is also barred from the royal museum of Epsilon Hydra 7, persona non grata on Betazed, and wanted dead on Myrmidon for stealing the crown of the First Mother. Vash hasn't been to Earth for twelve years, and decides not to return there, deciding instead to go to Tartaras 5, where the ruins of a Rokai provincial capital have been uncovered.

Quark tries to tempt Odo with a suit of finest Andoran silk, a ring of pure sorax, a complete set of Tanesh pottery – and a latinum-plated bucket to sleep in. Quark's cousin is called Stol.

7: 'Dax'

US Transmission: 13 February 1993
UK Transmission: 3 October 1993
Writers: D.C. Fontana, Peter Allan Fields,
from a story by Peter Allan Fields
Director: David Carson
Cast: Gregory Itzin, Anne Haney, Richard Lineback,
Fionnula Flanagan

A group of aliens with a detailed knowledge of the station's security procedures unsuccessfully attempt to kidnap Dax, and then produce an arrest warrant for the Trill. She is wanted on Klaestron 4 to face charges of murder and treason, the alleged events having taken place when Curzon Dax was a mediator there. Curzon is accused of arranging an ambush to kill the general he was friends with. Sisko realises that although an extradition treaty exists between the Federation and Klaestron no such protocol is in place involving Bajor, and so he is able to defer matters to a Bajoran arbiter. However, Dax refuses to say anything in her defence, and Ilon Tandro, the general's son, is adamant that Jadzia Dax must answer for the crimes of Curzon Dax. Sisko tries hard to prove that Jadzia Dax and Curzon Dax are two entirely separate people, but the argument will be difficult to prove conclusively. Sisko sends Odo to Klaestron, who tracks down the widow of the general. She comes to Deep Space 9 to testify that Dax is innocent and, to her son's disgust, that Jadzia was silent only because she and Curzon had an affair.

Stardate: 46910.1

Strange New Worlds: Thirty years ago there was a civil war on Klaestron 4.

New Life Forms: The Klaestrons are allies of the Cardassians.

Some years ago an Argosian lieutenant threw a drink in Sisko's face (he still has a scar from Curzon Dax's ring-finger as the Trill tried to restrain him).

Quark's Bar: Serves Raktajino (Klingon coffee).

Notes: An interesting story, with its trial scenes faintly reminiscent of Data's in 'The Measure of a Man'.

Miles and Keiko have gone to Earth to celebrate Keiko's mother's hundredth birthday (so women would seem routinely to give birth at a very late age in the 24th century). Sisko has known Dax for twenty years. Curzon died two years ago: new host Jadzia is 28. The competition to become a host is intense as it is a great honour. Hosts tend to receive their symbionts in their mid-twenties. Ninety-three hours after the 'joining' process the symbiont and host are biologically interdependent (see, however, 'Invasive Procedures'). Jadzia Dax says that her blood type, metabolism and brain-wave patterns are very different from Curzon's. She has degrees in exobiology, zoology, astrophysics and exoarchaeology (premier distinction). Sisko describes Curzon Dax as being very interested in women and perhaps a little too fond of his drink.

Dax thinks that some of DS9's technology came from the Romulans.

8: 'The Passenger'

US Transmission: 20 February 1993
UK Transmission: 10 October 1993
Writers: Morgan Gendel, Robert Hewitt Wolfe,
Michael Piller, from a story by Morgan Gendel
Director: Paul Lynch
Cast: Caitlin Brown, James Lashly, Christopher Collins,
James Harper

Kira and Bashir come to the aid of a ship damaged by fire. Within is a Kobliad scientist who killed others to prolong his life and the security officer who hunted him for twenty years. The prisoner, Rao Vantika, tries to strangle Bashir, but he dies before he can be transported to DS9. The officer, Ty Kajada, is convinced that the man still lives. An autopsy shows that Vantika's corpse is quite lifeless, but the station computer is purged, and Quark is liaising with a man who could indeed be Vantika. Vantika has in fact survived the ship's destruction via a microscopic device under his nail that allowed his coded neural patterns to be transmitted into Bashir's brain, but the criminal's plan is soon exposed.

Stardate: Not stated.

Strange New Worlds: Rigel 7 had its computers purged by Rao Vantika.

New Life Forms: The Kobliad. They are a dying race of humanoids and need deuridium to stabilise their cell structure, prolonging their life span. The Federation has been supplying deuridium, but even the new deposits in the Gamma Quadrant aren't enough to service the entire population.

Bashir says that synaptic pattern displacement is unique to Vulcans.

Technology: Vantika used drugs and prisoners to extend his life (in some undefined way).

Technobabble: 'Confirm that each distribution amplifier is at one hundred per cent efficiency . . . And that won't mean a thing if the power wave guide outlets fail. Double check them.'

Quark's Bar: Also serves *iced* raktajino (see 'Dax').

Dialogue Triumphs: Bashir on tricorders: 'Very accurate with live people, not so accurate with dead ones.'

Bashir on himself: 'I just seem to have a talent, I suppose. A vision that sees past the obvious, round the mundane, right to the target. Fate has granted me a gift, Major – a gift to be a healer.'

Notes: A good Bashir story that just about keeps you guessing. And it's nice to see *Trek* using Iggy Pop song titles, too.

The first of two stories to feature Starfleet security officer Lieutenant George Primmin. Bashir's access code is 4121.

9: 'Move Along Home'

US Transmission: 13 March 1993
UK Transmission: 17 October 1993
Writers: Frederick Rappaport, Lisa Rich,
Jeanne Carrigan-Fauci, from a story by Michael Piller
Director: David Carson
Cast: Joel Brooks, James Lashly, Clara Bryant

A new race from the Gamma Quadrant come to DS9 – and head straight for Quark's. When the Wadi are cheated they ask Quark to play a game of their own, involving four counters on various levels. Meanwhile, Sisko, Dax, Kira and Bashir awake in a strange and ever-changing environment, their lives seemingly in danger. When Quark is told of the missing officers he begins to suspect a correlation between the game he is playing and the fate of the others – and is horrified when asked to sacrifice a counter. When he has lost the Wadi are happy to depart: the whole game was just an illusion.

Stardate: Not stated.

New Life Forms: The Wadi, first encountered three weeks ago in the Gamma Quadrant. They like playing games, and try to impress Quark with some klon paegs (sticks) and alpha-currant nectar (a 'priceless' juice). (Thankfully they have a load of gems, too.)

Their (semi-real-life) game is called chula, a combination of three-dimensional chess with dice and *The Crystal Maze*. A girl called Chandra appears in the second shap (level), a skipping game. The third shap involves choking smoke and a drink antidote. The fourth features the lights that 'kill' Bashir; the fifth (thialo) requires a sacrifice so that the two other players may live (and indeed take a short-cut to the last move). Shap six, an earthquake, is as far as we see.

Quark's Bar: Sisko eats Ferengi lokar beans at Quark's. Andolian brandy is also available at Quark's (especially if the staff have just been caught cheating).

Notes: An excellent and intriguing episode which cleverly uses its surrealism to present a very alien culture. Apparently there are some people out there, just released back into the community, who think this is the worst episode of the season.

Baggy clothing is fashionable again on Bajor. Captain B. McCullough is the author of *First Contact Procedures for Starfleet* (revised edition).

10: 'The Nagus'

US Transmission: 20 March 1993
UK Transmission: 24 October 1993
Writers: Ira Steven Behr,
from a story by David Livingston
Director: David Livingston
Cast: Lou Wagner, Barry Gordon, Lee Arenberg, Tiny Ron,

Wallace Shawn

A Ferengi conference on the Gamma Quadrant, attended by the business leader Grand Nagus Zek, takes place at Quark's. The Nagus informs the assembly that Quark is to be the next Grand Nagus, a decision greeted with outrage, particularly from Zek's son Krax. Almost immediately Quark is threatened and pressurized by his fellow Ferengi, and when Zek dies Grand Nagus Quark makes Rom his body-guard. However, Rom and Krax are about to murder Quark when Zek returns: he only feigned death to test his son and, as he expected, he's not handled the situation at all well. Quark is pleased to emerge from the affair with his life, and will ensure that his brother never forgets this particular act of betrayal.

Stardate: Not stated.

Strange New Worlds: Tarahong, a planet whose people Quark calls 'incredibly gullible'. It is stated that Quark betrayed his cousin Barbo to the authorities there after selling them defective warp drives (see the Sixth Rule of Acquisition). Barbo has recently been released from a detention centre on Tarahong. There are cargo ports on Volchok Prime and Arcybite mining refineries in the Clarus system. The soothing harmonies of the tides on Balosnee 6 can cause hallucinations. Krax and Rom claim that the Nagus had started trading talks with Stakoron 2 in the Gamma Quadrant regarding its rich deposits of mizainite ore, but this was part of a ruse to kill Quark. The Gratitude Festival is Bajor's biggest holiday. Jake wants to visit the fire caverns there.

New Life Forms: An Andorian freighter is due in for a maintenance check with a shipment of anti-grav tractors. 'Tiny-eared' is a Ferengi insult, and infection of the timpanic membrane can be a chronic condition for Ferengi. When notable Ferengi – such as the Grand Nagus – die, the body is automatically vacuum-sealed, desiccated and sold in glass containers as 'prize collectables'. Grand Nagus Zek describes Rizean females as 'voluptuous'. Maihar'du, Zek's servant, is a Hupyrian, and like all Hupyrians he is devoted to his master.

Technology: Ferengi locator bombs home in on a victim's pheremones.

Technobabble: 'Sorry I'm late, but the transporter in Ops needed a minor adjustment in its upper molecule-imaging scanner.'

Ferengi Rules of Acquisition: First Rule: Once you have their money you never give it back.

Sixth Rule: Never allow family to stand in the way of opportunity.

Quark's Bar: The Grand Nagus is particularly fond of chilled tube worms.

Dialogue Triumphs: Punchline to a joke of Quark's: 'And so the Andorian says "Your brother? I thought it was your wife!"'

Quark: 'Tell me, is the Grand Nagus here on business or pleasure?' Krax: 'Is there a difference?'

The Nagus: 'I'm old. The fire dims. I'm just not as greedy as I used to be.'

Notes: Funny and involving.

Miles has returned from Earth: Keiko is due to stay there for another fortnight. Dax and Sisko play Jokarian chess. Dax has been a mother three times and a father twice. The Nagus feigned death by entering a Dolbargy sleeping trance.

11: 'Vortex'

US Transmission: 17 April 1993
UK Transmission: 31 October 1993
Writer: Sam Rolfe
Director: Winrich Kolbe

Cast: Cliff DeYoung, Randy Oglesby, Gordon Clapp,
Kathleen Garrett, Leslie Engleberg, Majel Barrett

One of Quark's money-making scams goes badly wrong as a
Miradorn twin is killed by a criminal wanted in the Gamma
Quadrant. The remaining twin swears revenge, but Odo is fascinated by the captive's tales of the shape-shifting Changelings.
The man, Croden, is wanted on Rakhar, but he tells Odo that he
knows where a colony of Changelings live, producing a shape-
changing pendant. When Sisko asks Odo to return Croden home
they evade the waiting Miradorn ship, and Odo discovers that
the Changeling colony is actually an asteroid containing
Croden's daughter, Yareth, held in stasis for her own protection. Although disappointed, his sense of justice is outraged by
what he hears of Croden's own world, and he undertakes to
ensure that the girl is looked after. The Miradorn ship is destroyed and Croden faces up to his own people.

Stardate: Not stated.

Strange New Worlds: Rakhar in the Gamma Quadrant, the
oppressive world from which Croden hails. In the same sector
is a nebula known as the Chamra Vortex which contains millions of asteroids. The vortex is also riddled with volatile pockets of gas known to the Rakhari as toh-maire.

New Life Forms: Miradorn twins like Ah-Kel and Ro-Kel are
two halves of one being and cannot function well when one is
dead. They have a valuable item that has probably been stolen
from a Vanoben transport, although they claim to have purchased it from an Altorian trader.

Rakhari such as Croden appear to be polygamous. He carries a Ferengi phaser and calls Odo's species Changelings. He
claims that there were Changelings on Rakhar centuries ago,
but they were persecuted and driven out. They were a proud,
moral people who refused to 'assimilate' (i.e. hold a humanoid
appearance). Croden thought that the stories about the

Changelings were merely myths as he hadn't actually seen one before. A Rigelian freighter helps disguise Odo and Croden's departure in a runabout.

Technology: The shape-changing pendant that Croden has isn't anything to do with the Changelings but was instead bought from an Akari merchant. It is the key to Yareth's stasis chamber.

Quark's Bar: Langer is one of the best drinks at Quark's. The large-throated alien often seen propping up the bar is finally given a name – Morn.

Dialogue Triumphs: Quark to Odo: 'You think the whole universe is plotting around you, don't you? Paranoia must run in your species, Odo. Maybe that's why no one has ever seen another shape-shifter – they're all hiding.'

Notes: An excellent story, although sloppy editing means that the splendid make-up used to create the Miradorn's cohorts is barely visible in the finished episode. The tale moves from the double-crossing shenanigans at the beginning to a possible exploration of Odo's origins and a tender portrayal of a political 'subversive'. The ending is excellent.

The Vulcan science vessel is the *T'Van*.

12: 'Battle Lines'

US Transmission: 24 April 1993
UK Transmission: 7 November 1993
Writers: Richard Danus, Evan Carlos Somers,
from a story by Hilary Bader
Director: Paul Lynch
Cast: Camille Saviola, Paul Collins, Jonathan Banks,
Majel Barrett

Kai Opaka comes to DS9, and Sisko invites her to take a trip to the Gamma Quadrant in a runabout. The Kai, pondering a prophecy and its relevance to herself, becomes interested in a moon on the other side of the wormhole. The craft she, Kira and Sisko are travelling in is attacked by an artificial satellite, and it crashes, killing the Kai. Sisko and Kira are immediately embroiled in the factional fighting that plays across the moon's surface – and are shocked to discover that the Kai seems to have returned to life. Similarly, dead members of the Ennis and Nol-Ennis factions are continually 'resurrected': the two factions were exiled to the moon, which they – and now the Kai – can never leave. Although the origins of the conflict are lost, and death no longer has any meaning, the anguish and pain of combat continue. The Kai decides that it is her destiny to try to establish peace between the Ennis and the Nol-Ennis.

Stardate: Not stated.

Strange New Worlds: The lunar penal colony, surrounded by a satellite web, in an uncharted binary star system containing various planets, approximately 25 moons and an asteroid belt. (The sixth planet has three moons, the third has one – the penal colony – and the seventh seems to have none.)

Technology: The combatants, and the resurrected Kai, have a biomechanical 'presence' at the cellular level that directly controls their metabolic processes. These artificial microbes are environment-specific, meaning that the people can never be killed on the moon but will die if they leave it.

Dialogue Triumphs: 'When you cease to fear death the rules of war change.'

Dax: 'I've never heard of a differential magnetomer. How does it work?' O'Brien: 'I'll let you know as soon as I finish making one.'

Notes: The death of the Kai sets up many of the conflicts that pepper the end of this season and beyond, and the story itself is absorbing.

Kai Opaka had never even left Bajor before. It is again stated that DS9 is 70,000 light years from the Gamma Quadrant (as in 'Emissary', cf. 'Captive Pursuit'). The fastest Federation starship would take over sixty-seven years to get there without the wormhole. Although Opaka stays on the moon she says that her and Sisko's pagh will cross again.

The runabout *Yangtzee Kiang* is destroyed during this story.

13: 'The Storyteller'

US Transmission: 1 May 1993
UK Transmission: 14 November 1993
Writers: Kurt Michael Bensmiller, Ira Steven Behr,
from a story by Kurt Michael Bensmiller
Director: David Livingston
Cast: Laurence Monoson, Kay E. Kuter, Gina Philips,
Jim Jansen, Jordan Lund, Amy Benedict

The Bajoran government has asked Sisko to mediate a land dispute between two rival factions – the Paqu and the Navot – which could trigger a civil war. His job is not made any easier by the fact that the leader of the Navot is a girl little older than Jake. Meanwhile, O'Brien pilots Bashir to a Bajoran village in need of medical assistance: its story-telling leader, the Sirah, is dying. O'Brien finds himself greeted as the new storyteller, a vital role as it is the tales that repulse the Dal'Rok, an energy monster that appears once a year. O'Brien's own attempts at telling the tales end in failure, and he is glad to be able to hand over to the young man who has dedicated himself to becoming the new Sirah.

Stardate: 46729.1

Strange New Worlds: The border between the Paqu and the Navot is the Bajoran river Glyrhond, which is in one of the harshest areas of the planet. The Cardassians diverted the flow of the river for use in mining operations during the occupation.

New Life Forms: The Dal'Rok is a cloud-creature that supposedly threatens a Bajoran village every year after the harvest. It can only be repelled by five nights of story-telling by the Sirah. In actual fact, the Dal'Rok is created by a fragment of one of the orbs from the celestial temple giving physical form to the villagers' fears. Over the years the Sirah had used the creature and the stories to unite the village.

The Paqu avoid contact with outsiders.

Ferengi Rules of Acquisition: Ninth Rule: Opportunity plus instinct equals profit.

Quark's Bar: The Navot leader says that Cardassian replicators make a fine larish pie. Quark serves those attending Sisko's mini-conference with two Bajoran synthales, a glass of Gamzain wine (see also 'Q-less') and a Trixian bubble juice ('for the little lady'). Kira asks for a double stardrifter at Quark's.

Future History: Nog says that they stopped playing baseball on Earth hundreds of years ago (see 'If Wishes Were Horses'). Jake says that Buck Bokai (see 'The Big Goodbye') was the greatest-ever pitcher.

Notes: 'If he dies, we all die.' There's some great interplay between O'Brien and Bashir in this charming story of the responsibility of leadership (especially its effects on the young) and a new take on the old 'land and the people are one' theme.

In the station's hierarchy Bashir is superior to O'Brien.

14: 'Progress'

US Transmission: 8 May 1993
UK Transmission: 21 November 1993
Writer: Peter Allan Fields
Director: Les Landau
Cast: Brian Keith, Nicholas Worth, Michael Bofshever,

Terrence Evans, Annie O'Donnell, Daniel Riordan

While Nog and Jake endeavour to turn a surplus of useless condiment into latinum, Kira is ordered to remove a Bajoran farmer from a world that he refuses to leave. Landing on Jeraddo, Kira finds herself drawn to Mullibok, but she cannot convince him that it is in the best interest of Bajor that he go. Mullibok is injured during an attempt at forced evacuation, and Kira decides to stay and look after him, knowing that her work for the Bajoran government is over. Sisko arrives on the moon, and appreciates her dilemma, but reminds Kira of the bigger picture. Full of regret, Kira oversees the farmer's departure.

Stardate: 46844.3

Strange New Worlds: Jeraddo is the fifth moon of Bajor. Its core is about to be tapped in Bajor's first attempt at large-scale energy transfer.

New Life Forms: The Lissepian captain trades with the Cardassians. Kira describes Mullibok as walking like a carnivorous Rastapod. Mullibok says that Kira sounds like a two-headed Malgorian.

Technology: Even O'Brien has never seen a self-sealing stem bolt before. Nog and Jake acquire 100 gross of them.

Quark's Bar: Quark has over 5000 wrappages of Cardassian yamok sauce (surplus to requirement due to the massive reduction in Cardassians coming to his bar).

Notes: 'She didn't offer a word of explanation, sir. She simply removed her uniform and started . . . building.' An excellent tale that illustrates how well the writers develop and mature Kira in this first season: with the Kai's help in 'Battle Lines' she comes to realise the pent-up anger within her that she still feels towards the Cardassians; here, she perceives that she's now on the side of the oppressors (or, at least, the side with the power). There's an excellent ending as the viewer is left to decide on the fate of Mullibok and his relationship with Kira. The gripping moral dilemma is cleverly balanced by the sheer fun of Jake and Nog's financial dealings.

Mullibok grows katterpods (a type of bean) on Jeraddo. The unit of area on Bajor is the tessipate: Jake and Nog buy seven tessipates of land (or 'dirt' as Nog refers to it). When Kira was young a 'nasty old tree' grew outside her bedroom window.

15: 'If Wishes Were Horses'

US Transmission: 15 May 1993
UK Transmission: 28 November 1993
Writers: Nell McCue Crawford, William L. Crawford, Michael Piller,
from a story by Nell McCue Crawford, William L. Crawford
Director: Robert Legato
Cast: Keone Young, Michael John Anderson

In rapid succession three fantasies are turned into flesh: Rumplestiltskin, baseball ace Buck Bokai, and a subservient Dax who is smitten with Julian. A sinister space wave formation is also causing some concern – a previous similar disruption destroyed an entire system when an attempt was made to probe it. The 'fantasies' reveal themselves to be an alien race from the Gamma Quadrant on an extended exploration of the galaxy. They like humans, but have difficulty with their concept of imagination. The sub-space phenomenon turns out to be a relatively harmless thoron field.

Stardate: 46853.2

New Life Forms: The nameless, powerful aliens. A Baneriam hawk is a bird of prey. A Gunji jackdaw is an ostrich-like bird.

Bashir's (Failed?) Conquests: A junior lieutenant at the reception for Captain Stallios and a Betazoid envoy (a 'barely adequate' substitute for Dax). And a (submissive) fantasy version of Dax.

Dialogue Triumphs: 'Too many people dream of places they'll never go, wish for things they'll never have, instead of paying adequate attention to their real lives.'

Odo: 'You're disgusting'. Quark: 'It's a living!'

'It's snowing on the promenade.'

'Ladies and gentlemen . . . And all androgynous creatures.'

'This imagination of yours – it's a tough concept for us to get a handle on, Ben!'

Notes: 'It seems we're letting our imagination run wild.' A great comedy episode (Odo's fantasy is Quark confined), with some surprisingly nasty moments (Kira's pyro-nightmare).

Ships have tended to avoid the Denorios Belt for many years (see 'Emissary'). There is a strain of Larosian virus going about. A similar sub-space rupture was reported in the Hanoli system in the 23rd century. The system was destroyed after a Vulcan ship detonated a pulse wave torpedo.

Herman 'Buck' Bokai was a baseball player with the London Kings. In 2036 he beat Joe DiMaggio's consecutive home run streak (see 'The Big Goodbye'). He was part of the team that won the world series in 2042. By this stage baseball was declining as a spectator sport (only three hundred people watched this game).

Quark appreciates art and has a large collection of Tartaran landscapes.

16: 'The Forsaken'

US Transmission: 22 May 1993
UK Transmission: 4 December 1993
Writers: Don Carlos Dunaway, Michael Piller,
from a story by Jim Trombetta

Director: Les Landau
Cast: Constance Towers, Michael Ensign, Jack Shearer,
Benita Andre

Lwaxana Troi comes to DS9 as part of a delegation of Federation ambassadors. Sisko asks Bashir to look after them, but Julian becomes irritated by their constant complaints. Only Lwaxana is happy: she thinks that Odo is her type of man. Meanwhile, a probe comes through the wormhole and O'Brien downloads its data into DS9's computer. The personality of the station's computer system begins to change, actually allowing O'Brien to do what he wants but also seeming to create little disasters to keep him in Ops. One such 'accident' traps Lwaxana and Odo in a turbolift, causing the constable great concern as he is due to return to his liquid state. O'Brien concludes that the station's problems are being caused by an inquisitive non-biological life form within the station's computer systems, and so he leaves it to 'play' in a subroutine where it can cause no further damage. Bashir's quick-thinking at last wins the respect of the ambassadors.

Stardate: 46925.1

Strange New Worlds: Lwaxana Troi recommends the fourth moon of Andevian 2 at dawn. Nehru Colony, New France Colony and Corado 1 Transmitter Array are mentioned with regard to establishing a computer database on wormhole activity.

New Life Forms: The non-biological life form (nicknamed Pup by O'Brien) that infects DS9's computers via a probe from the Gamma Quadrant.

The Federation Ambassadors, on a fact-finding mission to investigate the wormhole, comprise an Arbazan woman, a Bolian man, a Vulcan male, and the Betazoid Lwaxana Troi. Odo describes Lwaxana's attentions as being like those of a Wanoni tracehound.

Dopterians are relatives of Ferengi. Odo does not eat.

Technology: The probe is made out of corundium alloy.

Dialogue Triumphs: Lwaxana Troi to Odo: 'On this station you are the thin beige line between order and chaos.'

Odo on romance: 'Procreation does not require changing how you smell or writing bad poetry or sacrificing various plants to serve as tokens of affection.'

Bashir on the Federation ambassadors: 'Nothing makes them happy. They are dedicated to being unhappy and to spreading that unhappiness wherever they go. They are the Ambassadors of Unhappy!'

Notes: A story that defines Lwaxana Troi like no other with some wonderful scenes between Mrs Troi and Odo that are funny and ultimately very touching.

Curzon Dax often assigned Sisko to looking after VIP guests. (Sisko once hit one. Despite his grumbles, Julian on the other hand will be recommended for a commendation.) Odo has based his hairstyle on that of the Bajoran scientist assigned to him in the research labs (see 'The Alternate'). He used to imitate chairs and razor cats to entertain people. O'Brien once had a puppy.

Lwaxana Troi's latinum hair brooch has been in her family for thirty-six generations and is described as being 'priceless'. Lwaxana Troi indicates that she made love to DaiMon Tog in 'Ménage à Troi'. She has dark 'ordinary' hair and lots of wigs: she says that before Odo no one has ever seen her with her 'real hair' before.

17: 'Dramatis Personae'

US Transmission: 29 May 1993
UK Transmission: 5 December 1993
Writer: Joe Menosky
Director: Cliff Bole
Cast: Tom Towles, Stephen Parr, Randy Pflug, Jeff Pruitt

Kira refuses to allow a Valerian transport to dock with DS9, but Sisko countermands her order. Although the Valerians have in the past supplied dolamide to the Cardassians there is no evidence that this practice is continuing. The Klingon vessel *Toh'Kaht* returns from the Gamma Quadrant a month early and promptly explodes. The treachery and in-fighting revealed by the ship's logs begin to mirror events on DS9 as Kira tries to get Odo on her side and O'Brien becomes very protective of Sisko. Odo remains unaffected, and traces the amplifying force back to energy spheres found by the Klingons in the Gamma Quadrant.

Stardate: 46922.3

Strange New Worlds: The Klingons decided that the fifth planet of a system within the Gamma Quadrant was unworthy of a colony.

The Valerian transport *Sherval Das* has visited Fahleena 3, Mariah 4 and the dolamide purification plant on Ultima Thule.

New Life Forms: The Saltah'na are the ancient race who created the energy spheres found by the Klingons on the planet in the Gamma Quadrant. They contained a telepathic archive describing a power struggle that seemingly destroyed their civilisation.

The Valerians ran weapons-grade dolamide to the Cardassians during the occupation of Bajor, and often trade with the Federation.

Technology: Dolamide is used in power-generators, reactors and short-range transporters. If pure enough it can be used to make weapons.

Quark's Bar: Quark prepares a Modela aperitif for Dax.

Notes: This is about as limp as *DS9* gets, but it's still pretty good. It feels like a *TNG* plot, complete with silly ending, forced upon its younger brother, although the end result is very dark indeed. Oddly, to see the crew of DS9 at each other's throats is more disturbing than the *Next Generation* equivalents ('Sarek', 'Power Play', etc.) and, of course, an awful lot more difficult to spot.

Keiko has taken eleven children to see a grain-processing centre at Lasuma on Bajor. Dax mentions a time when Curzon and Benjamin were cornered by a party of Kaleans on Aldeira 3. Dax was decorated after his first mission by a Vulcan admiral.

18: 'Duet'

US Transmission: 12 June 1993
UK Transmission: 11 December 1993
Writers: Peter Allan Fields,
from a story by Lisa Rich, Jeanne Carrigan-Fauci
Director: James L. Conway
Cast: Harris Yulin, Robin Christopher, Norman Large,
Tony Rizzoli, Ted Sorel

A transport ship delivers a passenger in need of medical assistance. Kira discovers that the Cardassian patient suffers from Kalla-Nohra Syndrome, which could only have been acquired as a result of a mining accident at the Gallitep forced labour camp. She immediately has him arrested as a war criminal, although the Cardassian claims to be Aamin Marritza, a clerk who's never been to Gallitep. He's suffering from Pottrik Syndrome, which is very similar to Kalla-Nohra and is treated with the same medication. Bashir, however, confirms that Marritza is suffering from Kalla-Nohra. After questioning, Marritza – in a cell next to a troublesome Bajoran – admits that he was at Gallitep, but disputes Kira's version of history. There were no mass executions. Photographic evidence from the camp unexpectedly indicates that Marritza is in fact Gul Darhe'el, the brutal commandant known as the Butcher of Gallitep. He now begins to taunt Kira with the details of his crimes – but when Sisko discusses the matter with Gul Dukat he is informed that Darhe'el died some years ago. The prisoner's body contains large amounts of dermatiraelian plasticine, a dermal regenerative agent used to maintain skin resilience after cosmetic alteration. Marritza changed his appearance to that of Darhe'el five years ago. When Marritza came to DS9 he was hoping to be captured and executed, as he can no longer bear what he saw at the camp. A mere cowardly clerk, he was too frightened to oppose what happened, but now he wants his own people to examine their consciences. As Marritza is led away he is stabbed by the Bajoran prisoner, who still thinks him to be the Butcher of Gallitep.

Stardate: Not stated.

Strange New Worlds: At first Marritza claims to have been a military file clerk on Kora 2.

New Life Forms: Marritza comes to DS9 in a Kobheerian freighter.

Quark's Bar: Marritza says that the replicated sem'hal stew could do with some yamok sauce. Shame Quark got rid of his surplus (see 'Progress'). Odo gives a Moraltian seev-ale from Quark's private stock to calm Kira's nerves.

Dialogue Triumphs: 'What you call genocide, I call a day's work.'

Notes: 'How can there be war crimes when there hasn't been a war?' The pinnacle of the season, a tightly plotted and allusive tale that could be 'about' the Simon Wiesenthal Centre, the modern Nazis' re-writing of World War Two or even Bosnia. Although the juxtaposition with the previous episode is less than ideal, with Kira seeming to go behind Sisko's back to get what she wants, the strength of the script and the performances more than make up for this. Harris Yulin excels as the coward who personalised the guilt of an entire race. This powerful and absorbing drama is also very Roddenberryesque: Kira realises, just before the clever twist ending, that his being a Cardassian is not reason enough to want to kill him.

At Gallitep mothers were raped in front of their children, husbands beaten until they were unrecognisable, and old people buried alive when they could no longer work. Kira, as a member of the Shakaar resistance group, helped to liberate the camp, and says that survivors of Gallitep have always been a symbol of strength and courage for Bajorans. Darhe'el died from a massive coleibric haemorrhage six years ago, and when the mining accident occurred he was on Cardassia receiving the Proficient Service Medallion.

Kira started fighting at the age of twelve. When Jadzia was young she used to break windows with other youths at night.

Odo once played Kalevian montar with Gul Dukat. Dukat cheated.

19: 'In the Hands of the Prophets'

US Transmission: 19 June 1993
UK Transmission: 12 December 1993
Writer: Robert Hewitt Wolfe
Director: David Livingston
Cast: Robin Christopher, Philip Angum, Louise Fletcher,
Michael Eugene Fairman

The events surrounding the selection of the new Kai on Bajor spill on to DS9 when Vedek Winn, the leader of an orthodox sect, accuses Keiko of blasphemous teaching in DS9's school. Winn is a leading contender to become the next Kai, and she seems to be stirring up trouble deliberately. The Bajorans on the station become increasingly hostile to Starfleet and the school, despite Sisko's attempt to discuss matters with Vedek Winn and the more moderate Vedek Bareil, the man most likely to be the next Kai. The school is bombed and O'Brien and Odo uncover a plot to murder Vedek Bareil on Deep Space 9 but, for the moment at least, Winn is not directly implicated in the subterfuge.

Stardate: Not stated, although it is noted that they've been on DS9 for seven months.

Technology: The wormhole is formed by unique self-sustaining particles called verterons. Cabrodine and infernite are easily obtainable explosives.

Technobabble: Apparently you need an EJ7 interlock to close a security seal. An EJ7 has an independent tritanium source.

Ferengi Rules of Acquisition: A paraphrase of the Seventh Rule is 'Keep your ears open'.

Dialogue Triumphs: 'One must never look in the eyes of one's own gods.'

Keiko: 'I'm not teaching any philosophy. What I'm trying to teach is pure science.' Kira: 'Some might say pure science, taught without a spiritual context, *is* a philosophy, Mrs O'Brien.'

Notes: 'The teacher has dishonoured the celestial temple. If she does not recant, I cannot be responsible for the consequences.' *DS9* does the Rushdie affair, although Keiko is too belligerent to be a likeable 'martyr' to humanism. The long-overdue conflict between a tolerant, atheistic Federation and the deeply spiritual, sometimes fanatical Bajorans comes in an episode thick with the intrigue of the Papal succession.

Vedek Winn's orthodox sect is not named, but Kira seems to have some sympathy for her views. Winn does not quite have enough support in the Vedek Assembly to become the next Kai.

Miles is fond of jumja sticks, lollipops made from the sap of the jumja tree. Bariel grows a plant called felorum bromiliads on Bajor.

Deep Space Nine

Second Season

26 45-minute episodes

Created by Rick Berman, Michael Piller,
based on *Star Trek*, created by Gene Roddenberry

Executive Producers: Rick Berman, Michael Piller
Co-Executive Producer: Ira Steven Behr
Producers: Peter Allan Fields, Peter Lauritson (20–34)
Associate Producer: Steve Oster
Supervising Producers: James Crocker, David Livingston
Consulting Producer: Peter Lauritson (35–45)
Line Producer: Robert della Santina (26, 36)
Story Editor: Robert Hewitt Wolfe (23–45)

Regular Cast: Avery Brooks (Commander Sisko), Rene Auberjonois (Odo), Siddig el Fadil (Dr Bashir), Terry Farrell (Lt Dax), Cirroc Lofton (Jake Sisko), Colm Meaney (Chief O'Brien), Armin Shimerman (Quark), Nana Visitor (Major Kira) Max Grodénchik (Rom, 20, 22, 26-27, 30), Marc Alaimo (Gul Dukat, 20, 24, 27, 39-40), Rosalind Chao (Keiko O'Brien, 22, 24, 30, 32-33, 44), Hana Hatae (Molly O'Brien, 22)/ Hana White (Molly O'Brien, 33), Aron Eisenberg (Nog, 22, 29, 45), Andrew Robinson (Garak, 24, 37, 41-42)

20: 'The Homecoming'

US Transmission: 25 September 1993
UK Transmission: 3 April 1994
Writers: Ira Steven Behr,
from a story by Jeri Taylor, Ira Steven Behr

Director: Winrich Kolbe
Cast: Richard Beymer, Michael Bell, Marc Alaimo, Leslie
Bevis, Paul Nakauchi

Kira hears that the great Bajoran resistance fighter Li Nalas,
believed dead, is being held at a Cardassian labour camp. Sisko
agrees that the man needs rescuing – if only to provide some
hope for Bajor, currently awash with the in-fighting of the religious factions and threatened by the terrorist group the Circle.
Although successfully rescued, Li proves to be not quite the
great leader everyone was expecting – his daring exploits and
military prowess during the Cardassian occupation are all hugely
exaggerated – and he tries to leave the station unnoticed. Sisko
is adamant that Li can still have a role in Bajor's future, but is
shocked when Minister Jaro makes Li DS9's new liaison officer. Kira is called home.

Stardate: Not stated.

Strange New Worlds: The Cardassian labour camp is on Hutep.
Kira disguises her rescue mission by claiming that she is going
to Lamenda Prime to bring back mineral fragments.

New Life Forms: Quark states that a Zubbite freighter was
smuggling defective isolinear rods to Bajor. Kira's ship is disguised as a Lissepian transport (see 'Progress'). Li Nalas tries to
stow away on the Tygarian freighter *Nanak* heading for the
Gamma Quadrant (the Tygarian captain is a reptillian humanoid).

Technobabble: 'I could modulate the engine's power emissions,
reconfigure the deflector shield grid, instal field buffers about
the sub-space emitter coil . . .'

Ferengi Rules of Acquisition: Seventy-sixth Rule: Every once
in a while, declare peace (as Quark says, 'It confuses the hell
out of the enemy').

Quark's Bar: Has a drink called a Black Hole.

Notes: With the exception of the thrilling 'Escape from Stalag Cardassia' sequence, this is a quiet episode to introduce the season. The story of the reticent hero Li Nalas is fascinating, and there's some lovely humour when Kira pretends to be a prostitute.

Since the death of the Kai (see 'Battle Lines') there have been religious riots on the Southern islands of Bajor. One extremist group has become particularly dominant: the Alliance for Global Unity, otherwise known as the Circle. They believe in 'Bajor for the Bajorans', and that other species are inferior and should leave the planet.

Cardassian Supreme Directive 2645 covers the return of Bajoran prisoners of war. Li is made Nayvark (see 'The Circle') and (for the moment) assigned to DS9 as liaison in place of Kira.

Kira's quarters contain some sort of shrine. She claims to have a consignment of rulat seeds for the (fictitious) Gul Morain when intercepted by a Cardassian ship. Jake has decided to ask out Layra, a Bajoran girl. Sisko orders a raktajino, a Jackaryne peel and a hyperberry tort.

The crew have been on DS9 for about a year.

21: 'The Circle'

US Transmission: 2 October 1993
UK Transmission: 10 April 1994
Writer: Peter Allan Fields
Director: Corey Allen
Cast: Richard Beymer, Stephen Macht, Bruce Gray,
Philip Anglim, Louise Fletcher, Mike Genovese, Eric Server,
Anthony Guidera

Kira seeks solitude in Vedek Bareil's monastery on Bajor, and finds herself being increasingly drawn to the man. Sisko tries to establish why the Bajoran military are so slow in moving against the Circle, especially as they have reason to believe that the terrorist group is being armed by the Cardassians. Kira is captured by the Circle, who are led by Minister Jaro, but is rescued by Sisko and the others. However, the Bajoran military have ordered that all non-Bajorans should leave the station: the Circle are about to take DS9 by force.

Stardate: Not stated.

Strange New Worlds: It is stated that Bajor brought architecture to 'countless planets'. Circle headquarters are in caves beneath the Bajoran Perichean peninsula.

New Life Forms: The Krisari are said to have supplied the Circle with their weapons, despite not even having a military themselves.

Dialogue Triumphs: Jaro, leader of the Circle: 'They can't even agree it is a government so they call it "provisional". It's just another word for "powerless".'

Notes: There is some lovely comedy as everyone and their dog come to say goodbye to Kira, which balances the clever politics and intrigue on display elsewhere. The sequences with Bareil and Kira in the monastery are beautiful.

Amongst the various functions and abilities of the Nayvark is the reception of guidance from the prophets. As previously hinted, the Vadek would appear to be the head of an order (Jaro belongs to Winn's order). The third orb, which resides in the monastery, is known as the Orb of Prophecy and Change (presumably at least some orbs have been returned since 'Emissary': see also 'The Storyteller'). Kira has always dreamt of seeing one of the Tears of the Prophets.

Sisko reports to Admiral Chekote at Starfleet Command.

Dax has borrowed Kira's epitalic skin lotion. Kira's favourite synthale is Budda. When she was young she was a very bad painter.

22: 'The Siege'

US Transmission: 9 October 1993
UK Transmission: 17 April 1993
Writer: Michael Piller
Director: Winrich Kolbe
Cast: Steven Weber, Richard Beymer, Stephen Macht,
Philip Anglim, Louise Fletcher, Katrina Carlson

DS9 is evacuated, but Sisko isn't giving up that easily. A surprise will be waiting for the 'conquering' Bajoran troops in the form of a small number of armed personnel hiding in the service conduits. Meanwhile, Kira and Dax hope to deliver the revelations regarding the Cardassians' involvement in the Circle to the Chamber of Deputies. They crash on Bajor, but manage to get to the chamber, where they confront the scheming Winn and Jora. Winn distances herself from the coup when the Bajoran soldiers are ordered to return from DS9, but Li is shot whilst saving Sisko's life.

Stardate: Not stated.

Strange New Worlds: When DS9 is evacuated, the *Rio Grande* heads towards the Hanolin colony, and the *Ganges* towards the Kurat system.

Ten years ago Li hid some sub-impulse raiders on Lunar 5.

New Life Forms: Li Nalas mentions frightened Cardassian voles. Vulakoo are edible spider-like creatures common on Bajor's moons.

Insect bites can interfere with the biochemical connections between Trill hosts and symbionts.

Technology: The Circle flood the conduits with poisonous anestascene gas.

Ferengi Rules of Acquisition: Thirty-first Rule: Never make fun of a Ferengi's mother. (Quark's making this one up, surely?)

Dialogue Triumphs: Dax (very frightened, crawling through caves): 'What's that? Is that a spider or a dog?'

Notes: 'Off the hook, after all.' Given that the conclusion to most *TNG* two-parters suck, this, the conclusion to *DS9*'s first three-parter, should have been a stinker. In fact, it's marvellous, with some great build-up scenes winding up to a gripping climax. It's a cosmic *Die Hard* again, only this time with lots of people. Keiko whinges interminably, as usual.

The *Orinoco* is introduced as the *Yangtzee Kiang*'s successor.

The Vadek Assembly elects the Kai.

Dax describes 'her' second host, the male Tobin, as having 'Barely a sex life and no imagination, but he knew phase coil inverters like no one else'. Kira says that a year ago (she must mean more than a year – see 'The Homecoming') she was living in a camp like the lunar colony. O'Brien claims to like combat rations – the only thing he misses from the Cardassian front lines.

23: 'Invasive Procedures'

US Transmission: 16 October 1993
UK Transmission: 24 April 1994
Writers: John Whelpley, Robert Hewitt Wolfe,
from a story by John Whelpley
Director: Les Landau
Cast: John Glover, Megan Gallagher, Tim Russ,
Steve Rankin

DS9 has been hit by a violent plasma disruption and has been temporarily evacuated – just the backdrop needed by the desperate Trill Verad, who forces Bashir to remove Dax from Jadzia's body and transplant the symbiont into himself. Sisko reminds Mareel, Verad's partner, that he won't be the same person after the operation, implying that his feelings for her might change. Quark affects an ear complaint as part of an audacious rescue plan, and, with Verad's Klingon thugs overpowered and Mareel preferring the original Verad, the symbiont is returned to Jadzia.

Stardate: 47182.1

Strange New Worlds: Mareel says she grew up on the streets of Kafka 4.

New Life Forms: A 'mindless Tigla' would appear to be a Klingon sacrificial animal.

Notes: The juxtaposition with the previous episode is unfortunate, both stories involving a skeleton crew and Quark avoiding evacuation. (Far better if it was stated that the rest of the crew still haven't returned after the events of 'The Siege'.) The story itself is interesting enough, and Quark gets to be a real hero (and villain).

The Symbiosis Evaluation Board is mentioned (see 'Playing God'), Jadzia claiming that it is no disgrace not to be chosen. Only one in ten applicants becomes a Trill host, and neither Jadzia's parents nor her sister underwent symbiosis. Verad, however, feels condemned to a life of mediocrity. A Trill host, once joined, usually dies within hours without the symbiont (for no adequately explained reason, Verad survives).

Sisko says that Dax has eight life times of memories (see 'Shadow Play', 'Equilibrium'), but names only Jadzia, Curzon and Tobin (see 'The Siege'). Sisko and Curzon Dax first met on Galileo Station, enjoyed a trip to the caves of Bole and spent months aboard the *Livingston* (during which time Science Officer Krystanovich had eight helpings of Andorean redbet). Dax attended Sisko's 'bachelor party' and wedding.

Mareel gives O'Brien some Synarian egg broth, and Quark is able to break open a Degorain locking mechanism.

O'Brien has two brothers.

24: 'Cardassians'

US Transmission: 23 October 1993
UK Transmission: 1 May 1994
Writers: James Crocker,
from a story by Gene Wolande, John Wright
Director: Cliff Bole
Cast: Marc Alaimo, Robert Mandan, Terrence Evans,
Vidal Peterson, Dion Anderson, Sharon Conley,
Karen Hensel, Jillian Ziesmer

Rugal, a Cardassian orphan brought up by Bajorans, comes to
DS9, and savagely attacks Garak. Gul Dukat gets to hear about
this, and offers to trace the boy's natural parents, although Garak
is very suspicious of his motives. Dukat was in charge of the
evacuation of Bajor, and the Cardassians would never 'accidentally' leave anyone behind. Dukat finds out that Rugal is
the son of an important Cardassian politician, and demands his
return. Garak leads Bashir to the Bajoran records involving the
many Cardassian 'war orphans', and it becomes clear that Dukat
has set up the return of the boy to discredit one of his enemies
and to paint himself in a more positive light prior to a Cardassian
tribunal which will investigate the occupation of Bajor. However, Sisko is still left with the impossible decision, and he concludes that Rugal should be sent to Cardassia.

Stardate: 47177.2 (which would place this story *before* 'Invasive Procedures').

New Life Forms: The O'Briens and Rugal eat (or, rather, poke
at) a stew of Cardassian Zabu meat.

Quark's Bar: Bashir drinks Tarkalian tea; Garak drinks Racassa
juice ('The odour is unmistakable').

Notes: 'Family is everything.' An excellent exploration of orphans and deep-seated prejudice, with a noble Cardassian politician, Sisko on the horns of a dilemma, and 'plain, simple

Garak' becoming more mysterious by the minute. One minor quibble: Keiko loses yet more viewer sympathy by not only insensitively inviting the young Cardassian boy round but making them all eat Cardassian food. (Miles lost a lot of friends during the wars (see 'Tribunal' and *TNG*'s 'The Wounded'), and the boy doesn't like Cardassian fare anyway.)

Ten million Bajorans were murdered by the Cardassians during the occupation. Gul Dukat's command post – DS9 – was known as Terek Nor. A number of young Cardassians were left behind when the forces withdrew from Bajor, who are now cared for as orphans on Bajor.

Orphans have no status in Cardassian society. Cardassian civilian leaders have no direct authority over the military.

The teachings of the Bajoran prophets would seem to preclude physical punishment for children.

Molly O'Brien is now four, and is staying with the Petersons (see also 'Tribunal').

25: 'Melora'

US Transmission: 30 October 1993
UK Transmission: 8 May 1994
Writers: Evan Carlos Somers, Steven Baum, Michael Piller,
James Crocker, from a story by Evan Carlos Somers
Director: Winrich Kolbe
Cast: Daphne Ashbrook, Peter Crombie, Don Stark,
Ron Taylor

Ensign Melora Pazlar comes to DS9. Being an Elaysian she is crippled by what is normal gravity for humans. As Bashir gets to know her better he decides that he can offer her the chance of a 'normal' life, but it will mean that instead she will be an invalid on her own world. The treatment begins, and seems to be successful, but Melora comes to the conclusion that the price is too great. She asks Julian to stop the treatment.

Stardate: 47229.1

Strange New Worlds: There is a very low surface gravity on Pazlar's planet.

When Julian was 10 his father was a Federation diplomat on Averaia 2.

New Life Forms: Melora is the first Elaysian member of Starfleet.

Dax once knew a hydrogen-breathing Lowthra who fell in love with an oxygen-breather.

Delvak is a Vulcan composer (their equivalent of Philip Glass, we think).

Technology: Both Melora Pazlar's usual anti-grav units and Federation cargo-lifts are incompatible with Cardassian architecture.

Technobabble: 'It's a computer model of an elevated neural output from the brain's gross motor cortex. It's stimulating acetylcholine absorption to increase tensile strength.' (Accurate, but it sounds like technobabble.)

Bashir's (Failed?) Conquests: Some serious romance with Melora.

Ferengi Rules of Acquisition: Sixteenth Rule: A deal is a deal.

Quark's Bar: Is now facing some competition from the new Klingon restaurant that has just opened on the Promenade. (Julian orders racht, a double serving of glacht (no sauce) and a side order of zim'kagh: Melora, who can speak Klingon, says that the racht are half-dead and so the fat Klingon gets some live ones.)

Quark serves Fallit Kot, whom he betrayed, a home-cooked meal starting with baklova soup, followed by jumbo Vulcan molluscs sautéed in rumbolian butter.

Notes: As noted in the dialogue, this is a reworking of Hans Christian Andersen's mermaid tale that deals cleverly with issues regarding disability, and bravely ensures that Melora is as tough and flawed as any 'normal' character. Like the little mermaid she is only 'disabled' when out of her natural environment. It would have been very right-on to have had an Elaysian on board the *Voyager*.

Melora Pazlar arrives on the *Yellowstone*. She has a cane made from the wood of a garlannsk tree. Only a 'handful' of Elaysians have ever left home. Dax hasn't seen a wheelchair for over 300 years. Nathanial Terros did some work over thirty years ago on low-gravity species. Although his work on neuro-muscular adaption was sound in principle there seemed to be no practical application, but Bashir is able to 'update' his work with great success.

One hundred and fifty years ago Dax had a steady relationship within Starfleet, but few 'sub-space relationships', as they are called, prove long-lasting.

Quark owns 42 of the 80 Rings of Bulgis. Kot has just been released from a prison camp for hijacking a shipment of Romulan ale. Before Julian became a doctor he thought that he might be able to make a career out of tennis (see 'Rivals').

26: 'Rules of Acquisition'

US Transmission: 6 November 1993
UK Transmission: 15 May 1994
Writers: Ira Steven Behr,
from a story by Hilary Bader
Director: David Livingston
Cast: Helène Udy, Brian Thompson, Emilia Crow, Tiny Ron,
Wallace Shawn

The Grand Nagus returns to Deep Space 9 with an opportunity for Quark to negotiate in the Gamma Quadrant. Meanwhile a new waiter, Pehl, is proving himself to be a huge asset to Quark. But Pehl is really a female Ferengi, and despite her superb business knowledge, Quark's discovery of her gender makes their working together impossible.

Stardate: Not stated.

New Life Forms: The Dozie, from the Gamma Quadrant: a red-skinned alien with black and white pigment markings. 'Very serious when it comes to profit.' There is also the first mention of the Dominion, a great power in the Gamma Quadrant.

Ferengi Rules of Acquisition: There are 285 Ferengi Rules of Acquisition. These include 'Never place friendship before profit' (twenty-first); 'Wise men can hear profit in the wind' (twenty-second); 'It never hurts to suck up to the boss' (thirty-three); 'The bigger the smile, the larger the knife' (forty-eighth); 'Free advice is seldom cheap' (fifty-ninth); 'The riskier the road, the greater the profit' (sixty-second).

Dialogue Triumphs: Dax: 'Is that how you really like your women? Naked and submissive?' Quark: 'You find such a lifestyle appealing?'

Kira, on Ferengi: 'They're greedy, misogynistic, untrustworthy little trolls.'

Notes: 'If you're going to pretend to be a man, act like one. Take the profit!' A good comedy episode with one priceless silent sequence featuring Quark, Rom and Pehl like some Ferengi version of the Three Stooges.

No sleeping on the Promenade is one of Odo's rules. Curzon Dax was a fine Taango player (a Ferengi game of chance). Jadzia has inherited the gift and improved on it.

Ferengi women have smaller ears than the males. Brizene Nitrate is a fertiliser badly needed on Bajor. Tulleberry wine is a Dozie drink. Quark once overheard Dax describe her childhood bedroom to Kira, and recreated it for her in the holosuite. It wasn't very accurate but Dax says it was the thought that counted.

The Grand Nagus gooses Kira. Twice.

27: 'Necessary Evil'

US Transmission: 13 November 1993
UK Transmission: 22 May 1994
Writer: Peter Allan Fields
Director: James L. Conway
Cast: Katherine Moffat, Robert MacKenzie

Quark is hired by a Bajoran woman to find a box hidden on DS9 since the Cardassian occupation. Quark finds the object, and a list of names within, but is shot by an accomplice of the woman. Investigating, Odo is reminded of the crime which began his career as the station security officer. The murder of a chemist, Vetrick, was never solved, though Odo always suspected the man's wife. Kira also remembers the events, having been present on the station working for the resistance when Odo saved her from Gul Dukat's attentions. Establishing Vetrick's widow's interest in the list (blackmail – the list contains names of known collaborators), Odo confronts Kira who confesses to murdering Vetrick, albeit in self-defence.

Stardate: 47282.5 (five years after Vetrick's murder).

Ferengi Rules of Acquisition: One Hundred and Thirty-ninth Rule: Wives serve, brothers inherit.

Dialogue Triumphs: Odo: 'You're not as stupid as you look.' Rom: 'I *am* too!'

'*Everyone* has to choose sides, Constable.'

'Justice, as the humans like to say, is blind. I used to believe that.'

Notes: 'I have no intention of becoming a Cardassian agent.' A piece of dramatic, oppressive *film noir* (complete with Raymond

Chandler-style voice-over). Without a doubt the best episode of *Deep Space 9* to date, and an episode that shows just how far the *Star Trek* universe has come as a regular member of the crew is shown to be a murderer. The ending is very enigmatic.

Magnasite drops are corrosive enough to eat through duranium. Quark is shot with a 'compressed tetrion beam weapon'. The lunar prison on Meldra 1 has a temperature of 200 degrees in the shade. The station's store used to be the chemist shop owned by Vetrick.

Gul Dukat first met Odo at the Bajoran centre of science two years before the murder of Vetrick. The Cardassian high command was invited to 'view' the shape-shifter, and were highly impressed with a 'Cardassian neck trick' he was forced to perform. Odo left the centre and came to DS9 to learn more about life, and ended up as a sort of wandering arbitrator: being seen by both Bajorans and Cardassians as a neutral, he would solve petty disputes. Dukat's motives in making him an investigator are, of course, neither straightforward, nor have the interests of justice at heart.

'First drink on the house' is an old ('dreadful') Cardassian tradition. Kira says she likes Pirellian ginger tea. Five years ago she told Odo she was working for the underground and came to the station to commit sabotage, but her real target was Vetrick and the list of collaborators. She paid Quark for an alibi and killed Vetrick in self-defence. (She says . . .)

28: 'Second Sight'

US Transmission: 20 November 1993
UK Transmission: 29 May 1994
Writers: Marek Gehred-O'Connell, Ira Steven Behr,
Robert Hewitt Wolfe,
from a story by Mark Gehred-O'Connell
Director: Alexander Singer
Cast: Salli Elsie Richardson, Richard Kiley, Mark Erickson

On the fourth anniversary of his wife's death, Sisko meets the mysterious Fena, a woman who fascinates him. However, she disappears before anything can develop. The station is playing host to egotist terraformer Gideon Seyetik who is about to attempt his greatest feat, re-igniting a dead sun. When the DS9 crew have dinner with Seyetik, Sisko is alarmed to find that Fena is Seyetik's wife, though she seems not to recognise the commander. The woman is revealed to be a member of a telepathic race, Fena being a projection of Sisko's memories of his wife. Sadly, Seyetik is killed during the successful climax of his career.

Stardate: 47329.4 (four years and a day after the Wolf 359 massacre).

Strange New Worlds: Terosa Prime is mentioned. Blue Horizon was one of the planets terraformed by Gideon Seyetik. Sisko and Jake have visited it. Epsilon 119 (a dead star) is Seyetik's current project.

New Life Forms: The Alaana, a 'psycho-projected telepath' race who mate for life.

Picard Manoeuvre: Sisko does it.

Dialogue Triumphs: 'It's hard to talk man-to-man to a woman!'
'Nothing of worth was ever created by a pessimist.'

Notes: 'That's one of the great things about this station. You never know what's going to happen next.' An attempt to soften Sisko's hard-edged character which achieves little, mainly due to a lack of plot.

The Runners is a Bajoran constellation. Sisko normally drinks Raktajino (see 'The Passenger') but after meeting Fenna tries Taroltan tea with a twist of lemon instead. Dax thinks Andorian tutaau is delicious.

According to Nog, the three signs of being in love are ignoring your food, lack of concentration and smiling all the time.

Seyetik's ship is the *Prometheus*. Julian once saw some of
Seyetik's paintings at the Central Gallery on Logobis 10. Seyetik
has had nine volumes of his autobiography published.

G'traak was a Klingon poet; his *Fall of Kaang* is required
reading at the academy.

29: 'Sanctuary'

US Transmission: 27 November 1993
UK Transmission: 12 June 1994
Writers: Frederick Rappaport,
from a story by Gabe Essoe, Kelley Miles
Director: Les Landau
Cast: William Schallert, Andrew Koenig, Michael Durrell,
Betty McGuire, Robert Curtis-Brown, Kitty Swink,
Deborah May, Leland Orser, Nicholas Shaffer

DS9 becomes a temporary home to the Scria, an alien race from
beyond the wormhole who are searching for their mythical
home, Kintana. The Scrians have a history that parallels the
Bajorans', and believe that Bajor may indeed be Kintana. They
wish to be allowed to settle there and Kira presents their case to
the provisional government, but it is rejected. The Scria leave
to continue their search for a homeworld.

Stardate: 47391.2

Strange New Worlds: Draylon 2, near Sophela Prime. A temperate world with good farming prospects, Sisko's proposal for
the Scrian homeworld.

New Life Forms: The Scria, whose language and syntax is
unknown to the universal translator. A female-dominated society, they may be a Bajoran splinter group. Three million Scria
are situated on the other side of the wormhole and were held in
slavery for eight hundred years by the Terrogerands (until the

latter were conquered by members of the Dominion). The Scria have flaky skin. Their legendary home, Kintara, is 'a planet of sorrows'.

Dialogue Triumphs: 'It's bad enough you hang around the station not buying anything, you have to start fighting too.'

Notes: 'Fifty years of Cardassian rule has made you all frightened and suspicious. I feel sorry for you.' Rather wordy and dull, although the message of the oppressed forgetting their suffering to oppress others is worthy.

Varani is a famous Bajoran musician. Kira gets him a job playing in Quark's bar (much to the latter's chagrin as his music is so beautiful customers stop drinking and gambling to listen). The Scria call the wormhole the Eye of the Universe. Deep Space 9 has space for 7,000 inhabitants.

Plix Tixtaplick is a Regrunian criminal, wanted in seven star systems for illegal weapons sales.

30: 'Rivals'

US Transmission: 1 January 1994
UK Transmission: 19 June 1994
Writers: Joe Menosky,
from a story by Jim Trombetta, Michael Piller
Director: David Livingston
Cast: Chris Sarandon, Barbara Bosson, K. Callan,
Albert Henderson

While O'Brien becomes more and more enraged at his rivalry with Bashir over a racket game, Quark faces competition from suave conman Martus, who's chanced upon a gaming device that's all the rage. To compete, Quark sets up a heavily publicised match between Bashir and O'Brien, but the game goes O'Brien's way – so much so that the participants realise that O'Brien has gained phenomenal good luck. Indeed, the balance of luck right across DS9 has changed, with disastrous results. It's only when Martus' games are deactivated that things get back to normal.

Stardate: Not stated.

Strange New Worlds: The Flota asteroid belt is ripe for mining. The Elorian system and Pythro 5 are mentioned.

New Life Forms: We hear of the Pythrons, and meet an Elorian, who are humanoids and great listeners. Plygorian mammoths are big.

Ferengi Rules of Acquisition: Forty-seventh Rule: Don't trust a man wearing a better suit than your own.

One Hundred and Ninth Rule: Dignity and an empty sack is worth the sack.

Notes: This is rather ordinary, apart from Chris Sarandon's stellar, attention-grabbing turn as Martus, and Bashir's rather suspicious finger signal to O'Brien when he enters the racketball court.

10,000 Iziks is a lot of money. 2,000 will buy passage out of DS9, 500 if you go cargo. The Bajoran fund for orphans is administered by monks (see 'Cardassians'?). Quark's brother used to be teased about his small earlobes. On his Naming Day, Quark substituted his presents with vegetables. Quark bribed the Cardassians for DS9's exclusive gambling contract.

O'Brien built DS9's racketball court. Fifteen years ago he played the game five hours every day. He's probably not over 38. Bashir was captain of the Starfleet medical racketball team in his final year, when they took the sector championships, Bashir beating a Vulcan in the final.

31: 'The Alternate'

US Transmission: 8 January 1994

UK Transmission: 26 June 1994
Writers: Bill Dial,
from a story by Jim Trombetta, Bill Dial
Director: David Carson
Cast: James Sloyan, Matt McKenzie

Visiting a planet which may have been home to a people similar to his own, Odo picks up a biological sample, along with a piece of religious architecture. On returning to DS9, the sample is released, and a dangerous creature roams the station. Odo's mentor – the Bajoran who first found him, Dr Mora Pol – is visiting. When the remains of the original creature are found, it becomes clear that it is Odo himself who is wreaking havoc at night, transformed into a wild shape-shifting mass by contamination from the sample. Dr Mora Pol helps to return Odo to his normal self.

Stardate: 47391.7

Strange New Worlds: We hear of Kosla 2, where Plegg lives, but the world of the shape-shifters, six light years from the wormhole in the Gamma Quadrant, is unnamed.

New Life Forms: A multicellular life form that needs more carbon dioxide than there is in Earth's atmosphere.

Ortas sing.

Quark's Bar: Aractean gin is a beverage.

Notes: This is okay, but the budget's clearly been spent on the splendid animation rather than on the hugely obvious painted planetary backdrop.

Dr Mora Pol was assigned to Odo after he was found. Odo's first transformation was to copy his home beaker. It took Pol a while to discover Odo was sentient. Odo's rejuvenation period is sixteen hours. Sisko's father died after an illness.

The trip from Bajor to DS9 takes five hours. The late, great Plegg was a Ferengi salesman of renown.

32: 'Armageddon Game'

US Transmission: 29 January 1994
UK Transmission: 3 July 1994
Writer: Morgan Gendel
Director: Winrich Kolbe
Cast: Darleen Carr, Peter White, Larry Cedar, Bill Mondy

Bashir and O'Brien are helping two alien races, who have come to terms after a long war, to dismantle the deadly Harvesters, biological weapons of mass destruction. Assassins burst in, and the two men narrowly escape, landing on a remote landscape with few provisions. O'Brien is infected by the Harvesters. But their hosts tell the crew of DS9 that their friends were killed by a security device, showing them footage of the deaths. Only Keiko fails to believe it, knowing her husband's coffee habits too well. The DS9 crew rescue Bashir and O'Brien just as their hosts, who wanted all knowledge of the Harvesters wiped out, have arrived to kill them.

Stardate: Not stated.

Strange New Worlds: T'Lani Prime. T'Lani 3's population was decimated by the Harvesters.

New Life Forms: The T'Lani, with double-peaked hair, and the Kelleruns, with single peaks, species previously at war who share ridged ears.

Technology: Harvesters are biomechanical weapons. An inversion field blocks sub-space communications.

Ferengi Rules of Acquisition: Fifty-seventh Rule: Good customers are as rare as latinum: treasure them.

Notes: The rather *Red Dwarf*-ish plot of this episode involves Sisko instantly acting on Keiko's sheer hunch regarding her husband's death, and then frantically trying to prop its credibility up with a routine spectroscopic analysis of a cup of coffee . . . Is this the sort of thing they always do at accident inquiries? Or is every beverage automatically analysed as it's drunk? Sorry, don't believe a word of it.

Altorean chowder and tulleberry crêpes are foodstuffs. The Cardassians used to mine supplies left behind with pressure grenades. Bashir was once in love with the ballerina Paris Delon, whose father was administrator of a medical complex in Paris, but he didn't take up the man's offer of a career there, and the romance ended.

33: 'Whispers'

US Transmission: 5 February 1994
UK Transmission: 10 July 1994
Writer: Paul Robert Coyle
Director: Les Landau
Cast: Todd Waring, Susan Bay, Philip LeStrange,
Majel Barrett

O'Brien races away from DS9 in a runabout, dictating his record of the odd circumstances that made him flee the station. Ever since he got back from a conference, his wife and friends have treated him oddly, not trusting him, barely concealing their unease. He's been denied access to security matters, and assigned the most ordinary tasks. Only Odo, who has also just returned, seems unaffected, but when it turns out that he's in on the plot too, O'Brien runs for it, convinced that the whole thing is something to do with the dark plans of the Paradan government. He finds their agents, but is astonished to also find himself, the original O'Brien. The one we've been following is a replicant, designed to assassinate a rebel delegation at a forthcoming conference on DS9. The DS9 crew rescue the original O'Brien, and the replicant dies heroically, saving them.

Stardate: 47581.2

Strange New Worlds: The Paradas system is on the other side of the wormhole. Parada 2 is the site for peace talks. Parada 4 is the largest planet in that system, with seven moons.

New Life Forms: The Paradas are a grey, ridge-headed, small-mouthed people, who've been at civil war for twelve years. Their smell changes with their moods.

Ferengi Rules of Acquisition: One Hundred and Ninety-fourth Rule: It's always good business to know about your customers before they walk in your door.

Notes: A great reversal of the usual paranoia plot.

The runabout *Mekong* is seen for the first time. Gupta and Roman are Starfleet admirals. O'Brien likes coffee, Jamaican blend, double strong, double sweet. His birthday is in September. His mother died two years ago, and his father remarried last Spring. He built sub-space transceivers when he was a boy. He likes Frikando stew, endive salad, and Wheatflon dessert.

34: 'Paradise'

US Transmission: 12 February 1994
UK Transmission: 17 July 1994
Writers: Jeff King, Richard Manning, Hans Beimler,
from a story by Jim Trombetta, James Crocker
Director: Corey Allen
Cast: Julia Nickson, Steve Vinovich, Michael Buchman
Silver, Erick Weiss, Gail Strickland, Majel Barrett

Their runabout subject to a loss of power, Sisko and O'Brien beam down to a world where a group of Federation citizens, led by a woman called Alixus, live a simple, untechnological life. Initially, they're welcomed, but their efforts to contact DS9 are gradually met with hostility. Meanwhile, Kira and Dax search for their friends. Unwilling to submit to Alixus' rules, Sisko is punished in a metal box that heats up in the sun, while

O'Brien finds that the power losses are not natural, but are caused by a technological device. As Kira and Dax arrive to rescue their friends, the community is rocked by the news that Alixus sabotaged their ship, then set up the power drain to keep them here. Still, they choose to keep to their way of life, even when Alixus is taken away by the visitors from DS9.

Stardate: 47573.1

Strange New Worlds: An unnamed planet in the Aurelius system.

Gamelan 5 (see *TNG*'s 'Final Mission') is mentioned.

Technology: We hear of Thorium grease. A duonetic field inhibits energy flow.

Future History: Gulinka was a famous football player ('Ooh-ah-Gulinka'?).

Notes: This is suitably disturbing, a nightmare of being shipwrecked with Margaret Thatcher, but Sisko is put through things that would be beneath Picard or even Kirk's dignity, without any real heroic pay off. That's disturbing for different reasons.

The runabouts were commissioned two years ago. The *Gazo* is a Romulan vessel. The USS *Crocker* is mentioned. The *Santa Maria* was an M1 Transport.

O'Brien learnt his engineering skills on the Cardassian front. He's not good with plants. He can knock out somebody painlessly. On Earth, Dax met a Hopi who could do rope tricks. Sisko and his brothers worked in their father's vegetable garden. Sisko is a bad poker player (he finds bluffing very difficult), and Admiral Mitsuya always beats him.

35: 'Shadowplay'

US Transmission: 19 February 1994
UK Transmission: 24 July 1994

Writer: Robert Hewitt Wolfe
Director: Robert Scheerer
Cast: Philip Anglim, Kenneth Mars, Kenneth Tobey,
Nolan Thornton, Trula M. Marcus, Martin Cassidy

Dax and Odo find an inhabited valley on the second planet of a
system in the Gamma Quadrant. Odo decides to investigate the
mysterious disappearance of many of the townsfolk, and discovers that the people are all holograms who believe themselves
to be alive. The disappearances are being caused by malfunctioning machinery. There is only one human living in the area,
and he pleads with Dax to do the necessary repairs. Dax and
Odo then leave the town in peace, knowing it to be the last
reminder of a world before the Dominion invaded.

Stardate: 47603.3

Strange New Worlds: The holographic society is a representation of life on the planet Yadeera Prime some 30 years ago,
just before the Dominion took over.

Quark's cousin Cono has just robbed a museum on Cardassia 5.

New Life Forms: Cono escaped on a Tellarit freighter.

The people Odo and Kira find in the Gamma Quadrant have
heard of the Changelings, but like Croden in 'Vortex' they believe them to be mythical.

Technology: Omicron particles are very rare, and block scanner and tricorder functions. Such particles are only created by
certain matter/anti-matter reactions.

DS9 uses colour-coded isolinear rods: white for engineering
systems controls, red for library and information storage, and
blue (unspecified).

Notes: 'It's all an illusion – an illusion I created.' DS9's take
on the 'Do holograms know they're not real?' theme also echoes the strange alien-young girl relationship seen in *The Next
Generation*'s 'Thine Own Self'. It's all charmingly done but

barely original.

Dax mentions 'seven life times' (see 'Invasive Procedures', 'Equilibrium'). Quark has another cousin (see 'Q-Less') called Cono. Jake is fifteen: Nog is a little older. O'Brien's father wanted him to be a musician, and so he practised the cello every day (see 'The Ensigns of Command'). He was accepted for (but never attended) the Aldebaran Music Academy at the age of seventeen.

Kira and Bereil disagree over the interpretation of the Eighth Prophecy. Bareil's suggestions for further things to discuss include the Ilvern katterpod crop (see 'Progress'), a new nature reserve in the Intaspool Province, and the standings in the Springball Championship. Both Kira and Bareil used to play springball. Kira played with her brothers at the Singa Refugee Camp; Bareil was at Relika.

36: 'Playing God'

US Transmission: 26 February 1994
UK Transmission: 12 February 1995
Writers: Jim Trombetta, Michael Piller,
from a story by Jim Trombetta
Director: David Livingston
Cast: Geoffrey Blake, Ron Taylor, Richard Poe

O'Brien is dealing with an 'outbreak' of Cardassian voles, and Dax is assessing Trill host candidate Argin. Dax's reputation as a 'breaker' of candidates is well known, but Argin is shocked by Jadzia's behaviour. However, more important matters are afoot – their runabout returns with some space 'seaweed', which begins to eat away at the station. However, analysis indicates that it could be a proto-universe, and Sisko cannot sanction its destruction. Dax and Argin are able to dispose of the thing safely by taking it back through the wormhole.

Stardate: Not stated.

Strange New Worlds: Dax's male wrestling friend has to be at Coladea 4 by tomorrow.

New Life Forms: Cardassian voles are a problem on DS9: they hid in areas of the station only recently returned to. They are attracted by electromagnetic fields.

The runabout brings back a sub-space interphase pocket, stellar 'seaweed' that could be a proto-universe, complete with life signs.

Technobabble: Apparently the wormhole is full of verteron nodes that affect the mini-universe.

Ferengi Rules of Acquisition: Quark says number 112 is 'Never have sex with the boss's sister', but he's probably just ruminating over his own past misfortunes.

Quark's Bar: Is situated on level seven section five.

Dialogue Triumphs: Quark to Dax: 'Don't play with my ears – unless you're serious about it.'

Sisko: 'Phasers on stun, Mr O'Brien. I want those voles taken alive.'

Later: 'And take those phasers off stun, Chief. No more Mr Nice Guy.'

Quark describes his current position: 'Tending bar out here in Wormhole Junction while the big boys fly past me at warp speed.'

Notes: The best Dax story yet. It's a shame the sub-plot about the voles is abruptly forgotten half-way through as some thoughtful contrasts are established between killing them as vermin, the machinations of the Borg as remembered by Sisko, and the fate of the tiny universe. Perhaps the production team were wary of creating the *DS9* equivalent of tribbles. The ending is sadly unsatisfactory: just what did they do with the mini-universe when they reached the Gamma Quadrant?

Five thousand host candidates qualify in the Trill symbiosis program each year, with only three hundred symbionts available on average. Dax is famous for 'breaking' host initiates. Over the past two hundred years Dax has personally eliminated 57 host candidates from the program. Curzon Dax was Jadzia's assessor: he recommended that her initiate period be terminated. She was very quiet and had little knowledge of life beyond the symbiosis program at the time: the rejection prepared her, ironically, to become Dax's next host (see 'Equilibrium'). Jadzia Dax enjoys partaking in a 'brutal, but fun' form of wrestling. She recommends the citrus blend from the replicator, but actually wants a Ferengi black hole for herself. She 'collects' forgotten composers, and asks the computer in the runabout to play something by Frenchat, a self-exiled Romulan. She taught the Klingon chef a Klingon song that even he did not know. Jadzia is a level three pilot (Argin is level five). Dax's host before Curzon would seem to be called Lila (flatly contradicted by 'Equilibrium').

When Quark was very young he worked for a District sub-Nagus. Jake says he's in love with Mata, a Dabo Girl (see 'The Abandoned').

Bashir and the Trill host Argin have just come from Starbase 41.

37: 'Profit and Loss'

US Transmission: 19 March 1994
UK Transmission: 19 February 1995
Writers: Flip Kobler, Cindy Marcus
Director: Robert Wiemer
Cast: Mary Crosby, Michael Reilly Burke

Quark's former lover, the Cardassian Professor Natima Lang, returns to DS9 – and the years have not dimmed the Ferengi's desire. She resists his advances at first, impatient only for her ship to be repaired so that she and her two students can be on their way. However, the Cardassians want them tried on various charges of subversion, and send a battle ship to back up their point, with Garak acting as an intermediary. The Bajoran government order Sisko to hand the Cardassians over: in return six Bajoran prisoners will be released from Cardassia. Lang realises that she still cares for Quark, and the Ferengi comes up with an escape plan. He begs Odo to release Lang and the students, who does so, knowing the terrible fate that awaits them. On their way to their ship they are confronted by a phaser-carrying Garak, but he allows them to go when he realises that his exile on DS9 will not be so easily terminated. Quark sadly says goodbye to Lang, and Garak implies that the influence of Lang and the others is of value because he loves Cardassia.

Stardate: Not stated.

Strange New Worlds: Personal cloaking devices are illegal on Bajor (needless to say Quark has one).

New Life Forms: Garak says that General Yeree has decided to execute his brother for treachery against the Trellonian government.

Ferengi Rules of Acquisition: Quark is about to quote the Two Hundred and Twenty-third Rule but is interrupted by Lang.

Notes: 'I love you, Quark. I've always loved you. Even when I hated you.' A wonderful Quark love story is a million times less tacky than it sounds. It actually explores the non-money-grabbing side to the character only previously hinted at, and the viewer's expectation that at some point the capitalist punch line will come is entirely subverted. Add in some excellent scenes with Odo and Garak, the latter dramatically concluding that he's been exiled in disgrace for long enough, and you have a gem of a story.

Cardassia seems to be slipping from the control of the military. Professor Lang no longer drinks Samarian Sunsets (see

'Conundrum') because they remind her of Quark. She believes that her teaching of political ethics will 'change the future of Cardassia'. Before Odo came to DS9 she was a correspondent with the Cardassian Information Service, and saved Quark's life when he sold food to the Bajorans. She was with him when he installed his first holosuite, but left the station seven years ago (which contradicts information given in 'Emissary' regarding how long Quark's been on DS9).

O'Brien has lent *I, the Jury* by Mickey Spillane to Odo (in electronic form, of course).

38: 'Blood Oath'

US Transmission: 28 March 1994
UK Transmission: 26 February 1995
Writer: Peter Allan Fields
Director: Winrich Kolbe
Cast: John Colicos, Michael Ansara, William Campbell, Bill Bolender, Christopher Collins

Three old Klingons arrive on DS9, searching for their old friend Dax. Long ago, the four of them swore an oath to avenge the death of the Klingons' first born children at the hands of the Albino, a Klingon villain. Dax, even in her new body, takes the oath seriously, and, having gained the old warriors' trust, joins them in their assault on the Albino's compound. Much stealthy trickery and violent action later, the villain is killed in battle, along with two of the Klingons, and Dax has honoured her oath.

Stardate: Not stated.

Strange New Worlds: The Earth-like fourth planet of the Cicara system, where the Albino hides. We hear of Deus 4, where his ex-wife lived, and Gal Vontere, where the band of revengers first met him. Curzon Dax negotiated with Koloth on the Korvach Colony.

New Life Forms: Depradeders are either a species or a class of person, led by the Albino, eighty years ago. The Toohimiras is sickly.

D'har is a martial discipline; both Kor and Koloth are masters. Breshtanti ale and backbon are drinks, a goptu being a Klingon goblet. A part of their anatomy is the Keyvons. On a related topic, to have K'ojol Makt is to have impertinent courage. A bat'telh weighs 5.3 kilograms, and is made of composite backenite.

Technology: Tetryon particles neutralise phasers. Ridimite is a hard material.

Future History: The battle of K'laak d'kel brakt was a Klingon victory over the Romulans one hundred years ago, in which Kor was involved.

Notes: This is a wonderful kung fu movie, exciting and giving Dax loads to do, further establishing her character. The three Klingons are clearly meant to be those of the same name from the original series, thus indicating that our changing image of the Klingons is purely a matter of perception. Their personalities have changed a bit as well. Cop out ahoy!

Dax was the godfather of Kang's son, also called Dax. Curzon was decorated many times for diplomacy, and opened the door to Klingon/human peace.

The Iyengeran Strategy is sneaky.

39: 'The Maquis, Part One'

US Transmission: 23 April 1994
UK Transmission: 5 March 1995
Writers: James Crocker, from a story by Rick Berman, Michael Piller, Jeri Taylor, James Crocker
Director: David Livingston
Cast: Bernie Casey, Tony Plana, Bertilla Damas, Richard Poe, Michael A. Krawic, Amanda Carlin, Michael Rose,

Steven John Evans

A Cardassian freighter is destroyed by a bomb while leaving DS9. The Maquis, a Federation militia from the Demilitarised Zone between Federation and Cardassian territory, claim responsibility. Sisko's old friend Cal Hudson, Federation liaison to the DMZ, arrives on DS9, and claims that the Cardassians will exploit the bombing. Gul Dukat asks Sisko for help in restraining the Maquis. Then Dukat is kidnapped by the Maquis. Pursuing him, Sisko discovers that Hudson is the Maquis leader.

Stardate: Not stated.

Strange New Worlds: We hear of the Regulan system, and of the Volon Colonies in the DMZ, including Solkod 4, where Ropol City is, Galador 2 and Ferrius Prime. The Badlands is a stretch of space on the Cardassian border where there are plasma storms.

New Life Forms: Bolians, Bardesans, Galadorians, Luceptians, Kotakians, and Galamines, who have twice-human brain size and transparent skulls, are all mentioned.

Technology: Cobalt thorium devices are bombs. Gala-class phaser banks are a Federation weapon. Kalendine and rhodinium are common Cardassian ship materials. Mercassium is a synthetic material found in Federation ships.

Ferengi Rules of Acquisition: Two Hundred and Fourteenth Rule: Never begin a business negotiation on an empty stomach.

Dialogue Triumphs: Kira: 'When I kiss a man good night, I like to know where I'm kissing him.'

Notes: This has the special DS9 quality of complex political intrigue, and Marc Alaimo (Dukat) is as wonderful as ever, the grey ethics of the series personified.

Three hundred year old Vulcan port is a drink. The

Cardassians are given intense mind-training from the age of four. Gul Dukat was commander of DS9 for ten years. He's a commander of the second order, and has seven children.

Sisko is an old friend of Commander Calvin Hudson, the Starfleet attaché to colonies in the DMZ (within Cardassian territory, that is). They went to the Mazurka festival in New Berlin, where Sisko wore lederhosen. He still has the hat.

Kira lived under Cardassian rule for twenty-six years (so she's about twenty-eight). The Vulcans have a warrant out on Quark. They also have a Bill of Rights.

40: 'The Maquis, Part Two'

US Transmission: 30 April 1994
UK Transmission: 12 March 1995
Writers: Ira Steven Behr, from a story by Rick Berman,
Michael Piller, Jeri Taylor, Ira Steven Behr
Director: Corey Allen
Cast: Bernie Casey, Tony Plana, John Schuck,
Natalia Nogulich, Bertila Damas, Michael Bell,
Amanda Carlin, Michael Rose

Hudson claims that the Cardassians are smuggling arms to their colonies in the DMZ, and then leaves. Investigating a female Vulcan who tried to buy arms from Quark, Sisko finds the Maquis base and Dukat, who's shocked to find out that the Cardassians are about to use him as a scapegoat for the smuggling operation. The Maquis are planning to destroy a Cardassian weapons dump beneath a civilian settlement. Sisko and crew intercept the Maquis ships, and halt their plans, but Hudson escapes.

Stardate: Not stated.

Strange New Worlds: Bolon 3, Umeth 8 and Hotken 7 are all in the DMZ, as is the Cardassian world Brima.

New Life Forms: The Agreans farm wheat. Both the Zeppelites (grey ridge-heads with fish-like faces) and Lucethians were Cardassian intermediaries, but only the latter were caught.

Ferengi Rules of Acquisition: Third Rule: Never spend more for an acquisition than you have to.

Dialogue Triumphs: Quark: 'Vulcans are a species that appreciate good ears.'
Dukat: 'Will you stop talking and shoot them?'

Future History: There is no poverty, crime or war on Earth.

Notes: This doesn't end as well as it began, but that's always the way with *Trek* two-parters, and Dukat is still great fun.

Hudson and Sisko swore to be captains by thirty and admirals by forty. The Cardassians are run by their Central Command. Legate is a Cardassian rank (see also 'Second Skin'). Dukat can shield his thoughts from a Vulcan mind-meld. Cardassian trials decide the verdict before the public spectacle of the trial itself (see 'Tribunal').

41: 'The Wire'

US Transmission: 7 May 1994
UK Transmission: 19 March 1995
Writer: Robert Hewitt Wolfe
Director: Kim Friedman
Cast: Jimmie F. Skaggs, Ann Gillespie, Paul Dooley

When Garak starts to exhibit unusual behaviour, he's reticent about letting Bashir investigate, until he passes out in incredible pain. It turns out that he's been implanted with a Cardassian pain device by his former employers, the Cardassian secret police, who he left in disgrace. Seeking to cure him, Bashir visits Garak's old superior, who disputes the many different tales Garak tells of why he was given the device, but won't tell the doctor the truth. He does, however, give Bashir the information he needs to heal the Cardassian. Death is, it seems, too good for Garak.

Stardate: Not stated.

Strange New Worlds: We hear of Erowath (a Cardassian colony), Mared 2 (who have advanced technology), Rigel 4 (where hydroponics conferences are held), and Lidonia 3 (where one may buy plants).

New Life Forms: Galitogens don't acknowledge time and make good sweaters. The Algorian mammoth has a hearty constitution.

Technology: Triptecederin is a powerful anaesthetic. Tennis rackets are made of nilimite alloy. Sizing scanners are used by tailors.

Quark's Bar: Saurian brandy is a drink, Idanian spiced pudding is a food. Kanar is a Cardassian alcoholic drink.

Dialogue Triumphs: Garak on Quark's: 'I'm not really in the mood for noisy, crowded and vulgar today.'

Bashir does Bones: 'I'm a doctor, not a botanist.'

Notes: This goes on a bit, and it's becoming more and more clear that we're supposed to accept Garak as our token camp character, on the evidence that he's a tailor . . . Well, thanks, that does a lot for the cause, especially since he's about as macho as any other Cardassian. What next, a Vulcan hairdresser?

The Obsidian Order is the Cardassian secret police, similar to the Romulan Tal Shi'ar (see also 'Second Skin'). The Cardassians use mechanised infantry. Garak claims to have been both a Gul in the military and a member of the Obsidian Order, and gives several contradictory explanations for his exile. His implant protects 'certain information' and makes him resistant to torture, and was given to him by Inabrun Tain, head of the Obsidian Order. Garak's first name is Eelim.

The post-central gyrus is part of the Cardassian brain. Great Cardassian novels include *The Never-Ending Sacrifice*, a repetitive epic that Bashir found dull, concerning seven generations of a single family, and *Meditations on a Crimson Shadow* by Prioch, science fiction concerning a Klingon/Cardassian war.

Bashir's middle name is Subatoi. He and Garak have lunch once a week. Odo monitors Quark's sub-space communications via a bug in his quarters. Quark and Garak have never done business before. Dax has never been a good gardener: Curzon had a go, but had no luck, as with his relations with women.

42: 'Crossover'

US Transmission: 14 May 1994
UK Transmission: 26 March 1995
Writers: Peter Allan Fields, Michael Piller,
from a story by Peter Allan Fields
Director: David Livingston
Cast: John Cothran Jr, Stephen Gevedon, Jack R. Orend,
Dennis Madalone

An accident in the wormhole takes Kira and Bashir into a parallel world where the Bajorans, Cardassians and Klingons have defeated a pacifist Earth, and DS9 is run by Kira's dominatrix double. Bashir is put to work with a cowed O'Brien under a vicious Odo, while Kira is courted by her other self. The visitors manage to convince an amoral privateer version of Sisko to rebel, and escape back to the wormhole as an uprising rocks the station.

Stardate: 47891.1

New Life Forms: Drathan puppyliks are pets. Samhorans are an intelligent species.

Bashir's (Failed?) Conquests: He goes after Kira, to her horror, on the shuttle.

Dialogue Triumphs: Mirror Kira on her other self: 'Find this . . . attractive young woman some quarters.'

Notes: This has to be the horniest episode of DS9, with the characters taking a trip to the Land of Fan Fiction, and Kira fancying herself rotten while Bashir gets enslaved. Nana Visitor enjoys herself as a flamboyant mixture of Cleopatra and Mae West. You still have to be bad and unreal to be gay in *DS9*, but we're getting there . . . Even if the ending is hugely simplified.

Kira meditates every day. Bashir learnt from a Samhoran teacher. Tor Joran is a Bajoran composer, not one of the Baldaric masters of the last century. Kira has never heard of James Kirk, but Bashir read about the events of 'Mirror, Mirror' when he was at the Academy.

In the mirror universe, one hundred years ago a reformed Spock turned the Earth Empire towards pacifism. The Klingon/Cardassian alliance won the war against them. In this universe, Odo is an authoritarian collaborator, Quark a kind-hearted rebel, Sisko an amoral privateer, O'Brien a forelock-tugging victim, Garak a ruthless torturer, and Kira a bisexual dominatrix. So no change there, then!

43: 'The Collaborator'

US Transmission: 21 May 1994
UK Transmission: 2 April 1995
Writers: Gary Holland, Ira Steven Behr,
Robert Hewitt Wolfe, from a story by Gary Holland
Director: Cliff Bole
Cast: Louise Fletcher, Philip Anglim, Bert Remsen,
Camille Saviola, Charles Parks, Tom Villard

The new Kai is about to be elected, and the leading candidate is Vedek Bareil. But he is troubled by visions of a cleric who hanged himself, having given away the location of a rebel base during the occupation. Then a quisling Bajoran minister returns from exile on Cardassia. Vedek Wynn gives him sanctuary, because he claims that it was actually Bareil who was the traitor. Wynn gets Kira to investigate her lover. She discovers that it was actually Kai Opaka who gave the information that led to a massacre, but Bareil refuses to clear himself of the charge, not wanting to soil the office of Kai. Wynn thus becomes the new Kai.

Stardate: Not stated.

Strange New Worlds: The Di Kean monastery is on Bajor.

Ferengi Rules of Acquisition: Two Hundred and Eighty-fifth Rule: No good deed ever goes unpunished.

Notes: A lovely script, which takes us, with the knowledge of audience expectation and *realpolitik* wit that *DS9* is known for, to the point of thinking that, because Kira's lover is only a semi-regular, he's got to leave the series. Complicated human relations and compromises such as these are places where *Trek*, in either form, never went. But why does nobody mention Odo's collaboration? Hugely preferable to the worst excesses of *ST:TNG*'s space opera.

The Ilvian Proclamation sentenced all Bajoran collaborators to exile. Kai Opaka's son was killed in the Kendra Valley Massacre. Talina is another Vedek. Bareil was Kai Opaka's choice to be next Kai. A Vedek can grant sanctuary.

44: 'Tribunal'

US Transmission: 30 April 1994
UK Transmission: 9 April 1995
Writer: Bill Dial
Director: Avery Brooks
Cast: Caroline Lagerfelt, John Beck, Richard Poe,

Julian Christopher, Fritz Weaver, Majel Barrett

The O'Briens are going on holiday, but Miles is captured by
Cardassians and awakes on Cardassia Prime. He is about to go
on trial, although he does not know on what charges – and his
defence counsel is only interested in how gracefully he will
admit the error of his ways. Odo is able to attend the tribunal,
and O'Brien is accused of supplying twenty-four photon war-
heads to the Maquis. The preliminary evidence on DS9 does
seem to indicate that Miles authorised the removal of these
weapons, but he has in fact been framed. Sisko applies a good
deal of political pressure and O'Brien is released.

Stardate: Not stated.

Strange New Worlds: On Cardassia, guilt is decided before
the trial commences. The trial – the first time a defendant hears
the charges – is therefore purely a public spectacle at which the
defendant sees the error of his or her ways. Clemency is never
granted. O'Brien is held at the central prison on Cardassia Prime.

Volden 3 is said to be on the Cardassian side of the DMZ.

Technology: The Cardassians need liderian for their warp
drives.

Notes: *DS9*'s version of 'Chain of Command', only not that
good.

O'Brien and Boon served together on the *Rutledge* (see 'The
Wounded'). Miles and Keiko were going on their first holiday
in five years, leaving Molly (now aged five) behind with the
Petersons (see 'Cardassians'). O'Brien asks the computer to
play something by Minizaki shortly before the Adeki-class
Cardassian patrol ship hoves into view. The *Enterprise*, the
Prokofiev and the *Valdemar* have been ordered to the border of
the demilitarized zone.

Odo was made an officer of the Cardassian Court four years
ago (see 'Necessary Evil'). O'Brien's trial is the longest in

Cardassian history.

45: 'The Jem'Hadar'

US Transmission: 7 May 1994
UK Transmission: 16 April 1995
Writer: Ira Steven Behr
Director: Kim Friedman
Cast: Molly Hagan, Alan Oppenheimer, Cress Williams,
Michael Jake, Sandra Grando, Majel Barrett

While exploring a beautiful world in the Gamma Quadrant, Sisko and Quark are attacked by a telekinetic woman, Eris, who is running from the Jem'Hadar, feared troops of the Dominion. Soon all three are captured by the powerful lizard soldiers, who inform Sisko that the Founders – the rulers of the Dominion – will no longer allow ships from the other side of the wormhole into their territory. The colony of New Bajor is destroyed by the Jem'Hadar. Thanks to the skills of Quark and Eris an escape is possible, and a huge rescue operation is mounted. However, in the process the Galaxy-class starship *Odyssey* is destroyed by the Jem'Hadar. Back on Deep Space 9, Eris is exposed as a Dominion spy, but she transports to safety. Sisko ponders the threat of the Jem'Hadar.

Stardate: Not stated.

Strange New Worlds: The planet the team land on in the Gamma Quadrant seems to be like Earth during the early Devonian period, with lots of plant life, fish and insects, but no predators or large animals. The atmosphere is seventy-seven per cent nitrogen, twenty-one per cent oxygen, two per cent carbon dioxide. The water contains traces of copper, nickel and a little berithium. The planet reminds Jake and Benjamin of a camping trip they took with Jennifer on Itamish 3 (Jennifer taught Jake how to water-ski).

Karil Prime was offered entry into the Dominion, but the people refused. The Dominion sent in the Jem'Hadar.

New Bajor in the Gamma Quadrant had an impressive irrigation system.

New Life Forms: The Jem'Hadar, tall lizard soldiers of the Dominion. The Jem'Hadar are looking forward to fighting some Klingons, and have already heard of the bat'telh. The Ferengi have been trying to open up trade negotiations with the Dominion for a year. Eris says that 'The Dominion decides that you have something that they want. And they come and take it, by negotiation or by force.' Eris's people are telekinetic, which attracted the attention of the Dominion. The Founders are the semi-mythical rulers of the Dominion (see 'The Search').

A Bolian freighter is due at DS9 in two days' time.

Ferengi Rules of Acquisition: One Hundred and Second Rule: Nature decays, but latinum lasts for ever.

Dialogue Triumphs: A terrified Nog, when a ship approaches the runabout: 'Computer: evasive manoeuvres! Fire phasers! Launch torpedoes! Escape pods!'

Quark, on why 'hoo-mans' don't like Ferengi: 'The way I see it, humans used to be a lot like Ferengi: greedy, acquisitive, interested only in profit. We're a constant reminder of a part of your past you'd like to forget . . . But humans used to be a lot worse than the Ferengi. Slavery, concentration camps, inter-stellar wars – we have nothing in our past that approaches this kind of barbarism. You see, we're nothing like you. We're better.'

Notes: 'You have no idea what's begun here.' The introduction of the meanest *Trek* aliens since the Borg is carried out with some skill, although the story ultimately falls down on its predictable plotting and design. The Jem'Hadar move well but look little different to any other race of *Trek* aliens, and their ships, although powerful, are similarly conventional. Still, the episode promises great things for the future.

Jake is doing a school science project on Bajoran katterpods (see 'Progress'). Quark has some ointment for his ears – they sometimes react to 'nature'. He is still trying to persuade Sisko to allow him to sell products over the station monitors: these include Andorean jewellery, Vulcan edic pins and Bolian crystal-steel.

Captain Keo had worked with Dax before. The Dominion hoped to use Eris to spy for them against the Federation, although they already have a lot of information from various sources.

'If the Dominion come through the wormhole, the first battle will be fought here, and I intend to be ready for them.'

APPENDIX

Deep Space Nine

Third Season

45-minute episodes

Created by Rick Berman, Michael Piller,
based on *Star Trek*, created by Gene Roddenberry

Executive Producers: Rick Berman, Michael Piller
Co-Executive Producer: Ira Steven Behr
Producers: René Echevarria, Peter Lauritson
Co-Producer: Steve Oster **Supervising Producers:** Ronald
D. Moore, David Livingston **Line Producer:** Robert della
Santina **Executive Story Editor:** Robert Hewitt Wolfe

Regular Cast: Avery Brooks (Commander Sisko), Rene
Auberjonois (Odo), Siddig el Fadil (Dr Bashir), Terry Farrell
(Lt Dax), Cirroc Lofton (Jake Sisko), Colm Meaney (Chief
O'Brien), Armin Shimerman (Quark), Nana Visitor (Major Kira)
Andrew Robinson (Garak, 48, 51, 53, 64–67), Rosalind Chao
(Keiko O'Brien, 49, 56), Max Grodénchik (Rom, 49, 60), Marc
Alaimo (Gul Dukat, 53, 55), Majel Barrett (Lwaxana Troi, 56),
Aron Eisenberg (Nog, 60), Tim Russ (Tuvok, 65)

47: 'The Search, part 1'

US Transmission: 26 September 1994
Writers: Ronald D. Moore,
from a story by Ira Steven Behr, Robert Hewitt Wolfe
Director: Kim Friedman
Cast: Salome Jens, Martha Hackett, John Fleck,
Kenneth Marshall

Simulations indicate that a Jem'Hadar attack would result in a massacre. Sisko leads his team into the Gamma Quadrant in an experimental cloaked craft, the *Defiant*, hoping to find the Founders of the Dominion. While Odo is compelled to travel to a planet in a nearby nebula, Sisko and Bashir come under attack.

Stardate: 48212.4 (eight months after Quark's trade agreement with the Coroma).

Strange New Worlds: A rogue class-M planet in the Omarion Nebula which holds a strange fascination for Odo. Callanon 7, an unmanned Dominion relay station.

New Life Forms: The Coroma, Quark's business partners in a deal involving tulleberry wine. Their currency is the Direk.

The Vorta, the Coroma's contact with the Dominion, are mentioned.

Technobabble: Cloaked ships emit a slight sub-space variance at warp speed.

Picard Manoeuvre: One of the Jem'Hadar does it!

Notes: 'No one is expendable!' A new focus, *DS9* going 'out there' for just about the first time in an attempt to turn Sisko into a 'proper' *Star Trek* captain. The Jem'Hadar attack on the *Defiant* is breath-taking, and there are some great Odo/Quark scenes. Various racist undertones concerning Odo are also explored. A promising new direction.

Dax has a new haircut. Bajoran jewellery is made from diamide-laced beritium. Deep Space 9's shields have perimeters of approximately 300 metres. The *Defiant* was designed five years ago as the flagship for a new fleet of warships to fight the Borg, though various technical deficiencies caused the project to be shut down. It is officially designated as an escort vessel. It also contains a cloaking device loaned by the Romulans (along with its operator, sub-commander T'Rul).

Sisko's fascination with ancient African tribal art is mentioned. He has spent two months at Starfleet undergoing debriefing over the events of 'The Jem'Hadar'. Quark is bribed into going into the Gamma Quadrant with the Sceptre of the Grand Nagus. Curzon used to tell Sisko never to volunteer for anything.

48: 'The Search, part 2'

US Transmission: 3 October 1994
Writers: Ira Steven Behr,
from a story by Ira Steven Behr, Robert Hewitt Wolfe
Director: Jonathan Frakes
Cast: Salome Jens, Natalia Nogulich, Martha Hackett,
Kenneth Marshall, William Frankfather, Dennis Christopher,
Christopher Doyle, Tom Morga, Diaunté, Majel Barrett

The shuttle arrives back at DS9 to discover a newly formed alliance between the Dominion and the Federation. Tensions on the station increase as the Jem'Hadar arrive in force. Meanwhile, Odo meets his fellow Changelings. Investigating a tunnel on the planet, Kira discovers a vault where Sisko's away team are being held, wired up to an image enhancer which is feeding them the illusion of being back on DS9. Odo's race are revealed to be the Founders of the Dominion.

Stardate: None given (begins six days after the events of part one).

New Life Forms: Odo's race the Changelings: the Founders of the Dominion.

Another member of Eris' race from 'The Jem'Hadar' is seen.

Dialogue Triumphs: 'To become a thing is to know a thing.'
Odo: 'If you'll excuse me, I have to return to my bucket.'
Garak: 'After years of hemming women's dresses, a little

action is a welcome change!'

'Being an outsider isn't so bad. It gives you a unique perspective. It's a pity you've forgotten that.'

Notes: 'Life is full of surprises, Commander.' Unfortunately, this episode isn't! Obvious from the word go, a story similar to the *Red Dwarf* episode 'Back to Reality' (and three or four *Next Generation* episodes) is signposted with large arrows marked 'plot device' all over the place. The action sequences are great, Jon Frakes' direction is faultless and much of the script is witty, but as with so many two-parters this is a big letdown.

Garak says that 'Enemies make dangerous friends' is an old Cardassian saying. Quark misquotes Martin Luther King's 'I have a dream' speech concerning various races coming together in his bar to gamble.

49: 'The House of Quark'

US Transmission: 10 October 1994
Writers: Ronald D. Moore,
from a story by Tom Benko
Director: Les Landau
Cast: Mary Kay Adams, Carlos Carrasco, Robert O'Reilly,
Joseph Ruskin, John Lendale Bennett

Quark gets into a fight with a drunken Klingon, who accidentally falls on to his own blade. Quark claims that he killed Kozak in self-defence, hoping that the notoriety will improve the fortunes of his bar. Quark is questioned by DeG'or, who claims to be the dead Klingon's brother, and Grilka, Kozak's widow. She takes Quark to the Klingon Homeworld, where he learns that the House of Kozak has no male heir. Because Quark stated that Kozak died honourably, the High Council are unable to make a special dispensation. DeG'or hopes to receive control of the House of Kozak in order to pursue a seat on the Council.

Grilka marries Quark, which makes him head of the House, and the Ferengi exposes DeG'or's dubious financial dealing, which has accelerated the decline of the House of Kozak. Confronted by the evidence, DeG'or challenges Quark to a duel but is shown to be a coward. Grilka, granted a special concession, divorces Quark and becomes head of the House of Kozak.

Stardate: Not stated.

New Life Forms: O'Brien complains that three Korvarian freighter captains wanted to use the same docking port.

Ferengi Rules of Acquisition: Quark makes up rule number 286, saying it should be 'When Morn leaves, it's all over.'

Quark's Bar: Is very quiet, until the Klingon dies there.

Dialogue Triumphs: Quark, pondering his empty bar: 'I should have gone into insurance. Better hours, more money, less scruples.'

Quark's way of dealing with the dead Klingon's family: 'I'll stand up, look them straight in the eye . . . And offer them a bribe.'

Notes: 'The House of Kozak is gone. For the time being it will be known as . . . the House of Quark.' Although the shadow of the Dominion palpably hangs over this episode there is some great comedy here, notably the clash between the Klingon and Ferengi cultures. Quark doesn't so much act out of character as reveal the hidden depths first indicated in last season's 'Profit and Loss'.

The Klingon Homeworld is called Qo'nos. The Brek'tol ritual allows the widow of a Klingon slain in combat to marry his victor. Klingon divorce seems to involve hitting the partner, making some sort of curse, and then spitting at them.

Keiko is seen doing bonsai. She has closed down the school, as the families of her last Bajoran students have relocated to Bajor, leaving only Jake and Nog.

Quark's father is or was called Keldar.

50: 'Equilibrium'

US Transmission: 17 October 1994
Writers: René Echevarria, from a story by
Christopher Teague
Director: Cliff Bole
Cast: Lisa Banes, Jeff Magnus McBride, Nicholas Cascone,
Harvey Vernon

Dax becomes obsessed by a piece of music she's never heard before and uncharacteristically loses her temper with Sisko. She sees hallucinations of a terrifying masked figure, and returns to the Symbiosis Commission on Trill. Sisko comes to believe that the hallucinations are the jumbled memories of a previous host, and discovers that the music was written by a Trill named Joran Bellar 86 years ago. When Dax is shown a picture of the composer she collapses. Computer files have been tampered with in an attempt to disguise the truth, so Sisko and Bashir contact Joran's brother Yullad, who believes that Joran – an 'unsuitable' candidate – accidentally underwent symbiosis. Joran Dax was killed – the symbiont being transplanted into Curzon – six months later, the authorities worried about what would happen to their society if it were widely known that up to fifty per cent of the population were capable of being 'joined'. Now Joran Dax's artificially repressed memories are returning, and Jadzia must accept and explore these if she is to survive.

Stardate: Not stated.

Strange New Worlds: Our first look at Trill. Dax says that she could have taken Sisko and Bashir on a tour of the Tenaran ice cliffs, which are presumably one of Trill's great attractions.

New Life Forms: We learn a little more about the symbionts:

they breed in huge expanses of interconnecting pools, and communicate by energy discharge. They are looked after by the Guardians, unjoined Trills dedicated to their care.

Bashir's (Failed?) Conquests: He offers Dax a bunk in his quarters on the *Reliant* (phwooarhh), only for the Trill promptly to fall asleep (boo).

Notes: 'If you want to know who you are, it's important to realise who you've been.' An entertaining and surreal glimpse into Dax's mind and the society of the Trills.

A Trill's isoboromene level is a count of a particular type of neurotransmitter that mediates the synaptic functions between host and symbiont. The symbiont is removed if the level drops to below forty per cent of normal. The Symbiosis Commission (of which the Symbiosis Evaluation Board – 'Invasive Procedures', 'Playing God' – is presumably a sub-section) state that a symbiont placed in an unsuitable host would lead to mutual death in a few days. In actual fact, there is little need for their stringent selection process (which perhaps partly explains some of the troubling aspects of Trill symbiosis that we have seen, most notably Riker's role in 'The Host'). However, there simply aren't enough symbionts to go round, and the Commission is worried about the creatures becoming mere desirable commodities.

Dax has had eight hosts, although the official records only show seven (as mentioned in 'Shadow Play': Sisko guesses – correctly as it turns out – that there have been eight in 'Invasive Procedures'). The last four are Tarisus, Joran, Curzon and Jadzia (the former three all being male). (Given that Tobin, mentioned in 'The Siege', was also male, then Dax's comment on having been a mother three times in 'The Nagus' must mean that her first, third and fourth hosts were female, which would just about tie-in with Dax's comment in 'Babel' that she hasn't been a woman for over eighty years. Lila – see 'Playing God' – was perhaps the host before Tarisus.) It's about four years since

Curzon died (a time consistent with that given in 'Dax'). Apart from Joran, none of Dax's hosts have any musical ability. Jadzia is unique in successfully re-applying to the Symbiosis Commission after initial rejection (see 'Playing God').

Sisko's father's restaurant was in New Orleans. When Bashir was young he was frightened of doctors. Curzon fell out of a tree once, and so Dax is very wary of top bunks.

51: 'Second Skin'

US Transmission: 24 October 1994
Writer: Robert Hewitt Wolfe
Director: Les Landau
Cast: Lawrence Pressman, Gregory Sierra, Tony Papenfuss, Cindy Katz, Christopher Carroll, Freyda Thomas, Billy Burke

The Bajoran Central Archives contact Kira regarding her time in the Ellenspur Detention Centre during the Cardassian occupation. Kira claims not to have been there, but Cardassian records indicate that she was held there for seven days, a fact confirmed by one of her fellow prisoners, who recognises her. When Kira goes to Bajor to investigate she is intercepted, and wakes up on Cardassia Prime. She has a Cardassian face, and is told that she is an undercover operative of the Obsidian Order named Eliana Ghemor. Ten years ago she was sent to infiltrate the Bajoran resistance, and now that she has returned her true memories will soon return. She cannot accept the idea, and begins to suspect that the whole thing has been arranged to trick her into giving Federation secrets to the Cardassians. In fact, the Order is trying to expose her 'father', a member of Central Command who has sympathies with Cardassian dissidents and believes that the Obsidian Order has too much power. Kira and Ghemor are rescued by Sisko, Garak and Odo.

Stardate: Not stated.

Strange New Worlds: Bashir has just returned from Klaestron 4 (see 'Dax'), where a new treatment for burns has just been developed.

New Life Forms: We briefly see Sisko masquerading as a Kobheerian freighter captain (see 'Duet'). Ghemor is offered political 'sanctuary' by the Nathamite government.

Once, when Kira was on long-range reconnaissance in the Vestri woods on Bajor, she shot a female harra cat, thinking it a Cardassian.

Dialogue Triumphs: Garak, on his life-saving clearance code: 'Oh, it's just something I overheard while hemming someone's trousers.'

Garak, to a Cardassian Kira: 'Major, I don't think I've ever seen you look so ravishing.'

Notes: 'Treason, like beauty, is in the eye of the beholder.' This just about avoids being a dull re-run of 'The Face of the Enemy': Kira doesn't wake up looking like any old alien but instead the very race she has dedicated her life to fighting. It's (another) good Garak story as, despite having saved his life, Ghemor warns Kira not to trust him! On the down side, it's all rather contrived, with a very convenient escape and a rather implausible emotional departure scene with Kira and her Cardassian 'father'.

Kira is from Dakor province. Both her parents died in Cardassian camps on Bajor (her mother died of malnutrition in the Singa refugee camp when she was three). Kira's mother was an icon painter. Hesperet is a Bajoran food best served warm.

52: 'The Abandoned'

US Transmission: 31 October 1994
Writers: D. Thomas Maio, Steve Warneck
Director: Avery Brooks

Appendix

Cast: Bumper Robinson, Jill Sayre, Leslie Bevis,
Matthew Kimbrough, Hassan Nicholas

Quark buys the wreckage of a transport ship that crashed within
the Gamma Quadrant for three bars of latinum from an old business contact. It contains nothing of interest apart from a baby
boy in a stasis chamber. The boy swiftly grows into a Jem'Hadar
warrior. He escapes from the medical centre on to the Promenade and wreaks havoc, but shows respect to Odo, knowing
him to be one of the Founders. Although Starfleet wish to examine the boy, Sisko allows Odo to oversee the young warrior
to see if the nature of the Jem'Hadar is immutable. The
Jem'Hadar 'kidnaps' Odo, hoping that they can go together to
the Gamma Quadrant, but is disappointed when Odo does not
act as he imagined a Changeling would. Sisko allows Odo and
the boy to go, and the Constable returns, knowing that his attempts to 'reform' the warrior have ended in failure.

Stardate: Not stated.

New Life Forms: Quark's business contact is a Bosli captain:
she is said to be heading for Riza.

Ferengi Rules of Acquisition: There is a Rule of Acquisition
covering the inspection of merchandise before purchase, although Quark doesn't quote it. Mata and Jake say that the 'First
Rule of Dabo' is 'Watch the wheel, not the girl'.

Notes: *DS9*'s equivalent of 'I, Borg' (bring back an immensely
powerful enemy in a less menacing form), only this time little
humanity can be seen in the 'monster'. Competently written
and directed, the story establishes an interesting contrast between Odo and the Jem'Hadar, both strangers in an alien world.
Odo's motivation is a powerful one: he knows what it's like to
be a laboratory animal, and hopes that the Jem'Hadar boy can
decide to turn against the Founders, just as he did. Against that,
the ending is very weak, and the whole story lacks a certain

finesse.

The Jem'Hadar boy has a very fast metabolic rate (he resembles an eight-year-old after two weeks), with a basic intelligence implanted in his DNA. A genetically engineered addiction to a certain type of enzyme – that cannot be replicated – ensures that the Jem'Hadar remain loyal to the Founders. The 'cloaking device' would seem to be a biological ability.

We see Jake's large-chested Dabo girlfriend Mata (see 'Playing God'), who is twenty years old. She is a Bajoran whose parents were killed during the occupation. She proudly informs Sisko that Jake writes poetry and plays a mean game of Dom-Jot (see *TNG*'s 'Tapestry').

Odo has new quarters – full of abstract statues – in which he hopes to explore new shapes and textures (see 'The Search'). He no longer uses his bucket – he returns to his liquid state in his room – although he keeps it to remind him how he once lived.

Starfleet sends the USS *Constellation* to take the Jem'Hadar warrior to Starbase 201.

53: 'Civil Defence'

US Transmission: 7 November 1994
Writer: Mike Krohn
Director: Riva Badiyi

O'Brien and Jake activate a Cardassian poison-gas booby-trap.

54: 'Meridian'

US Transmission: 14 November 1994
Writer: Hilary Bader
Director: Jonathan Frakes

The crew discover a planet in the Gamma Quadrant that shifts dimensions periodically, and Dax falls in love.

55: 'Defiant'

US Transmission: 21 November 1994
Writer: Ronald J. Moore
Cast: Jonathan Frakes

Thomas Riker arrives on DS9, secretly working for the Maquis and impersonating his 'duplicate'.

56: 'Fascination'

US Transmission: 28 November 1994
Writers: Ira Steven Behr, James Crocker
Director: Avery Brooks
Cast: Philip Anglim

A love epidemic hits the station.

57: 'Past Tense, part 1'

US Transmission: 2 January 1995
Writer: Robert Hewitt Wolfe
Director: Reza Badiyi
Cast: Jim Metzler, Frank Military, Dick Miller, Bernardo, Tina Lafford, Bill Smitrovich

Sisko, Dax and Bashir travel to San Francisco in the *Defiant*, but end up travelling back to the year 2024.

58: 'Past Tense, part 2'

US Transmission: 9 January 1995
Director: Jonathan Frakes
Cast: Jim Metzler, Frank Military, Dick Miller, Bernardo, Tina Lafford, Bill Smitrovich, Deborah Van Valkenurgh, Clint Howard, Richard Lee Jackson

Odo and Kira strive to rescue their colleagues.

59: 'Life Support'

US Transmission: 30 January 1995
Writer: Ronald D. Moore
Director: Reza Badiyi
Cast: Philip Anglim, Lark Voorhies, Ann Gillespie,
Andrew Prine, Louise Fletcher

Vedek Bareil is critically injured just as he is about to attend a crucial conference with the Cardassians.

60: 'Heart of Stone'

US Transmission: 6 February 1995
Writers: Ira Steven Behr, Robert Hewitt Wolfe
Director: Alexander Singer

Kira, hunting down members of the Maquis, becomes encased in a growing crystalline formation.

61: 'Destiny'

US Transmission: 13 February 1995
Writers: David S. Cohen, Martin A Winder
Director: Les Landau
Cast: Tracy Scoggins, Wendy Robie, Erick Avari,
Jessica Hendra

After a successful peace conference with the Cardassians Sisko is disturbed to hear of a Bajoran prophecy regarding the destruction of the wormhole.

62: 'Profit Motive'

US Transmission: 20 February 1995

Director: Rene Auberjonois

The Grand Nagus returns to DS9.

63: 'Visionary'

US Transmission: 27 February 1995
Director: Reza Badiyi
Cast: Annette Helde, Jack Shearer

O'Brien, ill with radiation poisoning, witnesses his own death and uncovers a Romulan plot.

64: 'Distant Voices'

US Transmission: 10 April 1995
Director: Alexander Singer
Cast: Victor Rivers, Ann Gillespie

Bashir, in a telepathically induced coma, has three hours to live.

65: 'Through the Looking Glass'

US Transmission: 17 April 1995
Director: Winrich Kolbe
Cast: Felicia M. Bell

Sisko, abducted by the mirror universe O'Brien, meets the equivalents of the Vulcan Tuvok and his wife.

66: 'Improbable Cause

US Transmission: 24 April 1995
Writers: René Echevarria, from a story by Robert Lederman, David R. Long
Director: Avery Brooks
Cast: Carlos La Camara, Joseph Ruskin, Darwyn Carson, Juliana McCarthy, Paul Dooley

Garak's shop explodes. When Odo investigates, he and the Cardassian are captured by Romulans.

67: 'The Die is Cast'

US Transmission: 1 May 1995
Writer: Ronald D. Moore
Director: David Livingston
Cast: Leland Orser, Kenneth Marshall, Leon Russom,
Paul Dooley

As the events from the previous episode conclude, Garak is forced to torture Odo while the Cardassians prepare to invade the Gamma Quadrant alongside the Romulans.

68: 'Explorers'

US Transmission: 8 May 1995

69: 'Family Business'

US Transmission: 15 May 1995

Star Trek: Voyager
First Season

45-minute and one 90-minute episodes

Created by Rick Berman, Michael Piller,
based on *Star Trek*, created by Gene Roddenberry

Executive Producers: Rick Berman, Michael Piller

Regular Cast: Kate Mulgrew (Captain Kathryn Janeway),
Robert Beltran (Chakotay), Tim Russ (Tuvok), Robert Picardo
(Doc Zimmerman), Robert Duncan McNeil (Tom Paris), Garrett
Wang (Harry Kim), Ethan Philips (Neelix), Roxann Biggs-
Dawson (B'Elanna Torres), Jennifer Lien (Kes)

1: 'The Caretaker'

90 Minutes
US Transmission: 16 January 1995
Writers: Michael Piller, Jeri Taylor,
from a story by Michael Piller, Jeri Taylor, Rick Berman

The *Voyager* and the Maquis ship it was pursuing are pulled
70,000 light years across space to a huge space array in the
Delta Quadrant. The array protects a race called the Ocampa
on a neighbouring planet, but the evil Gazons have their sights
set on capturing it. If Captain Janeway returns the two ships to
the Alpha Quadrant then the Ocampa will be destroyed.

2: 'Parallax'

US Transmission: 23 January 1995

3: 'Time and Again'

US Transmission: 30 January 1995

4: 'Phage'

US Transmission: 6 February 1995

5: 'The Cloud'

US Transmission: 13 February 1995
Writers: Michael Piller,
from a story by Brannon Braga
Director: David Livingstone
Cast: Larry Hankin, Angela Dohrmann, Sandrine,
Luigi Amodeo

The *Voyager* investigates a nebula which contains an injured alien.

6: 'Eye of the Needle'

US Transmission: 20 February 1995
Writers: Jeri Taylor,
from a story by Hilary Bader
Director: Rick Kolbe
Cast: Michael Cumpsty, Carolyn Seymour, Tom Virtue

A wormhole to the Alpha Quadrant is discovered, through which the *Voyager* can contact a Romulan ship, but it is too small to travel through.

7: 'Ex Post Facto'

US Transmission: 27 February 1995

8: 'Emanations'

US Transmission: 6 March 1995

9: 'Prime Factors'

US Transmission: 13 March 1995

10: 'State of Flux'

US Transmission: 20 March 1995

Metaphor and Trek

Paul Cornell

Star Trek: The Next Generation reacted to *Star Trek*'s adoption as the Official American Metaphor by taking its first hesitant steps into plot lines that explored the mechanisms of America, especially American foreign policy. The Klingons, who had been the Soviets, got more alien and became Islamic, albeit a very *Lawrence of Arabia*-Islamic. Like black separatists, they had to be encountered in the heart of America, as part of the Federation. The Federation was also contrasted with the Borg (the Japanese), the Cardassians (a canny mixture of Israeli and the new Russians), the Bajorans (the Palestinians), and, in a move which suggested that Roddenberry wasn't averse to pushing his metaphor to its logical end, the Ferengi (the evils of capitalism.)

Regrettably, the last case shows how much he was up against. Firstly, the design of the Ferengi instantly veered into the anti-Semitic. This seems to have had more to do with culturally developed images of greed than with actual prejudice. Secondly, the Ferengi were swiftly made into characters at the centre of the Federation, loveable rogues rather than avaricious pirates, and so the line was neatly drawn. You can try to be sympathetic to Islam if you like, but you can't knock the power of the Dollar.

As the Official American Metaphor, the show also started to assume a sense of responsibility over what it included. The serious treatment of ethical terrorism in 'The High Ground', which ends with the *Enterprise* happily flying away when the situation gets too complex for a neat solution, and had the honour of being banned by the BBC, was a good step in that direction. It tried to say that the metaphor was not complete, but that it was accurate in its incompleteness, that there were issues that the series, that America, failed to address.

Unfortunately, the series has continually fallen down over that other great exclusion, the lack of a gay presence anywhere. It's difficult to say that there should be a gay character in say, *The X-*

Files, because that's just a show about some particular people, but when a series sells itself as the liberal hope for the future of a whole culture, then it becomes hard to say that there *shouldn't*. 'Blood and Fire' – a first season AIDS allegory – was never made. *ST:TNG* finally addressed the issue as a metaphor within a metaphor, in the cowardly and distasteful episode 'The Outcast', and actively turned away from it in 'The Host'. There are ways of treating the issue that would have worked, just two male ensigns holding hands, or a mention of homosexuality as one of the things the Romulans kill their children for, but this, to the series' shame, was not to be. *Star Trek: Deep Space Nine* is trying to do better, but not very hard.

Where *Deep Space Nine* does score is that it reflects the turning inward of American policy as the country comes to terms with its internal troubles, and recognises that the outside world is a complicated place that a diplomatic or military solution can't always fix. The goal is now not to win, but to do one's best and muddle through. It's possible that the whole vision of *Trek* was shifted this way by casting Patrick Stewart as Picard. First he turned bullish and invasive lines into ponderous questions, and then he started to be given lines in that interrogative style. In effect, he introduced Europeanism, the idea of living with one's national neighbours just over the border, and thus being reserved, moderate, thoughtful, into *Trek*. We may have a lot to thank this one actor for.

In *DS9*, we're sitting above the Bosnia/Palestine/India/Vietnam that is Bajor, and we're trying not to interfere, but we're still intimately concerned with the place, every day. The original *Trek* – an American power fantasy of interfering and then running away – is not an option. Actions here have consequences.

The style of *DS9* is equally mature. Semi-regular characters proliferate, and the series often seems more like a serial. The conventions of American series television, often motivated by social forces (for instance, 'if a character dares to have a sexual relationship, their partner will instantly die or leave') have been overturned. The Official American Metaphor is at last starting to bite the hand that fed it.